GOD'S CENTURY

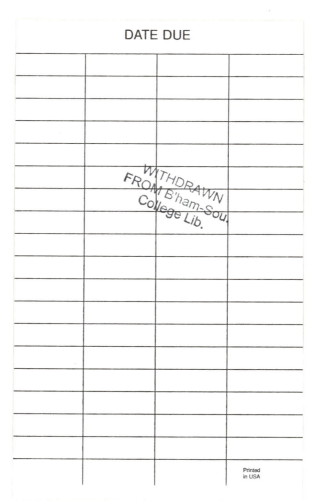

GOD'S CENTURY

Resurgent Religion and Global Politics

MONICA DUFFY TOFT

DANIEL PHILPOTT

TIMOTHY SAMUEL SHAH

W. W. NORTON & COMPANY
NEW YORK LONDON

W. W. Norton & Company has been independent since its founding in 1923, when William Warder Norton and Mary D. Herter Norton first published lectures delivered at the People's Institute, the adult education division of New York City's Cooper Union. The Nortons soon expanded their program beyond the Institute, publishing books by celebrated academics from America and abroad. By mid-century, the two major pillars of Norton's publishing program—trade books and college texts—were firmly established. In the 1950s, the Norton family transferred control of the company to its employees, and today—with a staff of four hundred and a comparable number of trade, college, and professional titles published each year—W. W. Norton & Company stands as the largest and oldest publishing house owned wholly by its employees.

Manufacturing by Courier Westford
Book design by Lovedog Studio
Production manager: Julia Druskin

Library of Congress Cataloging-in-Publication Data

Toft, Monica Duffy, 1965–
God's century : resurgent religion and global politics / Monica Duffy Toft,
Daniel Philpott, Timothy Samuel Shah. — 1st ed.
p. cm.
Includes bibliographical references and index.
ISBN 978-0-393-06926-6 (hardcover)
1. Religion and international relations. I. Philpott, Daniel, 1967–
II. Shah, Timothy Samuel. III. Title.
BL65.I55T64   2011
327—dc22

2010045967

This edition: ISBN 978-0-393-93273-7 (pbk.)

W. W. Norton & Company, Inc.
500 Fifth Avenue, New York, N.Y. 10110
www.wwnorton.com

W. W. Norton & Company Ltd.
Castle House, 75/76 Wells Street, London W1T 3QT

1 2 3 4 5 6 7 8 9 0

In Memory of

Samuel P. Huntington, 1927–2008

Contents

List of Tables

List of Figures

GOD'S CENTURY

Chapter One

THE TWENTY-FIRST CENTURY AS GOD'S CENTURY

HAD AN ENTERPRISING FORTUNE-TELLER PREDICTED FOUR decades ago that in the twenty-first century religion would become a formidable force in global politics, educated people would have considered him a laughingstock. In 1968, Peter Berger, one of the past generation's greatest sociologists, predicted that by "the 21st century, religious believers are likely to be found only in small sects, huddled together to resist a worldwide secular culture."[1] Similarly, in 1966 *Time* magazine printed starkly on its cover, "Is God Dead?," recalling German philosopher Friedrich Nietzsche's audacious assertions at the end of the previous century: "God is dead. God remains dead. And we have killed Him."

Global trends seemed to support these prophets of decline. Like dying supernovae, every major religion on every continent seemed to be rapidly losing its influence on politics, economics, and culture. More than that, they seemed "afloat on a receding wave of history," destined for oblivion.[2] Surging forward with seemingly unstoppable historical momentum were instead ideologies and doctrines that sought to replace religion as the source of people's loyalties. Apostles of nationalism, socialism, and modernization—such as Fidel Castro of Cuba, David Ben-Gurion of Israel, Gamal Abdel Nasser of Egypt, and the Shah of Iran—were men of the future. Mullahs, monks, and priests, with their dogmas, rites, and hierarchies, were creatures of an increasingly irrelevant past.

What came to be known as the "secularization thesis"—the prediction that religion would wilt before the juggernauts of the modern world—seemed

triumphant. Science, the thesis held, would expose the supernatural as super-
stition and reveal the truth of humanity's origins and makeup. Historical
inquiry would explain in similar fashion the true—and entirely human—
story behind events that the religious claimed to be miraculous and divinely
orchestrated. Democracy, free thought, and open expression would allow ordinary citizens to challenge the myths and dogmas by which church authorities
held people in servility and lent legitimacy to monarchy, aristocracy, and the
favorite pastime of the powerful, war. Industrialization, economic growth,
and technological progress would eradicate hunger, disease, and stunted
opportunity, the forces that lead people to turn to religion for answers. All of
this was hopeful. Religion's regress spelled humanity's progress.

Such thinking originated in the Enlightenment philosophical movement
of seventeenth- and eighteenth-century Europe. It included Thomas Jefferson, who edited his own version of the New Testament so as to omit all reference to the supernatural—heaven, hell, cross, and resurrection—and retain
only the gentle ethical wisdom of Jesus, from which he believed readers could
profit greatly. It also included Jean-Jacques Rousseau and other philosophers
of the French Revolution, who sought to kill off the monarchy and the Catholic Church and replace them with a system of secular thought and culture
centered on the nation. The thinking gained steam in the nineteenth and
twentieth centuries in the thought of Nietzsche, Charles Darwin, Karl Marx,
Sigmund Freud, Max Weber, and so many others. By the 1950s and 1960s,
the secularization thesis all but dominated the university, most elite sectors
in the West, and the views of Western-educated elites in Asia, Africa, and the
Middle East.

But the secularization thesis has proven a poor guide to global historical reality. Contrary to its predictions, the portion of the world population adhering to Catholic Christianity, Protestant Christianity, Islam, and
Hinduism jumped from 50 percent in 1900 to 64 percent in 2000. Globally
speaking, most people—79 percent—believe in God (a slight increase from
the late 1980s and early 1990s, which was 73 percent), and although in most
countries majorities agree that religion is private and should be kept separate from government, these majorities are increasingly slim in a number
of countries and the intensity of support for this separation has declined
in over half of the countries polled. In India, for example, the number of
people who "completely" agree on the separation of faith and government
dropped from 78 percent to 50 percent in just five years, from 2002 to 2007.[3]

Thus, over the past four decades, religion's influence on politics has reversed its decline and become more powerful on every continent and across every major world religion. Earlier confined to the home, the family, the village, the mosque, synagogue, temple, and church, religion has come to exert its influence in parliaments, presidential palaces, lobbyists' offices, campaigns, militant training camps, negotiation rooms, protest rallies, city squares, and dissident jail cells. Workplaces increasingly are the sites of prayer rooms and small-group Scripture studies. Even sporting events now feature conspicuous prayers by players and coaches, huddled together in supplication to the Almighty. Once private, religion has gone public. Once passive, religion is now assertive and engaged. Once local, it is now global. Once subservient to the powers that be, religion has often become "prophetic" and resistant to politicians at every level.

This book explains why this global transformation has occurred and what its implications are for today's politics. How and why has religion become publicly expressed and politically acceptable in so many parts of the world after a century of so many efforts to dethrone or displace faith as a source of political authority? What explains the diversity of political activities that the religious pursue? Why do some religious actors take up the gun through terrorism or civil war while others promote democracy, human rights, and reconciliation? The book also takes on the thorny and often heated question of what religion's political place ought to be. If religion is to have a seat at the political table, how big—and how elevated—should it be?

To see what is at stake in these questions, consider the following examples.

TWO OF THE MOST convulsive events for American foreign policy during the past generation have been the attacks of September 11, 2001, which led to the global "war on terror" and wars in Afghanistan and Iraq; and the Iranian Revolution of 1979, which resulted in a hostage crisis and a major realignment of Middle Eastern politics. Behind both events was an Islamic resurgence that has involved Muslims all over the world demanding regimes that actively promote Islamic law and morality both at home and around the world. Though the resurgence originated in the thought of Muslim intellectuals in the first half of the twentieth century, it did not become politically influential until the 1970s. Today, it contains diverse forms of politics, including social movements and political parties that favor democracy in places like Bangladesh, Indonesia, Mali, Senegal, and Turkey.

———————

IN 1990 A HINDU POLITICIAN took a well-publicized ride through India on a chariot—a powerful Hindu symbol—thus catapulting the Hindu nationalist Bharatiya Janata Party (BJP) to national prominence. In 1992, 150,000 Hindu-nationalist rioters burned to the ground a mosque in Ayodhya that was allegedly built on the site of the birthplace of the Hindu god Ram. In 1998 the BJP won the prime ministership of India, the world's largest democracy and a nuclear-armed state. All of this would have been unthinkable in 1947, when India achieved its independence. Founding father Jawaharlal Nehru and his Congress Party, which came to rule India for more than half a century, fully expected that economic modernization and democracy would bring about the decline of religion, at least in political life: the secularization thesis. Although today the BJP broadly respects the Indian constitution's basic separation of religion and state, its aggressive assertion that India is a Hindu nation has led it to pass laws that discriminate against Muslims and Christians, including state-level restrictions on religious conversion; to provoke riots and pogroms against Muslims and Christians in states such as Gujarat and Orissa; and to pursue a nationalistic foreign policy. The BJP lost national elections in 2004 and 2009 but has continued to exert power at the national level as well as in many of India's states. In Karnataka, for example, home to India's high-technology center of Bangalore, the BJP-controlled assembly succeeded in passing a ban on the slaughter of cows as recently as July 2010—ignoring protests from religious minorities.

———————

WHEN IT WAS FOUNDED in 1948, the new state of Israel was the product of decades of a nation's territorial struggle. The basis for "Zionism"— the brainchild of late nineteenth-century Austrian Jewish thinker Theodor Herzl—was the essentially secular idea of a homeland for the Jews based on principles of progressive social justice. This form of secular nationalism was opposed by Orthodox Jewish leaders, but adopted by secular statesmen such as David Ben-Gurion and Golda Meir. At Israel's founding, this secular vision of Israel's identity predominated. Since Israel's "miraculous" triumph over the vast armies of Egypt, Syria, and Jordan in the 1967 Six-Day War, however, a religious vision of Israel endorsed by devout Jews has been in the ascendancy. This vision is gaining ground in part thanks to demography: Ultraorthodox Jews have far higher reproductive rates than relatively secular citizens of Israel, and therefore constitute a rapidly growing proportion of the Israeli population. This fact poses significant challenges to the future identity and security of Israel, what it means to be a Jew, and the prospect of a final peace with the Palestinians.

———————

FOR OVER A CENTURY and a half, the Catholic Church did not get along well with Europe's advocates of democracy. Things had gotten off to a bad start in the French Revolution, when foot soldiers lopped off the heads of Catholic men in the name of the Rights of Man. European liberalism remained anticlerical, attacking the Church's schools, its appointment of bishops, and its governance of its affairs in many realms. The Church fought back. In his "Syllabus of Errors" of 1864, Pope Pius IX condemned "progress, liberalism, and modern civilization." Even in the early twentieth century, the Church declared voting in Italy a mortal sin, meriting eternal damnation. Dramatic, then, was the Church's embrace of human rights and democracy in the Second Vatican Council of 1962 to 1965. As a result, the Church, through its direct protest and its ability to mobilize its followers, became a driver of the global trend of autocratic regimes giving way to democracies. Most memorable was Poland, where Pope John Paul II held open-air pilgrimages before hundreds of thousands of people that led to the downfall of the Communist regime and sparked a chain reaction that ended the Cold War.

———————

HALF A CENTURY AGO, Buddhism was largely a religion of inward spirituality, personal transcendence, and political indifference. But then it took up politics. One face of this politics, known as "Engaged Buddhism," grafts age-old Buddhist concepts of peace and toleration with Western notions of human rights, democracy, and nonviolence. Engaged Buddhism has yielded fruit such as the activism of the Dalai Lama of Tibet; the courageous opposition of Burmese dissident Aung San Suu Kyi, and the leadership of the Indian convert to Buddhism B. R. Ambedkar, who was born an untouchable and rose to become a powerful government minister and opponent of India's caste system. But Buddhist politics also contains a domineering nationalist strand, as found in Sri Lanka, where the *sangha*, or religious community, is closely intertwined with the state and promotes Sri Lanka as a homeland for Buddhists, the religion of the Sinhalese majority group. The problem is that Sri Lanka is also home to the religious minority community of mostly Hindu Tamils. This uniting of nationalism and religion has provoked violent conflict with the minority Tamils, helping to fuel a decades-long civil war that reached a frightfully bloody conclusion in May 2009. Despite the government's "victory" over Tamil nationalists, profound tensions remain.

———————

IN 1976 THE DEMOCRATIC Party's candidate for president, Jimmy Carter, made it widely known that he was a "born-again Christian"—an augury that organizations like the Moral Majority and the Christian Coalition were to become formidable players in elections and policy debates in the United States. Conservative Christians attending church on Sunday morning would hear not just about salvation through faith in Jesus Christ, the importance of loving their spouse, and announcements for summer Bible camp, but also about the urgency of ending abortion, maintaining moral standards in the schools, protecting churches from government interference, and supporting Israel. In the past decade, this same constituency has widened its causes to include religious freedom, the war on AIDS, and the reduction of sex trafficking, all in a global context. With the election of a Democratic Congress in 2006 and Barack Obama in 2008, the Religious Right's influence is said to have waned, but it can hardly be counted out as an influential player.

———————

EVEN IN WESTERN EUROPE, widely thought to be secularization's ground zero, religious rumblings can be heard in such debates as whether French Muslim girls may wear head scarves to school, whether French Muslim women may publicly wear *burqas*, whether mosques in Switzerland can have a minaret, whether the preamble to a constitution for the European Union will mention Europe's Christian heritage, and whether Poland, Ireland, and Portugal will liberalize their abortion laws to match the rest of the European Union. Several heads of state, including British Prime Ministers Tony Blair and Gordon Brown, French President Nicolas Sarkozy, Italian Prime Minister Silvio Berlusconi, and German Chancellor Angela Merkel have remarked—mostly positively—about the rise of religion in recent years. Even Europe's most famous political philosopher, Jürgen Habermas, who built his intellectual career on decidedly secular foundations, has taken a strong and open interest in religion. He participated in a public dialogue with Cardinal Joseph Ratzinger, later to become Pope Benedict XVI, and even averred that Christianity was the source of Europe's values of human rights, tolerance, and democracy. "Everything else is postmodern chatter," he commented.

WHAT IS REMARKABLE ABOUT all of these cases—and we will be describing many others—is not only that religion has resurged in its political influence but that it has resurged with the help, rather than the opposition, of the very same forces that secularization theorists thought would spell its demise: democracy and open debate, rapid progress in communication and technology, and the historically unprecedented flow of people, ideas, and commerce around the globe. Democracy, it has turned out, has not killed religion through public exposure but has instead provided just the open arena in which Hindu nationalists, Turkish Muslims, and the Christian Religious Right in America can communicate their views and compete for power. Cell phones and computers are Al Qaeda's tools of the trade. It was by airplane that Pope John Paul II traveled around the globe to encourage (sometimes subtly) opponents of dictatorship. The television network Al Jazeera helps spread doctrines of radical revivalism throughout the Arab Muslim world. The Vatican has a sophisticated Web site, and Pope Benedict XVI recently acquired his own e-mail address. Today, the Internet enables religiously inspired ideas about politics to crisscross the globe at lightning speed. It is a consistent hallmark of today's most influential religious groups, in other words, that they combine aspects of modernity and religious orthodoxy into a new and potent blend.

In 1998, with uncommon scholarly humility, Peter Berger retracted his prediction of thirty years earlier:

> [T]he assumption that we live in a secularized world is false. The world today . . . is as furiously religious as it ever was, and in some places more so than ever. This means that a whole body of literature by historians and social scientists loosely labeled "secularization theory" is essentially mistaken.[4]

Berger's revised view is also our view: The twenty-first century is "God's Century." That is to say, religion has become and in all likelihood will continue to be a vital—and sometimes furious—shaper of war, peace, terrorism, democracy, theocracy, authoritarianism, national identities, economic growth and development, productivity, the fate of human rights, the United Nations, the rise and contraction of populations, and cultural mores regarding sexuality, marriage, the family, the role of women, loyalty to nation and regime, and the character of education.

If God is not dead, neither is the secularization thesis. In the past few years, a school of writers dubbed the "neo-atheists" has penned books with titles like *God Is Not Great*, *The God Delusion*, and *Breaking the Spell: Religion as a Natural Phenomenon* and *The End of Faith: Religion, Terror, and the Future of Reason*.[5] But their version of the thesis is somewhat different from that of their predecessors. They acknowledge that religion has not disappeared—at least not yet—and are alarmed by its persistence. They still believe that religion will eventually recede and hope that it will do so sooner rather than later—before it does more damage. Where they differ from the old secularization theorists most is in their moral assessment of religion, which, if anything, is even more splenetic, leading them to insist that religion is always and everywhere hard-wired to be irrational, violent, and repressive. In the view of Christopher Hitchens, for example, religion "poisons everything."

This version of the secularization thesis fares poorly, too, however. Religion can be violent and repressive, the source of civil war, terrorism, and laws that oppress women and minorities. But the last four decades have shown religion also to be a destroyer of dictatorships, an architect of democracy, a facilitator of peace negotiations and reconciliation initiatives, a promoter of economic development and entrepreneurship, a partisan in the cause of women, and a warrior against disease and a defender of human rights. These many faces of religious politics not only elude simple description but reveal the broader reality that religion's political influence is too little understood, partly because the instruments and frameworks widely used to interpret it remain far too crude.

If scholars, journalists, educators, and public intellectuals have come to realize by now *that* religion matters, they have only begun to understand *how* religion matters and whether it is likely to bring violence or peace, division or unity, progress or decline. But such an understanding is crucial for grasping contemporary global politics. Whether one is a maker of foreign policy, a business person conducting global commerce, a scholar of politics, economics, or culture, an advocate for economic development or human rights, a doctor fighting disease overseas, a translator, a missionary, or simply a world traveler, one cannot afford to ignore religion's resurgent political power in its almost infinitely varied manifestations.

Two Theses

Does recent historical evidence bear out our thesis about the resurgence of religion's influence on global politics? If so, why has a religious resurgence occurred at this point in history? Is this resurgence likely to continue into the future? If so, is this a worrisome or a welcome development? If religious politics takes many diverse forms, why do some religious groups promote peace or democracy while others take up the gun? And what lessons do the answers to these questions have for practical action? If, for instance, makers of American foreign policy were to understand better the importance of religion and the causes of religious behavior, how could they translate these insights into a foreign policy that would better secure America's freedom, security, and prosperity?

This book offers answers to these questions through two broad theses.

1. The first main thesis of the book is that *a dramatic and worldwide increase in the political influence of religion has occurred in roughly the past forty years.* It has been driven by religious people's desire for freedom—not just freedom as individuals to practice and express their faith, but freedom for their communities to assemble, worship, publicly profess their beliefs and programs, and, in the case of some religions, to convert others to their faith. The resurgent faiths have benefited from, rather than been hindered by, those forces that are most distinctive to the modern world—democracy, modernization in communication and technology, and globalization.

2. The second main thesis of the book offers an explanation for the wildly different politics of religious actors: why some fly airplanes into buildings while others destroy dictatorial regimes; why some strive to erect theocracies while others work to create peace settlements; why some engage in terrorism or civil war while others remain outside of politics altogether.

   While the influences behind these different forms of politics are many, we argue that two factors are more important than any others. *The first factor is the set of ideas that a religious community holds about political authority and justice, or what we call political theology.* Does a religious community believe violence to be justifiable? Can religious leaders legitimately hold political authority? Ought political authorities to give equal freedom to members of other faiths? These and many other questions are ones of political theology.

The second factor is the mutual independence of religious authority and political authority.[6] In liberal democracies, for instance, religion and state enjoy substantially separate spheres of authority. Even democracies vary, though. Most Scandinavian countries, as well as England, have established churches, while most other democracies do not, for example. In other countries, like Iran and Sri Lanka, the authority of the state is deeply enmeshed with the authority of the dominant religion, while religious minorities suffer varying degrees of disadvantage. In still others like Cuba and Egypt, the government exercises sharp control over all religious communities. The relationship that a religious actor enjoys with its government, along with its political theology, explains a great deal about what kind of politics it pursues, we argue.

RELIGION'S POLITICAL COMEBACK

Our first thesis, regarding the resurgence of religion over the last four decades, separates our view from other major schools of thought. Clearly, we take issue with the secularization thesis—though not as sharply as it might at first appear. For a long period of history, the secularization thesis had it right: religion's influence on politics was in global retreat from its former prominence and authority. During what Westerners call the Middle Ages, religious authorities in most parts of the world wielded a robust influence on their king, emperor, and laws of their realm, though not without nasty struggles at times. Then, from the seventeenth century up through the middle of the twentieth century, forms of politics progressively more hostile to religion unfolded, first in Europe and then in the rest of the world through colonization. By the 1960s, the secularization of politics had made such impressive gains in so much of the world that scholars like Berger and other chroniclers of the day like *Time* magazine had every good reason to think that this trend would continue. But then a global change occurred that few could have foreseen and that rendered the secularization thesis increasingly dubious.

So if we disagree with the secularization thesis, we also take issue with the opposite view, namely that religion has held steady in its political influence. If secularization is "the process by which sectors of society and culture are removed from the domination of religious institutions and symbols," as Berger has defined it, then it was for a long time a genuine reality in the politics of many countries and not simply an atheist phantasm or the illusion of those who could not see religion around them.[7] That is to say, religion's influence on politics has a history: three centuries of decline, then a comeback.

Such a grand thesis warrants nuance and qualification, which Chapter Three offers through its short history of the relationship between religion and politics. Here, an illustration will introduce our case. It involves a dramatic resurgence of religion in a setting that at one time, at least to outsiders, seemed dominated by secularism: twentieth-century Iran.

THE CASE OF IRAN

For several decades, the United States could not have had a better ally in Iran than Shah Reza Pahlavi. The setting was the Cold War, when a friend on the border of the Soviet Union, especially one rich in oil, was a precious asset. In 1953, the Central Intelligence Agency (CIA) placed the Shah in power by orchestrating the overthrow of the nationalist, left-leaning, but democratically elected Prime Minister Mohammed Mossadegh. Until the Shah himself was overthrown a quarter-century later, he remained unwaveringly loyal to the United States.

The Shah was also a poster boy for the secularization thesis. Much like monarchs in the Islamic Arab world to the west, the Shah built his rule on the ideas of nationalism and social and economic modernization. Through the revenues gained from the sale of oil, Iran would be transformed from a backward land of tribes and villages to a nation of cities and citizens. Women would enjoy equality and opportunity; everyone would enjoy a higher standard of living.

What about Iran's Shiite Muslim religion? The Shah's regime tolerated it as long as it was confined to the home and the mosque. Prior to his rule, religion had not been organized into a political program, certainly not since Iran had become a constitutional monarchy in 1906. Mossadegh, for instance, had been elected prime minister on a nationalist platform. Similar to Arab monarchs, the Shah allied himself with clerics who agreed with this vision while threatening and jailing more conservative and traditional clerics who advocated a political realm guided strongly by Islam. True, the Shah's approach did not measure up to U.S. ideals of human rights and democracy, especially religious freedom, but the U.S. could allow this because the Shah strongly supported its interests—or so America's grand strategists consistently believed.

What happened then in 1978 and 1979 was a set of events that took the U.S. foreign policy establishment utterly by surprise. After a year of major demonstrations by opponents of his regime, the Shah fled into exile in mid-January 1979. Two weeks later, Shiite cleric Ayatollah Ruhollah Khomeini returned from his own exile in France and was greeted with wild enthusiasm by several million Iranians. On April 1 of that year, Iranians voted to make their country a theocratic Islamic republic with Khomeini as supreme leader. The following November Iranian students took hostages at the American embassy and held them for 444 days. Theocratic Iran had become a hard-and-fast enemy of the United States.

Why did American foreign policy–makers fail to anticipate these events? Because they did not think religion mattered in world politics. James Bill, a scholar of Iran, tells the story of Earnest Oney, a CIA analyst who had proposed to his superiors a study of religious leaders in Iran. The response:

> His bureaucratic superiors vetoed the idea, dismissing it as "sociology." The work climate was such that he was sometimes condescendingly referred to by others in the government as "Mullah Ernie." It was not until the revolution and after his retirement that he was able to do his study on the force of religion in Iran. He did it for the agency on contract—*after* the force of religion had been felt not only in Iran but by America as well.[8]

Islam has lost little of its force and relevance. In the fierce clashes between conservatives and reformers following Iran's presidential elections on June 12, 2009, the mantle of Islam was sought passionately and sincerely by both sides. "In the battle to control Iran's streets," Neil MacFarquhar of the *New York Times* reported, "both the government and the opposition are deploying religious symbols and parables to portray themselves as pursuing the ideal of a just Islamic state."[9] For example, Mir Hussein Moussavi, the opposition leader, "demanded the kind of justice promised by the Quran and exhorted his followers to take to their rooftops at night to cry out, 'Allahu akbar,' or 'God is great.'" Such rhetoric was not mere expediency. Instead, Islam remains a fundamental touchstone of legitimacy in Iran. "If either the reformists or the conservatives can make reference to Islamic values in a way that the majority of citizens understand, they will win," according to Mohsen Kadivar, an Iranian scholar of Islamic studies. In the current context, no one questions *whether* Iran will be a religious state as in the 1979 revolution, but *how*.

Iran is not unique. Religion has been surging with new political force not only in Iran but around the globe.

THE CHARACTER OF THE RESURGENCE

Several themes characterize this resurgence. First, everywhere it took place it involved religious people and communities evolving from private devotion, enclosed in family, community, and place of worship, to public engagement, characterized by active efforts to influence constitutions, laws, and policy. No longer did religious communities reject politics as an unspiritual business but rather embraced political activism as a sacred calling. In some cases, by directing faith outward, believers recovered older forms of activism that had been temporarily submerged or forgotten. Elsewhere, they effectively invented new traditions and forms of religiously inspired political engagement. Religious communities commonly shifted from a strategy of changing cultural attitudes—regarding matters like family and the personal practice of faith—to one of changing laws, policies, and even regimes.

Second, one of the major causes of the religious resurgence was a crisis in secular ideologies. The religious revolution in Iran was caused in good part by the Shah's disastrous economic policies, which had brought inflation and shortages to Iran by the 1970s. In much of Africa and Asia, the euphoric nationalism that had spurred colonial independence movements in the 1940s, 1950s, and into the 1960s led to stagnation in the late 1960s and 1970s as founding fathers evolved into corrupt dictators and new states descended into civil war and persistent poverty. Take Algeria, for instance, where the same National Liberation Front that had fought heroically against France for independence in the 1950s and early 1960s had, by the 1970s, turned the country into a single-party dictatorship—socialist, secular, and stagnant—and sparked the eventual formation of the radical Islamic Salvation Front. Communist states, too, quite literally failed to deliver the goods, making Premier Nikita Khrushchev's 1956 boast to the West that "we will bury you" seem ever more vain. Though it may have seemed to Western scholars of the 1960s that secular ideologies were all that existed, populations around the world had begun to shop for other forms of legitimacy and were turning to sources that they had known all along.

A third theme of the religious resurgence is the quest of religious communities for freedom from state control. In the middle of the twentieth century, harsh and even brutal forms of state control were common, whether they took the form of anticlerical regimes in Europe and Mexico, the dictatorial secularism of Kemal Ataturk's Turkey and Arab monarchism, or regimes that sought to eradicate entire religions such as the Nazi government in Germany or Communist governments in the Soviet Union, Romania, Bulgaria, and China. Freedom, then, became a strong goal of Khomeini and his followers, of Muslim movements living under nationalist dictatorships in the Arab world as well as in Turkey and Indonesia, of Catholic and Protestant movements that have struggled against Communist regimes and right-wing military dictatorships alike, and of movements as diverse as Tibetan Buddhism, Burmese Buddhism, and Iranian Bahá'ís. This is not to claim, of course, that when these movements triumphed they necessarily favored free regimes or respected other religious minorities, as the Iranian case attests. It is only to claim that a major dimension of the religious resurgence has been the quest of religious communities to break free from the confines of secular forms of rule.

In pursuing freedom and political influence, in whatever form, religious communities have benefited from cooperation with modern forces like democracy, globalization, and technological modernization—a fourth theme of the resurgence. Resurgent religious movements themselves, to be sure, are not always democratic in their outlook. But political systems characterized by free speech and competition for power have not been generally detrimental to religious communities' pursuits. The BJP, for instance, made skillful use of India's democratic system of open expression and electoral competition. Democracies as diverse as Indonesia, Nigeria, Poland, and the United States have enabled religious politics, too. Religious movements are also at home with modern technology, communication, and transportation. Since 2004 the BJP has incorporated high-tech methods—such as text-messaging—into its campaigns, setting the pattern for subsequent contests. As noted earlier, Al Qaeda employs cell phones and computers in its operations.

Modern communication and transportation in turn propelled one of the most striking dimensions of the resurgence—the evolution of religious communities into transnational political actors. The Muslim Brotherhood spans multiple countries and communicates its ideas globally. Hindu nationalists in India are supported by equally ardent Hindus in the United States. National Catholic churches around the world were supported by the Vatican—though to different degrees—in their confrontations against dictatorships. Religious communities have spilled over the confines not only of the private and the local but also over the borders of the sovereign state.

Whether governments around the world like it or not, this resurgence of religion has meant that they would now have to reckon with religion in a way that they did not forty, fifty, or sixty years ago. After decades of preventing an Islamic political movement from winning power electorally through its army and its courts, the highly secularist government of Turkey finally allowed an Islamic party to govern, which it has done since 2002. Far from the days when religion was brutally suppressed under Mao's dictatorship and the Cultural Revolution of the 1960s, the government of China has come to accept the place of religion in Chinese society and sometimes even welcomes its contribution, though tentatively and far short of allowing it full freedom to operate. As Kim-Kwong Chan, a scholar of Chinese religion, has documented, local Chinese officials in the face of rampant opium addiction in some districts have turned to the only people they could find with a demonstrated ability to overcome it—Christian churches. (As Chan remarks, Communist officials reluctantly decided that the best weapon against opium addiction was precisely what Karl Marx famously condemned as the "opiate of the masses.")[10] In the United States, the rise of religion in politics has forced candidates for national office to speak the language of religion even if they do not belong to the wing of the Republican Party where the Religious Right finds its political home. It is a lesson that Democratic presidential candidates Bill Clinton and Barack Obama learned well but that Howard Dean and John Kerry did not. Even so, polls show a lingering "God gap" between the two parties: more Americans believe the Republican Party respects their faith and values than does the Democratic Party, and an overwhelming proportion of white evangelical Protestants—close to 70 percent—voted for Republican presidential candidate John McCain in 2008.

The resurgence is here to stay, we believe. This is because the conditions that encouraged it remain largely in place. No global retreat of religion into the private realm can be discerned. As much as ever, religious communities seek the freedom to express and practice their faith and to influence their societies. The conditions that have encouraged the resurgence—globalization, democratization, and modernization—persist and in many places grow wider. Of course, it is always possible that our own view of world history will be refuted by the next decade's events, just as secularization theory was in its time. But there is no sign of such a reversal on the horizon.

E X P L A I N I N G T H E W I L D L Y D I V E R G E N T P O L I T I C S O F T H E R E L I G I O U S

Our aim is to show not only that religion matters but also how it matters. Our second thesis is that a religious actor's political theology and its relationship to political authority explain much about why it takes on the kind of politics that it does—violent or peaceful, democratic or dictatorial, and the like. In Chapter Two, we explain both of these concepts in much greater depth.

Political theology is a matter of how religious actors think and promulgate their ideas. It makes a great deal of difference whether their doctrines call for a regime based on human rights and religious freedom, a regime that strongly promotes faith in every sphere of life, laws that respect religions other than their own, or the renunciation of the use of force. To some it might seem obvious that ideas matter. Yet it is striking how often both scholars and the media treat religious ideas and motivations as a by-product of some "underlying" force presumed to be more basic and compelling, whether it is economic deprivation, personal greed, stunted opportunity, resentment against colonialism, or a backlash against globalization.

Some scholars of the Iranian Revolution, for instance, account for it as a result of the growth of the middle class. But in fact it was also a theological revolution, rooted partly in religious ideas and motivations. An important development in motivating Shiites to seize state power was also a theological reinterpretation of the role of Imam Hussein, the seventh-century grandson of the Prophet Mohammed, from victim to hero-martyr. No longer were Shiites to be passive victims, the new thinking implied. Now, without contradicting their faith, they could fill Tehran's streets and demand and control a new regime, just as they in fact did in 1978 and 1979.

The other central influence on the politics of religious communities is the degree and kind of independence from political authority that they enjoy. The marginalized position that Shii Islam suffered under the Shah was crucial to its adoption of protest, violence, and overthrow as tactics, for instance. Though it is always speculative to imagine history differently, one can imagine devout Shiites taking up far more peaceful tactics in a setting of open communication and political competition.

Together, political theology and independence explain a great deal, as we show in Chapters Four through Seven. Each of these chapters examines a separate political pursuit of the religious. Chapter Four looks at religious actors' promotion of democracy. Chapter Five looks at religious terrorism.

Chapter Six focuses on the role of religion in civil war. Chapter Seven examines the influence of religious leaders on peace settlements and on political efforts to address the past injustices of war and dictatorship. In each chapter, we first show how the particular activity manifests our claim about religious resurgence—how religious actors have come to be far more active and engaged in politics. Then each chapter turns to political theology and independence to explain why some religious actors engage in the activity and some do not.

For example, Chapter Four looks at global democratization—the movement in which seventy-eight countries moved toward or became democracies between 1972 and 2009—and asks why some religious actors participated vigorously while others remained passive or even friends of dictators. The Catholic Church in Poland, Brazil, and the Philippines and Islamic movements in Indonesia, for instance, played a heroic role in their country's struggles for freedom, while the Catholic Church in Uruguay and Argentina and the Protestant hierarchy in East Germany played little positive role in their country's transition to democracy. Our argument is that those religious actors who promoted democracy most ardently were those who—even under dictatorship—both preserved a sphere of independence and embraced a political theology that favored foundational elements of modern democracy like religious freedom, separation of religion and state, and rule by the people.

The relationship between religion and violence is probably one of the most scrutinized aspects of religion and politics yet one of the least understood. In Chapters Five and Six, we explore the connection of religion with terrorism and civil wars, respectively. Data reveal that religious motivations underpin terrorism and civil wars far more extensively today than in the past and that an increase in religiously based violence began about four decades ago. The political theology of the actors matters as does the independence of these actors. Is violence and killing an acceptable form of political action, especially in states that repress religion and religious actors? To what extent are religious actors marginalized? Religious wielders of violence answer these questions in their domestic setting but under the influence of global processes. When modern religiously based terrorism emerged, it was linked in part to Iran's 1979 Revolution—a political, but also a theological, revolution. Today, the vast majority of terrorist acts, especially suicide attacks, have a religious dimension. Similarly, the proportion of civil wars with a religious tint jumped precipitously in the 1970s. Why? Because of the global resurgence of religion and also because domestic regimes failed to deliver on their secular promises of equality and development. Religion and religious actors offered a legitimate alternative to declining state authority. Some of these challenges resulted in nonviolent revolutions as in Poland, but in other corners of the world, terrorism and full-scale civil war seemed to offer the only means of challenging the state and achieving radical change, as in Afghanistan, Algeria, Russia, and Tajikistan, to name only a few examples.

Why some religious actors have brought civil wars to peaceful conclusions or have influenced their countries' choices for trials or truth commissions in dealing with past injustices is the subject of Chapter Seven. By and large, the religious actors most effective in pursuing peace and justice retained a healthy independence during the period of war or dictatorship, avoiding becoming either suppressed altogether or too cozy with either the regime or an oppositional faction. They usually embraced a political theology that stressed human rights, nonviolence, and social justice in the case of peace settlements and a political theology of reconciliation in the case of addressing past injustices.

Chapter Eight closes the book by identifying ten "rules" that our analysis yields for practice, particularly the conduct of American foreign policy. We advance these with a grain of caution, observing that several centuries and dozens of cases contain exceptions as much as they do rules. Most generally, the United States (and other Western governments) will pursue their policies of reducing terrorism and spreading democracy more successfully the more they come to understand the following: that religious communities are most likely to support democracy, peace, and freedom for other faiths, and least likely to take up the gun or form dictatorships, when governments allow them freedom to worship, practice, and express their faith freely and when religious communities in turn renounce their claims to permanent offices or positions of policy-making authority.

As the case of Iran illustrates so vividly, a major historical factor behind violent and oppressive political pursuits in the Muslim world in the latter part of the twentieth century was the marginalization of Islam by secular regimes in the middle of the twentieth century. Both terrorists and theocracies resulted. But not everywhere. Where Islamic parties preserved a measure of autonomy and where they have been open to democratic thinking, they have been influential forces for democratization and peace: Bangladesh, Indonesia, Malaysia, Mali, Senegal, and Turkey, and other countries reveal this alternative pattern. So, too, the lesson holds in the case of other religions. The United States and other Western states will most likely succeed in their foreign policy by encouraging regimes that treat religion neither as a prisoner nor a courtier but as a respected citizen and by supporting religious communities who struggle for just this kind of regime. But that will require first that American foreign policy–makers treat religion as something more than mere "sociology."

Throughout this chapter, we have made several large claims about religion, claims that we will explore more deeply in the pages that follow. In doing so we have used concepts and terms that seem straightforward enough in an introductory chapter but whose simplicity is in fact deceptive. The closer one looks at them, the more complicated they begin to seem. Even the concept of religion is not easy to define. Needing explanation, too, are *religious actor, political actor* (in relation to religion), *political theology,* and *independence of religious authority and political authority.* It is the job of Chapter Two to make these concepts—building blocks of the explanations to follow—clear and vibrant.

Chapter Two

BEHIND THE
POLITICS OF
RELIGION

A RELIGIOUS RESURGENCE HAS TAKEN PLACE. POLITICAL theology and the relationship between religious and political authority together explain a great deal about the radically varied behavior of religious actors. Behind these two major claims of our book lie some important concepts: religion, religious actor, political authority, political theology, and the relationship between religion and state. This chapter clarifies these.

THE DRAMATIS PERSONAE

The chief players in our drama are religion, religious actors, and political authorities. Though these figures are familiar in the public imagination, they are more complex than they appear and so demand closer scrutiny.

What Is Religion?

What is religion? Scholars and theologians have long debated the issue—seemingly without resolution. Is it a belief in God? That would mean that Buddhism and some strands of Hinduism, which do not incorporate such a belief, are not religions. Is it what the "big five" global religions—Judaism, Christianity, Islam, Hinduism, and Buddhism—have in common? But what exactly is that? And what of Confucianism? Or the Bahá'ís? And what about "nontraditional" religions like New Age spirituality or Scientology? Are they real religions? And is it possible to define religion so as not to include ideologies like nationalism and Marxism, which are not normally thought of as religions but which appear to share some of religion's characteristics?

Though no definition is perfect, we find philosopher William P. Alston's a useful one. Religion, he says, involves the following elements: (1) a belief in a supernatural being (or beings); (2) prayers or communication with that or those beings; (3) transcendent realities, including "heaven," "paradise," or "enlightenment"; (4) a distinction between the sacred and the profane and between ritual acts and sacred objects; (5) a view that explains both the world as a whole and humanity's proper relation to it; (6) a code of conduct in line with that worldview; and (7) a temporal community bound by its adherence to these elements.[1] Though not every religion includes all of these elements, all religions include most of them, such that we understand that religion involves a combination of beliefs, behavior, and belonging in a community.

Some scholars are skeptical that religion can be defined at all, claiming that all attempts to do so fail to distinguish religion from other beliefs that also define communities across time, inspire fervid and sacrificial loyalty, and carry political agendas. Consider nationalism. Nationalism is an ideology that prescribes a common political destiny for a people that shares a common culture, history, language, or race and place. It can take the form of healthy patriotism, as it has for the Polish people, whose national spirit has enabled them to survive centuries of partition and foreign occupation. It can sometimes take virulent and even ruthless forms, as it did in Nazi Germany. Sometimes nationalism combines with religion to form "religious nationalism"—contemporary Hindu nationalism in India, for instance. Sometimes nations command the absolute loyalty of their members, just as religions seem to do.

But nationalism and religion are not the same. Even where some religions are nontheistic (as in the cases of Theravada Buddhism, Confucianism, and Jainism), all religions by definition seek understanding of, and harmony with, the widest reaches of transcendent reality—the quality that distinguishes them from political ideologies such as Marxism or secular nationalism that are sometimes thought to be functionally equivalent to religion. Religions offer answers to universal questions about the origins of existence, the afterlife, and realities that transcend humanity; nations generally do not. Religious believers are not tied to one location by virtue of their faith; nationalism makes a claim precisely about the people who come from a particular territory. Most religions can be joined by virtually anyone. Some, like Christianity, Islam, and Buddhism, undertake global missionary efforts to expand their ranks. Nations, by contrast, though they sometimes forcibly assimilate minorities, do not call on humanity in general to convert to their identity. Serbs do not try to convince Frenchmen to become Serbs. One either is a member of a nation or one is not.

In sum, religion is something distinct, even if it sometimes shares characteristics with other forms of belief and belonging. In this book, we look mainly at the four largest world religions—Christianity, Islam, Hinduism, and Buddhism—as well as Judaism. All of these religions influence the politics of their members. But each of them also contains a great diversity of political pursuits. To understand how religion influences politics, then, we must look at a smaller entity—what we call a "religious actor."

Religious Actors

A maddening variety of people and organizations adopt political pursuits in the name of religion. Sometimes religious actors operate as individuals, either on their own, as a cleric or a member of an order of clerics, or by the authority they derive from a political or cultural position. In the late 1700s and early 1800s, English evangelical William Wilberforce fought for the abolition of the slave trade as a member of the British Parliament. Abdul Ghaffar Khan, a Muslim known as the "Pashtun Pacifist," was a contemporary of Gandhi who led a nonviolent movement against British rule in present-day Pakistan. Individual religious people also speak and act politically as voters, activists, intellectuals, journalists, propagandists, or dissidents, or through ordinary conversations.

At other times, believers act through a wide range of organized bodies. In Christianity, the church is the central organization, although its structure and hierarchy vary markedly from the Roman Catholic Church to the Eastern Orthodox Church to the manifold Protestant churches. In Buddhism, the most important association is the *sangha*, or community of monks or nuns. Jews have divided themselves into Reformed, Conservative, and Orthodox branches and Muslims into Sunnis and Shiites. But what these divisions mean, the sort of leadership they entail, and how each group is organized is not uniform within these traditions.

All of the major world religions include organizations of believers who advocate for political causes, at least as one of their pursuits. Examples are the Muslim Brotherhood, the National Association of Evangelicals, B'nai B'rith, the World Buddhist Sangha Council, and the Vishva Hindu Parishad

(World Hindu Council). Sometimes the religious form political parties, like the Christian Democrats in Europe and Latin America, the Justice and Development Party in Turkey, Jamaat-e-Islami in Pakistan, or the Bharatiya Janata Party (BJP) in India. Others, such as Al Qaeda, assume the form of transnational networks with no return address.

A single leader—a mufti, a chief rabbi, or a bishop—can communicate a political message on behalf of a religious organization. In some cases, a religious leader acts in isolation from a hierarchy, as did Mahatma Gandhi, who led a nonviolent movement for independence in India in the 1920s, '30s, and '40s. Still elsewhere, it is the mass of believers who send a political message, as did hundreds of thousands of Poles who thronged Pope John Paul II's open-air pilgrimages to Communist Poland in the late 1970s and the 1980s.

Few religious organizations are unanimous in their beliefs (though some cults come close), either because their members disagree or simply because they are decentralized. Even the Catholic Church, perhaps the most centralized of the major world religions by virtue of its pope and its bishops, contains many national and regional bishops' conferences, orders of priests and nuns, communities of lay people, advocacy organizations, thousands of theologians, universities, parishes, loosely affiliated political parties and organizations such as Catholic Relief Services, and a billion ordinary believers. For all such individuals and groups, political beliefs and messages are diverse in emphasis and sometimes at odds. During the 1970s, for example, the Catholic leadership in the Vatican had firmly proclaimed its support for human rights and democracy, but not every national Catholic Church followed suit. The Catholic Church in Chile was a strong opponent of the dictatorship of General Augusto Pinochet, but the Church in Argentina supported its own military dictatorship. Even this is too simple: The Chilean Church also contained unreformed traditionalists and the Argentine Church heroic dissidents like human rights activist Emilio Mignone. One can find both consensus and dissent within the global church, national churches, and at the individual level; and all the more so within religions that are far less centralized.

Our imperfect solution to this diversity of actors is to define a religious actor as any individual, group, or organization that espouses religious beliefs and that articulates a reasonably consistent and coherent message about the relationship of religion to politics. It is understood that this actor might well be a part of a larger religious entity and might be a collectivity whose members themselves are not unanimous.

This conceptualization contains an important implication for religious politics. Namely, it is not enough to ask the religious identity of an actor in order to discern his or her politics. Whether a voter, an activist, or a political party is Hindu, Muslim, or Orthodox Christian is partially important—but only partially. Every world religion also contains political diversity that is shaped by more localized influences. We take religious beliefs seriously but do not treat any one religion as a monolith.

Like religion itself, religious actors are generally not territorially bound, but transnational. Today, they frequently spill across the boundaries of states in membership and organization. Similarly, they span the fields through which modern political science approaches global politics: international relations (between states) and comparative politics (within states). Religion fits neither model, existing both within and across states. As a result, the political behavior of a religious actor in one state is often shaped by its confrères elsewhere. The national Catholic churches that opposed authoritarian regimes in Brazil, Chile, the Philippines, and Poland in the 1970s and '80s were strongly influenced by developments in the Vatican in the 1960s. Members of the Muslim Brotherhood in Iran, Iraq, Jordan, Kuwait, Palestine, and Syria were and are strongly influenced by their fellow members in Egypt, where the movement is based. Because religious actors cross borders and consist of populations that can exceed a billion people, they may usefully be thought of as active members of a "transnational civil society."[2]

Political Authorities

Political authorities, too, are among the chief dramatis personae in our story. A political authority is a person or body who rules a community according to its common good. One of this authority's quintessential attributes is its legitimate use of decisive force to uphold the laws of the community and its security against outsiders.[3] As we make clear in Chapter Three, religious actors have nearly always lacked this responsibility, even in times and places when they have acted in close association with political authority. In only a few cases has their authority so thoroughly fused with political authority that they have assumed its proper roles and responsibilities.

Almost always, religious authorities must chart their course of action in relation to distinct political entities. The politics of Buddhists in Burma or Tibet, for instance, takes the form of protest because they live under a regime that imposes sharp, authoritarian controls on the practice of their faith. In India, by contrast, open electoral competition provided the Hindu-nationalist BJP with the setting that both enabled and limited its influence. While holding the prime ministership from 1998–2004, it was forced to compromise and build coalitions, and it lost national elections in 2004 and 2009.

Depending on how political authorities make, enforce, and judge law, command armies and police forces, and proclaim gods, ideologies, national identities, and various ideas of morality and justice as legitimate for their realms, these authorities shape the contexts in which religious actors pursue (or are impeded from pursuing) their ends.

In its first three centuries, the Christian church lived under the authority of the Roman emperor, who claimed divine status and launched periodic waves of persecution against Christians. In this context, the early church fathers developed their political theologies as answers to questions such as: Can a good Christian serve in the emperor's army? Is the emperor himself a false god or is he a legitimate political authority, whatever his pretenses and heresies? In 313 C.E., when the Roman Emperor Constantine converted to Christianity, he radically altered Christians' entire political context. Now, as members of the established faith, they would ask: Under what conditions could a Christian ruler justly fight a war? Can heretics be coerced? What are the purposes and limits of political authority? As the political order changed, so too did the politics of the religious.

Similarly, Islamic revivalist intellectuals of the early and mid twentieth century such as Hassan al-Banna, Abul Ala Maududi, and Sayyid Qutb penned their ideas in response to the centuries-long decline of Islamic civilization at the hands of Western colonial powers and to Arab regimes who sought to imitate the West. When they wrote, Islam's influence on law, politics, and culture was at its lowest ebb since the time of Mohammed. Amid what they interpreted as *jahiliyya*—the state of ignorance that characterized the world prior to Islam—they reasoned about how to re-create Islamic social and political orders.

Al-Banna was an Egyptian intellectual and schoolteacher who became convinced that Western secularism was eroding the morals of traditional Islamic society. In 1928 he founded the Muslim Brotherhood in order to foster among ordinary Muslims a faith untainted by foreign adulteration. By the late 1930s, the organization contained 500,000 people. In 1949, at the age of forty-three, he was assassinated by an agent of the Egyptian government. Maududi was a theologian and journalist, born in British India in 1903, who founded the revivalist party Jamaat-e-Islami in 1941 and strove to make Pakistan an Islamic state after it attained its independence in 1947. Qutb was an Egyptian member of the Muslim Brotherhood who wrote extensively about how to revive Islam during the 1950s and 1960s. He famously arrived at his dark views of Western secularism—materialistic, violent, and licentious—as a student in the United States from 1948 to 1950 in which he observed the following at a church dance in Greeley, Colorado:

> Every young man took the hand of a young woman. And these were the young men and women who had just been singing their hymns! Red and blue lights, with only a few white lamps, illuminated the dance floor. The room became a confusion of feet and legs: arms twisted around hips; lips met lips; chests pressed together.[4]

Convinced that the West was decadent, and committed to preventing Islam from also falling into decadence, Qutb returned to Egypt. His views of the Arab regime were quite critical, and he began to promulgate radical views on Islam. The Egyptian government of Gamal Abdel Nasser reciprocated, branding him a criminal, imprisoning him, and finally executing him in 1966.

These Islamic revivalists are a strong example of how the politics of religious actors is shaped by the context created by political authority. The pages that follow are replete with other examples of how political authorities often create the problems and opportunities to which religious actors are compelled to respond.

Religion, religious actors, and political authorities, then, are the key players in our story. With them in mind, we turn to what we believe are the strongest influences on the political pursuits of religious actors: political theology and the relationship between religious authority and political authority.

POLITICAL THEOLOGY AND RIVAL IDEAS

Unlike the Islamic revivalists, some twentieth-century Muslims believed that a secular state such as Turkey or Algeria would best promote both Islamic belief and healthy politics. By contrast, other Muslims hold that only a caliph who fuses spiritual and political authority and governs the entire community of Muslim believers (*umma*) can embody the true meaning of the Quran. In another context, medieval and early modern European Christians thought that kings ruled by divine right—that God had selected them and mandated their rule. Philosopher Jean-Jacques Rousseau, for example, celebrated what he saw as Thomas Hobbes's accomplishment of bringing religion under the political authority of a sovereign state. Viewing India as their homeland,

Hindu nationalists call for restrictions on the religious freedom of Muslims and Christians. The "symphonic" partnership between church leaders and emperors and kings is a centuries-old doctrine in the Eastern Orthodox Church. For Dr. Martin Luther King and his followers, the Christian gospel demands equality for all the members of a political community and just as firmly demands the use of nonviolent means to attain it.

All of these are examples of political theology—the set of ideas that a religious actor holds about what is legitimate political authority.[5] Who possesses such authority? A king? A sultan? The people ruling through a constitution? To what degree and in what manner ought the state to promote faith? What does justice consist of? What is the right relationship between religious authorities and the state? What are the obligations of religious believers toward the political order? All of these questions deal with issues of political theology.

To say that political theology matters is to say that a religious actor's political stance is traceable, at least in part, to this set of ideas. Motivated by these notions, religious actors have undertaken to support, oppose, persuade, protest, rebel against, and sometimes pay very little attention to, political rulers. Religious actors arrive at their political theologies through reflection upon their religion's texts and traditions and its foundational claims about divine being(s), time, eternity, salvation, morality, and revelation. Contemporary circumstances, however, matter as well. In any particular context, political theology translates basic theological claims, beliefs and doctrines into political ideals and programs.

For instance, the early- and mid-twentieth-century Islamic intellectuals who called for religious revival desired to see a political order governed by a form of *sharia*—a word meaning "way" or "path" and denoting Islamic law—that they thought was consistent with the true message of Islam. Their ideas inspired an "Islamic resurgence" that gained political influence in the 1970s. In the 1950s, the Buddhist *sangha* of Sri Lanka argued that only a state-supported Buddhist homeland could embody the original meaning of Buddhism. This political form of Buddhism was a way of thinking that arose in the nineteenth century under British colonialism and in dialogue with American theosophists (practitioners of a late-nineteenth-century philosophical movement combining various religions to identify an underlying, universal harmony), continued to develop during the first half of the twentieth century, and sprung into action after Sri Lanka (then known as Ceylon) gained its independence in 1948. In developing the doctrine of religious freedom in the document *Dignitatis Humanae* at the Second Vatican Council, the Catholic

Church was influenced both by a renewed reflection on natural law and the New Testament and by its dialogue with the modern world. In the modern context, liberal democracies had become the best protectors of faith while Communist regimes and other forms of dictatorship had become its strongest adversaries.

Political theology can be arcane and scholarly. It is the stuff of medieval philosophers Thomas Aquinas and Moses Maimonides, who wrote from the Christian and Jewish standpoints, respectively. It can also be simple and popular, held by ordinary citizens and religious believers—for instance, the partly religious, partly political convictions of most Americans "that all men are created equal, that they are endowed by their Creator with certain unalienable Rights," in the words of the Declaration of Independence; that no single church should be nationally established; and that every citizen is entitled to religious freedom. Political theology sometimes begins with intellectuals and then migrates to the popular level, much as Al Qaeda's political theology, now held by a network of militants, descends from the writings of al-Banna, Maududi, and Qutb. Other times it grows up organically from experience and is later diagrammed by intellectuals. In seventeenth-century Europe, for instance, religious intellectuals began to articulate theologically rooted doctrines of religious tolerance in response to the overwhelming revulsion widely felt across the continent following a century and a half of bloody, convulsive war between Catholics and Protestants.

Some aspects of a political theology might be shared widely within a religion, while others may be held only by particular communities or factions. Muslims widely maintain that political authority should meet the standards of *sharia* but differ radically over its content. Mennonites and Methodists read the same Bible yet disagree over whether the state corrupts or promotes the common good.

Political theology also evolves. It is influenced by ancient, formative teachings, but also by historical development and evolving circumstances. The rise of Engaged Buddhism throughout Asia over the past half-century, for instance, has transformed at least some sectors of Buddhism from otherworldly political passivity to activism on issues such as human rights, democracy, and environmental protection. The fathers of the Christian Church during its first three centuries widely held a pacifist stance until, in the fourth and fifth centuries, St. Ambrose and St. Augustine developed a just-war doctrine that would dominate subsequent teachings on the matter in the Catholic Church and most Protestant denominations.

Likewise, one of the major themes in Islamic thought during the twentieth century has been the "opening of the gates of *ijtihad*," or the interpretation of holy texts by scholars, which had been closed in the twelfth century. The result was the development of new strains of political thought regarding how Islam should relate to the modern world. One strain was radical revivalist doctrines that called for concerted action to create cultures and regimes that promote Islamic law and morality. Another strain incorporated human rights, democracy, and progressive roles for women into the Islamic tradition.

Through disputes and developments over the course of history—in which partisans argue out of convictions about what they believe to be steady and eternal—political theology continually arrives at new syntheses and consensuses. Religious actors are both constrained by, and agents of, theological reinterpretation. This is true of the reinterpretation of theology in general and political theology in particular. The interaction of religious actors and political theology is indeed a major theme in the story of the past generation's religious resurgence. All over the globe, religious actors in all of the major traditions came to adopt doctrines that prescribed active engagement in political affairs, whether they were Catholic champions of liberation theology, who advocated justice for the poor in Latin America in the 1960s and 1970s, students in Egypt who joined the Muslim Brotherhood and began to agitate for political change in the 1970s, or the Religious Right in America, which also became organized in the 1970s.

To claim that political theology reflects the political activities that religious actors undertake is to claim that religious belief is powerful, autonomous, and not simply the by-product of nonreligious factors. Ideas shape politics. A religious actor is more likely to engage in certain forms of political activity (to lead or join a movement for democracy, for instance) the stronger it holds doctrines that favor those activities (a political theology that prescribes liberal democracy, for instance). It is important to understand that religious actors often arrive at their ideas before they undertake political activities and that these ideas, in turn, lead them to undertake these activities. Consider how ideas operate in three examples.

First, those national Catholic churches that challenged autocratic regimes in the 1970s and 1980s—in Poland, Brazil, and the Philippines, for example—did so only after first accepting and then acting on the teachings on human rights, politics, and religious freedom that the central Catholic Church in Rome promulgated in the Second Vatican Council of the mid-1960s.

Second, in the American colonies during the seventeenth and eighteenth centuries, for instance, Protestants like Isaac Backus and Roger Williams became convinced on theological grounds that political authorities ought to respect religious freedom, the right of every individual to adopt and practice his or her own religious beliefs. Their convictions derived in part from the stress on individual decision that arose from their Protestantism but also from their close reading of certain passages in the New Testament, such as Jesus' parable of the wheat and the tares, which suggests that believers and unbelievers should be allowed to coexist until God's final judgment (Matthew 13:24–30; 36–43).

The third example comes from Iran and Shiite Islam. In the 1960s and 1970s, Shiite clerics such as Ayatollah Ruhollah Khomeini and lay intellectuals such as Ali Shariati challenged the passivity of traditional Shiite teaching about politics and argued instead that it was a religious duty to overthrow unjust states and establish "Islamic government" in their place.[6] These clerics and intellectuals, along with scores of their students, then put this new interpretation into practice by overthrowing the Shah of Iran and establishing an Islamic republic. In the case of a group religious actor rather than an individual, political theology will shape its activities more strongly the more of its members hold it, the more strongly these members hold it, and the more that its top leaders, not just its rank and file, hold it.

Political theologies that are not liberal and democratic tend to favor a different sort of regime—a caliphate, a state that promotes religious law at the expense of religious freedom, or a state where the authority of state rulers and clerics are closely woven. Under the strong influence of Salafi Islam, a politically charged form of revivalism we explore further in Chapter Five, the government of Saudi Arabia mandates that all citizens be Muslims, prohibits the public practice of non-Muslim religions, and enforces Islamic morality through its Mutawwa'in, or religious police. In sharp contrast to Backus and Williams, this political theology stresses adherence to Islam on the part of the community and far less on the part of the individual.

Finally, a political theology may also simply be "regime neutral," in which case it is indifferent to the form a polity takes so long as the government supports, or at least does not impinge upon, the practice of the religious community. The Orthodox Church of Greece, for instance, adapted equally well to dictatorship and democracy during the 1960s and 1970s. Protestant evangelicals in Latin America, Africa, and Asia have been willing to live with a wide variety of regimes in the past generation. By contrast, religious actors that fight civil wars and support terrorism often hold a political theology that calls for a regime that strongly, overtly, and pervasively promotes the prerogatives and teachings of their religion even at the expense of other religions within the state's borders. In these and other respects, religious beliefs lie behind political behavior.

Political authorities also hold ideas that affect the atmosphere in which religious actors pursue their politics. These might include political theologies, which are derived from religious claims and events, but also take the form of ideologies, doctrines, and philosophies that have sources other than religion. On the basis of these ideas, political authorities have encouraged, buttressed, suppressed, or even sought to eradicate religious communities and their members. The ruling doctrines of the modern state have most often been secular ones, especially up through the 1960s. One form of secularism is relatively friendly to religion, holding that religion ought to be protected but not privileged through law. This form of secularism is found in the United States. Another form holds that the state ought to limit and regulate religion sharply, and has been embodied in the French Revolution and in parties carrying out its ideals in Europe and Latin America, as well as in the Republic of Turkey (founded by Kemal Ataturk in 1923), and its many Arab nationalist imitators. A stronger form of secularism seeks to eradicate religion or only to permit its frail shell, a form found in Communist regimes in the former Soviet Union, Mao's China, Bulgaria, Cuba, Romania, and many other countries. Though states only sometimes rule directly on the basis of religious ideas, they almost inevitably embody and promote ideas with strong implications for the fate of religious actors.

THE RELATIONSHIP OF RELIGIOUS AUTHORITY AND POLITICAL AUTHORITY

Over the centuries, in diverse corners of the world, religious authorities have adopted a wide variety of postures toward the kings, emperors, sultans, presidents, and constitutions under which they have lived. One stance is that of the martyr, who is willing to die rather than accept the state's direction of his or her conduct. Among those who are considered martyrs—at least by sympathetic members of their own religious communities—are the early Christians who died in the claws of the Roman emperor's lions; Thomas More, whom English King Henry VIII beheaded for his loyalty to the pope; and Sayyid Qutb, executed in 1966. A response to political authority very different from that of the martyr is that of German liberal Protestant theologian Adolf von Harnack, who wrote speeches for Kaiser Wilhelm defending Germany's attack on Belgium and its initiation of World War I in 1914. His position was almost indistinguishable from that of the state. Still a different response to political authority can be found in close partnerships between religion and state, ranging from theocratic Iran, where religious authorities vet presidents and members of Parliament; to Sri Lanka, where the *sangha* works closely with the state to promote a Buddhist homeland; to colonial Latin America, where Catholic prelates and colonial governments buttressed one another's authority in a "throne and altar" relationship; and to contemporary Russia, where the president and the Orthodox Church collaborate closely, even restricting the religious freedom of rival sects.

Different still are modern constitutional democracies in Europe, North America, South America, and parts of Asia and Africa, whose laws provide for a far greater separation of religion and state. But even these vary a great deal. The United Kingdom and most Scandinavian states each have established churches, ones that the state proclaims as official for the realm. Establishment usually means that the state exercises significant governance of the established religion. For instance, the British prime minister (in consultation with an appointments commission) appoints the Archbishop of Canterbury, the head of the Church of England. But it also means that the established religion holds certain political privileges. Several bishops in the Church of England hold permanent seats in the House of Lords. But unlike nondemocracies that establish official religion, these same countries also provide religious freedom. In contrast, the United States Constitution both precludes a nationally established church and institutes religious freedom.

The Importance of Independence

One of the crucial respects in which all of these examples differ is in the distance that religious actors and political authorities keep from each other. Does one dominate the other? Are they close partners? Or does each respect the other's separate sphere? The fact is, they are *independent* of each other to greater and lesser degrees. They also differ in the attitudes that religious and political authorities hold toward the degree of independence that they practice. Specifically, are they both satisfied with the status quo, or does at least one of them consider it illegitimate and desire to change it? The independence of religious and political authority is the second major factor that explains the kind of politics that religious actors adopt.[7]

Western philosophers, theologians, and jurists at least as far back as the Protestant Reformation have long considered the independence of religious and political authority to be a boon for both politics and religion. Protestants as well as many Catholics with soft loyalties to the pope celebrated the Peace of Westphalia of 1648, which, as we will argue in Chapter Three, was not only the founding moment of modern international relations but also a crucial moment in the history of religion's relationship to political authority. Due to Westphalia, the power of the transnational Catholic Church to assert temporal prerogatives over and against sovereign states was quelled. It was no wonder that Pope Innocent X condemned the Peace as "null, void, invalid, iniquitous, unjust, damnable, reprobate, inane, and empty of meaning and effect for all time."[8]

The independence of religion and state took an important step forward in the framing of the United States Constitution, the First Amendment of which made it the first legal document in the world both to enshrine religious freedom and to prohibit a nationally established church. In the 1800s, the independence of religion and state featured prominently in the writings of German philosopher G. W. F. Hegel and of Alexis de Tocqueville. In the early twentieth century, sociologists took up the concept as well. A classic example is Ernst Troeltsch, who, in *The Social Teaching of the Christian Churches*, argued that the separation of religion, society, and state characterizes modernity and was an arrangement by which churches could flourish and even influence politics and society.[9] Then, like Troeltsch, sociologists of the 1950s and 1960s also identified such separation—which they often called "differentiation"— as a feature of the modern world. But, in an important move, these scholars concluded far more pessimistically that distance meant decline. They saw it as part and parcel of the inevitable retreat and eventual extinction of religion in the face of science, enlightenment, bureaucratic rationality, pluralism, individual freedom, and the modern state.[10] What they propounded was the secularization thesis.

As the previous chapter showed, there are strong reasons to doubt the secularization thesis, especially in the realm of politics. While the independence of politics and religion may well be a feature of the modern world, it does not inevitably spell the decline of religion. Far from being a way station to annihilation, independence can be a haven in which religion can both flourish and influence politics. The United States and India illustrate this thesis best. Both have constitutions that strongly support religious freedom. Neither has an established religion, although India supports religion more directly than does the United States, even recognizing the authority of religious family law. But in both countries, an atmosphere in which religion and politics are independent in their authority coexists not only with the flourishing of religion but also with the active influence of religion on politics. In the case of the United States, conservative Protestants, Jewish groups, the Catholic Church, Mormons, and other religious people all powerfully influence politics through persuading voters and lobbying elected officials. As sociologist José Casanova influentially phrased it, religion can be public—engaged, influential, and involved in the political sphere—even in the modern world.[11] Independence, then, manifests both modernity and secularization but not necessarily the decline of religion.

But what exactly does it mean for religious and political authority to be independent? There are at least six dimensions in which religion and state might either keep a distance from each other's authority, respecting it and refraining from interfering with it, or become meshed with the other's authority, curtailing it or even collaborating with it. When independence is low, we can say that religious authority and political authority are "integrated"—a term that we will use repeatedly throughout this book. Today, virtually every state has at least some degree of distinction between religious and political authority; nowhere are they entirely unified. But states differ a great deal in the amount of independence of the two forms of authority.

Perhaps the most direct and obvious form of institutional enmeshment is a state constitution that grants monopoly or primacy to a particular religion. Pakistan's 1956 constitution, for instance, declares it to be an Islamic republic, affirming divine sovereignty and allowing no law "repugnant to Islam." In northern Europe, as mentioned earlier, several contemporary liberal democracies still maintain established churches. Other European states such as Germany and Spain grant strong financial and legal support to particular religious actors. Even France, one of the most notoriously "secular" states in Europe, provides funding to religious schools.

A second dimension of independence is the willingness of states to allow religious actors within their realm the freedom to carry out their activities, including worship, religious education, and public manifestations of belief. Certain classes of states deny religions this dimension of independence as a matter of principle. In their efforts to reshape human nature in their own image, Communist states repressed religion severely. The Soviet Union, for instance, destroyed both Christian churches and Islamic mosques throughout its territory and sought to replace religion with massive public works projects in celebration of the new Soviet individual. Post–World War II Arab nationalist regimes have typically banned a broad swath of Islamic organizations, permitting—and sometimes allying with—only those that strictly adhere to their policies and ruling ideology. Other considerations include whether the state gives minority religions the right to engage in missionary activity, or whether individuals enjoy the freedom to convert to such religions. Muslim states like Iran, Pakistan, and Saudi Arabia restrict these activities sharply. Do states allow religious education? The Polish Catholic Church's ability to maintain schools, camps, and other programs for children was an important source of its ability to resist Communism publicly and politically. In other countries, the state promotes religious education by financing it or even requiring it. Do states allow religious organizations to play a role in civil society through activities such as running hospitals, orphanages, and homes for the elderly, and providing services for the poor? Active support for the poor and the dispossessed is a means by which transnational Islamic organizations such as Jamaat-e-Islami and the Muslim Brotherhood maintain their independence and social power, for instance. Finally, do states allow religions to express themselves culturally, through dress, arts, and the media? Kemal Ataturk, founder of the Republic of Turkey in 1923, sought to modernize his country by thoroughly restricting the cultural expression of Islam. Still today, Turkey's Ministry of Religious Affairs regulates religious education, practice, observance, dress, and even distinctly religious matters like the content of Friday sermons in mosques and the editing of the *hadith*, key Islamic texts. The current French state's restrictions on Muslim girls wearing head scarves is analogous. In the 1870s, unified Germany's first chancellor, Otto von Bismarck, waged a *Kulturkampf* (or "cultural struggle") to curtail the influence of the Catholic Church over German culture. He arrested priests and bishops, closed monasteries and convents, and confiscated church property. In some integrated settings, the state might also regulate a certain religion's practices of marriage and burial.

Independence can be furthered or inhibited in other crucial respects. A third one is the freedom of a religious actor to determine its offices and leadership. Since the sixteenth century, both Protestant and Catholic churches have struggled to limit the power of kings and other heads of state to control their bishops or other top leaders. By the middle of the seventeenth century, most Protestant churches in England, Germany, and Scandinavia were strongly governed by their national king in an arrangement known as "Erastianism," while the Catholic Church in France was ever more controlled by its own king in a similar arrangement known as "Gallicanism." The achievement of significant freedom for churches to choose their own leadership had to await a future era. A state's control over the leadership of religious bodies is an important dimension of what we call integration in relationships between religious and political authority. Communist regimes during the Cold War, for instance, exercised a virtual veto over the leadership of Orthodox Churches in Russia and Eastern Europe, the Protestant Church in East Germany, and the Catholic Church in Hungary and Czechoslovakia.

A fourth dimension of religious freedom runs opposite the third. It is the degree to which religious officials hold standing prerogatives in the leadership of a polity. Rare today is the sort of integrated relationship in which religions enjoy a strong degree of such authority. It does exist, however—for example, in Iran, where a clerical Council of Guardians can veto legislation and vet candidates for Parliament, while a clerical Council of Experts chooses the supreme leader, the most powerful authority in the country.

State authority over religious finances is a fifth dimension of independence. A state that controls what money goes to a religious body will inevitably have a say in that body's activities. Such control can be suppressive, as it has been under Communist regimes. But it can also be collaborative. The Sri Lankan state, for instance, continues to finance the Buddhist *sangha*. Under conditions of strong independence, by contrast, the state neither restricts nor raises money for religious bodies. The United States approximates a model of such severance, although even it grants tax-exempt status to religious organizations, an indirect form of subsidy. Finally, financial authority can be contested. In sixteenth-, seventeenth-, and eighteenth-century France, monarch and church fought over the Church's rights to raise taxes and tithes, a battle in which the monarch increasingly gained the upper hand.

A sixth and final dimension of independence is a religious body's own transnational structure. The more a religious actor collaborates with its members and leaders outside its state's borders—in its appointments, policies, finances, education, and activities—the more independent it will be from its state's institutions. These relationships can in fact be a great source of power in the face of state suppression, equipping the religious community with allies and sources of support over and against its state. As we shall see in Chapter Four, in the "Third Wave" of democratization some national Catholic churches were empowered to oppose dictators in part by the outside support they received from the Vatican. Figure 2.1 summarizes the six dimensions of independence.

Together, these six dimensions are the defining building blocks of the "independence of religious and political authority." This concept partially

Figure 2.1

INSTITUTIONAL INDEPENDENCE OF RELIGIOUS AND POLITICAL AUTHORITY

Religious authority possesses institutional independence from political authority, and lacks institutional integration with it, to the extent that . . .

1. No single religious community enjoys primacy or a monopoly with respect to government endorsement, support, or privilege.

2. Religious actors within a state (some or all) enjoy the freedom to carry out their most distinctive activities—worship and other rituals, education, and public expression, the building of places of worship, missionary work, artistic expression, cultural expression and distinctive dress, and the conduct of civil society activities, including running hospitals, orphanages, services for the poor, and care for elders.

3. Religious actors enjoy the autonomy to create their offices and appoint their leadership.

4. Religious actors lack any standing prerogatives over the appointment of state officials or the making of public policy.

5. Religious actors enjoy autonomy in raising, governing, and spending finances.

6. Religious actors enjoy a transnational structure that strengthens their power vis-à-vis the state.

overlaps with but should not be confused with other familiar concepts such as establishment, in which one faith is declared the state religion. Certainly, the presence or absence of establishment is an aspect of independence. All else being equal, a state without an established church is one where religion and state are more independent (e.g., as in the United States). Yet, even established religions can vary greatly in the range and substance of powers that their established status confers. Established by state authorities in the nineteenth century, national churches in Finland, Iceland, and Norway retain a good deal of social standing and independence, despite the fact that most citizens do not attend church. This is due in part to the political support the churches showed for their countries' independence movements in the early twentieth century (Sweden abolished its established church in 1999.)[12] The Church of England, which also remains established today, derives far fewer powers from this privilege than it did four centuries ago, or than Islamic clerics do in Sudan, for instance. The establishment of religion can also be compatible with independence in other dimensions, such as a religion's autonomy or finances. Equally, disestablishment might accompany a lack of independence in other dimensions. It could be part and parcel of a regime's efforts to suppress religion altogether.

Religious freedom—the right of individuals and religious groups to practice their faith without interference—is another aspect of independence. Religious freedom may coexist with other respects in which state and religion are integrated. Vietnamese Catholics, for instance, enjoy broad freedom of public worship, but the Vietnamese Catholic Church is burdened by the state's significant control of its hierarchy. Religious freedom may even coexist with established churches, as it does in Denmark, Finland, Iceland, Norway, and the United Kingdom. In the United Kingdom, the Church of England is established in England but not in Scotland, Northern Ireland, or most of Wales, while in the entire state, Methodists and Muslims can worship freely.

Above all, the independence of religious and political authority should not be confused with the influence of religion on politics or with contact between religion and state. Religion might well be independent from the state in its basic authority yet affect the debates and policies of the state to a great extent. Again, the United States illustrates this paradox. It is simultaneously the state where religious authority is arguably the most independent in the world and the state whose religious actors are some of the most politically influential.

The independence of religious authority and political authority is difficult to measure precisely. Political and religious authority can be independent in some respects but not others and to different degrees for different religious communities within the same state. The Israeli government, for instance, grants Jews many important legal prerogatives that Muslims and Christians do not receive even though Muslims and Christians remain free to worship and practice their faiths. Neither independence nor its opposite, integration, is ever realized completely or perfectly. Still, relative to one another, relationships between religious and political authority can be judged to be independent to greater and lesser degrees. Political scientist Jonathan Fox and sociologists Brian J. Grim and Roger Finke have done a great service to scholars of religion and state by developing precise and thorough quantitative indices of assessing religion and state independence. Based on these indices, Fox finds that the United States possesses the least amount of "government involvement in religion" in the world. As might be expected, democracies show less government involvement in religion than nondemocracies. More surprising is the wide range of such involvement among democracies, those with the highest levels being Finland, Greece, and Israel.[13]

Types of Independence

The independence of religious and political authority can vary not only in degree, but also in kind: Is it consensual or conflictual? A consensual relationship is one that both religious actor and state regard as legitimate; each party is happy with the status quo. A conflictual relationship is one that at least one party wants to revamp; any consent it gives is either prudential and provisional or elicited by the other party's coercion. Independence and integration can each be either consensual or conflictual, resulting in the matrix of four types depicted in Figure 2.2.

Independence is high and consensual—Quadrant I of Figure 2.2—when religion and state enjoy autonomy from each other and are mutually content with this autonomy. A liberal democratic constitution that institutionalizes freedom of religion and disestablishment fits this category quintessentially. Most contemporary states in Europe, Latin America, North America, Australia, and New Zealand can be found here. It is also possible, but less common, for an authoritarian state to allow a religion its autonomy with the approval of both regime and religion. A few Latin American states of the mid-twentieth century fit this description, though only with respect to the Catholic Church and not to Protestant churches, which they restricted. Within this quadrant, as is true for all of the quadrants, there are varying levels of independence. Though virtually all liberal democracies fit within this quadrant, for instance, they differ significantly among themselves in their levels of independence.

Independence is high and conflictual—Quadrant II of Figure 2.2—when a religious community achieves significant autonomy but only through its firm resistance to a state that is determined to suppress it. It enjoys no legal or constitutional guarantee of its freedom. The Islamic party in Turkey has

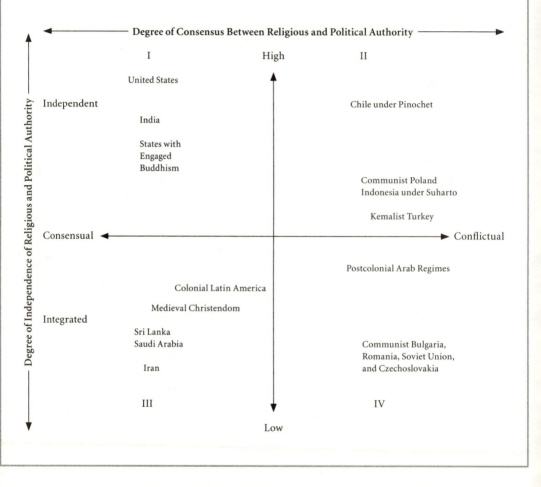

Figure 2.2

RELATIONSHIPS BETWEEN RELIGIOUS
AND POLITICAL AUTHORITY

Degree of Consensus Between Religious and Political Authority

Degree of Independence of Religious and Political Authority

I   High   II

United States

Independent   Chile under Pinochet

India

States with
Engaged
Buddhism
                                Communist Poland
                                Indonesia under Suharto

                                Kemalist Turkey

Consensual ←————————————————————→ Conflictual

                        Postcolonial Arab Regimes

            Colonial Latin America

        Medieval Christendom

Integrated
        Sri Lanka
        Saudi Arabia   Communist Bulgaria,
                                    Romania, Soviet Union,
        Iran   and Czechoslovakia

        III   IV

                Low

long fit this description. Despite the efforts of the secular Turkish state to sup-press it, including attempts to deprive it of electoral victories through regular military coups, the party has managed to survive. In part, the Islamic move-ment has done so by reinventing itself under new names: the Virtue Party, the Welfare Party, and now the Justice and Development Party. The latter incar-nation of the party has now held the dominant position in a coalition government, including the prime minster's office, from 2002 to the time of writing, although it still battles for its full legal rights to participate and continues to live under the constant threat of yet another military coup orchestrated by Turkey's secularist regime. Islamic movements under the dictatorship of Suharto in Indonesia (1967–1998) also experienced a conflictually independent relationship with the state. Virtually the only civil society movements that retained some independence under this regime, these movements were eventually able to become major players in the toppling of Suharto's dictatorship and the onset of democracy in the late 1990s.

Where the independence of religious and political authority is low, in some cases religious actors and the state will be content in their integration—Quadrant III of Figure 2.2. They enjoy a close relationship in which the state affords the dominant religious community extensive legal prerogatives, while the religious body legitimates the authority of the state. They might also engage in rivalry, but it is always over the terms of their integrated relationship. The struggles between the Catholic Church and various temporal rulers—the Holy Roman emperor, kings, and nobles—during the High Middle Ages in Europe (eleventh through fourteenth centuries) are a classic example. This was a time when the pope could adjudicate disputes and excommunicate kings and when bishops sat on the board of regents of their local king or noble. For their part, temporal rulers influenced the selection of bishops and enforced at least some of the Church's moral teachings through arms. Disputes would rage over the extent of each figure's authority and prerogatives but always within the context of an integrated relationship that both religious and political authorities regarded as generally legitimate. Colonial Latin American states, Spain and Portugal up through the 1970s, Iran, Saudi Arabia, and Sri Lanka also belong in this quadrant of consensually integrated relationships between religion and state.

Consensually integrated states (Quadrant III) reinforce the point that it is possible that two or more religious communities within a single state may practice very different kinds of relationships with the government. In Iran, for instance, Shiite Islamic leaders enjoy a consensually integrated relationship with the state while Bahá'ís are, to put it mildly, conflictually integrated (that is, suppressed). Likewise, in Sri Lanka the Buddhist *sangha* is consensually integrated with the state in a way that Hindu and Christian groups are not. In Russia, the Orthodox Church is consensually integrated while the Muslim minority is conflictually integrated. States like these are consensually integrated with reference to a dominant religious community. But it must not be forgotten that one or more weaker, often suppressed, religious communities exist in the same country.

The independence of religious and political authority can also be low and conflictual, as it is where states have dominated and altogether subordinated religious actors, depriving them of any meaningful autonomy. Though religious actors under such states may once have put up resistance, as did some martyrs in the Orthodox Church in the early days of the Soviet Union (1920s) or in the first years of the Cold War in Romania and Bulgaria (late 1940s), such dissent was quickly quashed. In these states, whatever freedom to practice their faith these religious actors came to enjoy was only what the regime would allow. Effectively, these regimes have "integrated" religion into their own authority. This represents Quadrant IV of Figure 2.2. The religion-state relationship in most Communist states fits this description as does the relationship between most modern nationalist Arab regimes and conservative Muslim groups within their borders—as in Iran under the Shah, as described in the previous chapter.

Relationships between religious authority and political authority rarely remain frozen in time; rather they change and evolve. This change might occur within a quadrant or across quadrants. After the collapse of the Soviet Union in 1991, for instance, Russia traveled from conflictual integration (the Soviet state's sharp control of religion) to the opposite corner, consensual independence (religious freedom for all), but then moved toward consensual integration as the government began to restrict the activities of non-Orthodox churches and Muslims in the mid-1990s. The longevity of the Justice and Development Party as the dominant coalition partner in the Turkish government from 2002 to the present represents a move from conflictual independence, in which the Islamic party was constantly struggling to exist, toward consensual independence, where it could operate and even govern. Still, the Turkish constitution's official secularism, the heavy degree to which the Ministry of Religious Affairs continues to regulate religion, and the military's ever-present threat of intervention keep Turkey out of the consensually independent quadrant. Turkey is still less than a robust liberal democracy, and, moreover, no stable consensus yet exists in Turkish society that religious actors should play an autonomous and influential role in its politics. These and other examples of changes in the relationship between religion and state are highlighted in Figure 2.3 below.

In subsequent chapters, we show that changes in the independence of reli-

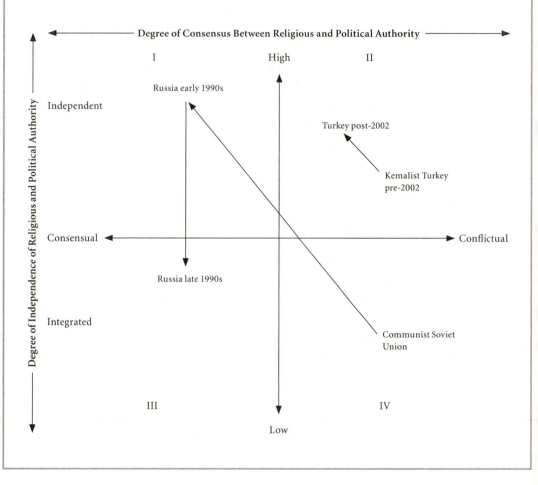

Figure 2.3

CHANGE IN RELATIONSHIPS BETWEEN RELIGIOUS
AND POLITICAL AUTHORITY

Degree of Consensus Between Religious and Political Authority

I   High   II

Russia early 1990s

Independent

Turkey post-2002

Kemalist Turkey
pre-2002

Consensual ◄—————————————————————► Conflictual

Russia late 1990s

Integrated

Communist Soviet
Union

Degree of Independence of Religious and Political Authority

III   IV

Low

gion and political authority as well as in political theology help to explain
the resurgence of religion's influence on politics over the past four decades.
One of the reasons that religious actors in both the developed and developing
worlds wield greater influence today than perhaps any time since the mid-
seventeenth century is that they also enjoy a far greater level of independence
from political authority in their self-governance and in their many pursuits
in society. They are free to think, speak, organize, and act more on the basis

of their own impulses, ideas, and interests and less on the basis of calculations about what the state will allow them to do. Many of the same features of modernization, democratization, and globalization that undermine the capacity of governments to act autonomously and effectively within their territories also enhance the capacity of religious organizations to act autonomously and effectively within and across national boundaries.

We aim to show, too, that the degree and kind of independence between religious and political authority help to explain what kind of politics a religious actor adopts. The most ardent and effective promoters of democracy are those in Quadrant II, the region of conflictual independence. Having eked out and defended a protected area of independence from an authoritarian regime that wants to suppress them, they seek a regime whose laws guarantee the practice of their faith—a regime that inhabits Quadrant I, consensual independence. Religious actors in Quadrant IV—conflictual integration—might also desire such freedom but are too suppressed to fight for it. In Quadrant III, religions that enjoy a consensually integrated relationship with their state are less likely to desire religious freedom because they are cozily supported by the state.

Along with the most effective agents of democratization, those religious actors who are most likely to mediate a peace agreement or to influence political choices for dealing with past injustices are found in Quadrants I and II, the region of consensual or conflictual independence. It is their ability to keep a distance from the government during a civil war or an authoritarian regime that empowers them and gives them the popular credibility to influence a peace process or a regime transition.

Civil wars and terrorism, by contrast, are likely to arise from the kind of religion-state relationship that exists in Quadrant III if, within the same country where one religion is integrated with the government, religious minorities or dissenters are shut out from consensual integration and marginalized. A major cause of the second civil war in Sudan in the 1980s and 1990s, for instance, was the Islamist regime's harsh version of *sharia* law and the resistance that it sparked among non-Muslim minorities in the south, including both Christians and animists. A similar story can be told about the civil war in Sri Lanka, where the push by some members of the Sinhalese majority for a state-imposed Buddhist homeland became an important cause of conflict with the mostly Hindu Tamil minority. In this dynamic, conflict arises between the alliance of the state and the dominant religious actor and the minority religious actor that has been sidelined and repressed.

POLITICAL THEOLOGY AND
INDEPENDENCE TOGETHER

Political theology shapes and is shaped by a religious actor's activities. These might include agitating against a dictatorship for a democratic regime; turning to violence to establish a state in which religion and state are integrated; advocating for a truth and reconciliation commission; pursuing terrorism; or engaging in any of the many activities through which religious communities and their leaders try to shape politics all over the world. The independence of religious authority and political authority then acts as a constraint or an enabler, determining how free a religious actor is to pursue its ends and what sort of incentives it faces. Together, then, political theology and the relationship between religion and state yield the diverse political pursuits of religious actors that subsequent chapters explore.

One might wonder, though: If political theology and the independence of religion and state shape the character of a religious actor's politics, then what shapes political theology and independence? By what historical processes do they come about? Every religious community's ideas and its relationship to political authority are shaped by the events and ideas of the community's founding, and then by centuries of schism, diaspora, growth, decline, conquest, subjection to conquest, persecution, migration, growth in institutional power, and the spread, rise, and ebb of membership. In the course of these trajectories, political theology and the independence of religious and political authority will evolve and even shape one another in complex ways. It is very difficult to generalize about these pathways. Our contention is only this: that given a certain political theology and a certain degree and kind of independence between religious authority and political authority, a religious actor will tend to adopt a certain kind of politics.

It is also important to clarify that political theology and independence are not the only shapers of the political activity of religious actors. Factors extrinsic to their religious character also matter, including their economic and demographic profile and the stability of the regime under which they live. Other factors that are more closely linked to their religious character besides political theology and independence also shape their pursuits. An example is the commitment level of a religious community's members— their reported beliefs, frequency of prayer, worship, other rituals, and other activities. Christian churches in South Africa, for instance, gained great strength in their struggle against apartheid from their members' religiosity.

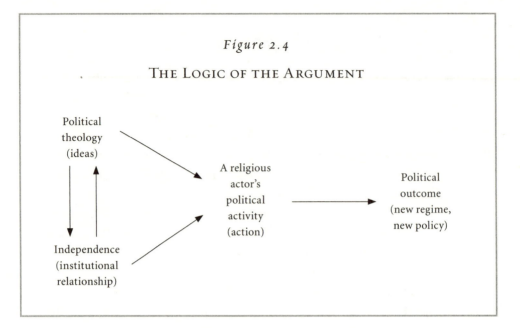

Figure 2.4

THE LOGIC OF THE ARGUMENT

The size of a religious actor and the structure of its organization will matter, too. Denominationally independent Protestant churches in Africa and Latin America rival mainline churches (Catholic, Anglican, and Presbyterian) in terms of numbers of believers, but they have been comparatively weak in promoting democracy and equal rights because of their less developed and more decentralized organizational structures. The Islamic movement in Turkey gains great strength from being organized into a political party. The quality of a religious actor's leadership will also make a significant difference. Bishop Desmond Tutu, Osama bin Laden, and the Dalai Lama have each strongly influenced the respective fates of South Africa's Truth and Reconciliation Commission, Al Qaeda, and Tibet.

A more complex influence is the relationship of a religious actor to a state's national identity. If a democratizing religious actor can align itself with the nation and portray its authoritarian regime as being at odds with the nation, then it will be empowered in its opposition. The Polish Catholic Church, integral to the identity of a Polish nation that survived when the Polish state was serially partitioned and conquered between 1795 and 1918, is just such an example. Similarly, a religious actor that opposes democracy can align itself with the national identity in favor of authoritarianism or against democratization. Prime examples can be found in the strategy of the Buddhist *sangha* of Sri Lanka and Hindu-nationalist organizations in India, as well as in the churches that rallied in support of extremist and violent forms of nationalism in the former Yugoslavia in the 1990s.

We will seek to highlight these other factors, both extrinsic and closely related to the distinct character of religious actors, where they are relevant. We also note that a religious actor's political activities are only one determinant of political events such as transitions from authoritarianism to democracy, civil wars, terrorism, the mediation of wars, and approaches to transitional justice. Clearly, many factors besides religion are influential—international and domestic, political, economic, cultural, ideological, and demographic. In politics, religion matters but is far from all that matters. Figure 2.4 illustrates the logic of the arguments in this book. The key outcome that we seek to explain is the one that appears in the middle of the chart—the political actions of religious actors. We argue that these are shaped by political theology and by the independence of religious actors in relation to the state, but also by other factors. In turn, the actions of religious actors are only one influence upon political outcomes.

The concepts developed over the course of this chapter are the basic building blocks of the arguments that follow. The dramatis personae will continuously enter and exit the stage. Most important, we argue that the interaction of these two key variables—political theology and the degree of independence between religious actors and political authority—offer the strongest general explanation of why religious actors act as they do: supporting or resisting democracy, terrorism, civil war, peacemaking, and the like. In the next chapter, we will see also how political theology and the independence of religious and political authority can help us to understand the dramatic history of religion in global politics—a history of increasing domination at the hands of the state from the Middle Ages up though the middle of the twentieth century, and then of a sharp political resurgence from then to today.

Chapter Three

THE RISE OF POLITICALLY ASSERTIVE RELIGION

SOME PEOPLE ARGUE THAT THE SALIENT FACT ABOUT RELI-
gion in the modern world is that it is "reviving" or staging a "comeback."
Citing the kinds of trends we noted in our introduction—religion's surging
influence in countries as diverse as the United States and Indonesia—they
argue that we are witnessing a global "resurgence" of piety and spirituality.
"God is back," *Economist* editors John Micklethwait and Adrian Wooldridge
elegantly put it. Despite more than one near-death experience, God not only
survives but thrives.

Others contend that religion continues to decline precipitously. They con-
cede that religion shows plenty of fight in some locales—lots of activism and
in some cases fanaticism. Those with this point of view, though, suggest that
religion's very activism and ferocity are signs of weakness, not revival. Terrorism represents a weapon of the weak, they claim, employed by fundamentalists overwhelmed by modernization who have no other means of resistance at
their disposal. Stubbornly, they insist that the ongoing onslaught of modernity means that God is as good as "dead."[1]

The purpose of this chapter is to clarify where we stand on this key question: What is the position of religion in today's world? More specifically, what
is religion's *direction* or *trajectory*? Is it one of revival? Or is it one of decline?

This is a crucial issue. If the "declinists" are right, you might as well throw
this book in the trash. Religion does not require your attention if it is on the
verge of dying. At most, its violent rigor mortis makes it a temporary and
occasionally destructive nuisance, not a subject for systematic inquiry.

If the "revivalists" are right, on the other hand, the situation is more complicated. They claim we are witnessing a global religious "revival," "resurgence," or even "revolution." Much of what we ourselves have been saying so far suggests that our sympathies lie more with this camp than with the "declinists." However, even if the "revivalists" are right and religion really is on an upswing, the claim of a global spiritual revival in itself says nothing about whether religion is surging in its *global political influence.*

But this is a book about global politics, written first and foremost for people interested in understanding the world's present and future political dynamics. Global trends in religious belief, behavior, and belonging—however important and interesting for understanding global society and culture—do not necessarily translate into noteworthy political trends or political outcomes. Compared to some other points in the recent past, more people may be praying in private, reading holy books, attending religious services, participating in Friday prayers, and wearing religious garments. Some religious movements, such as Pentecostalism, have probably experienced dramatic global growth in the last hundred years. Pentecostalism, in fact, is a movement that has gone from essentially zero adherents in 1900 to hundreds of millions of followers across the world today. There may be as many as forty times more Christians in sub-Saharan Africa today than in 1900. But about all these trends the State Department, Defense Department, and members of the U.S. National Security Council will ask: So what?

In this chapter, we tackle the "So what?" question head-on. We do not simply argue—like the "revivalists"—that religious dynamism has increased in recent decades. We cite some evidence of a general religious revival, but cite it only as a propellant of religion's political comeback. Instead, the focus of our argument is that major religious actors throughout the world enjoy *greater capacity for political influence* today than at any time in modern history—and perhaps ever.

Using the concepts we introduced in the last chapter, we present a historical narrative that has some points of agreement with the "revivalist" and "declinist" narratives of global religion but in the end tells a distinct story. Our narrative demonstrates that in the course of history major religious actors have experienced two kinds of shifts that have won them greater political power.

First, religious actors have come to enjoy greater *institutional independence* from political authorities. In the process of becoming less enmeshed in the structures of the state, many Buddhist, Christian, Hindu, Jewish, and Muslim actors have also won greater leverage over the state.

Second, many religious actors have exchanged relatively passive political theologies for *activist and engaged political theologies*. Rather than simply deferring to the "powers that be," religious actors have adopted political theologies that prescribe a divine obligation to be "prophetic"—that is, to mold politics and where necessary challenge political authorities to do God's will.

In other words, religious actors have experienced a shift in their proximity to political power and a shift in their theology of political power. The combined effect of these shifts, we argue, has been to enhance their political influence. Whether a spiritual "revival" is sweeping the world is hard to say. A more compelling and relevant claim is this: that religious actors have become increasingly able to wield political power within states as well as across states' borders.

BEFORE MODERNITY: THE FRIENDLY MERGER OF RELIGIOUS AND POLITICAL AUTHORITY

The history of religion's encounter with the state begins well before 1500. Consider here just a few examples.

+ The classical political system that existed in most Theravada Buddhist societies was organized with "the royal palace occupying the center of the realm." The palace was identified with Mount Meru, the center of the universe in Buddhist cosmology. In this political theology, the king, court, and government enact "cosmic roles."[2] Indeed, the monarch was considered a Bodhisattva, a future Buddha.[3] At the same time, there developed "an important symbolic bond between king and monk."[4] While there are stark contrasts between monk and king, "each definitely needs the other to be seen in the full splendor of his cultural role."[5] The order of monks, the *sangha*, in some ways "constituted a check on the king's power in the traditional Buddhist state."[6] At the same time, it was the duty of the king to support the *sangha* through the donation of land and the construction of monasteries and pagodas as well as to regulate the *sangha* through the adjudication of internal disputes and the punishment of wayward monks.[7]

+ When Mohammed and his followers established a distinct society in Medina in 622, one of its striking features was its unity: Mohammed was ruler and prophet, king and priest. Upon Mohammed's death, a "successor" or *khalifah* (caliph) was chosen, who exercised similar unitary authority. But "within the first century after Mohammed there was a growing cleavage between the religious and secular institutions. . . ."[8] The demise of the caliphate in 1258 due to the Mongol conquest of Baghdad caused Muslim political theorists to assign the religious scholars, or *ulema* (sometimes *ulama*), "an ever larger role in the government of Muslim communities as advisers and counselors to reigning princes." Sunni political theory "shifted slowly to deemphasize the Caliphate and to accept the reality of Sultan and scholar as the key figures in the Muslim political order."[9] Two mutually dependent sets of actors—the political figure of the sultan in consultation and cooperation with the *ulema*—became the essential underpinnings of Muslim society.

✦   In premodern India, the Laws of Manu declared that the king was a "great deity in human form."[10] The royal consecration ceremony (*rājasuya*) identified the king with Indra, the god of war, and even with Prajāpati, the Most High God. The king could lose his sacrosanct status, however, if he failed to safeguard the order of society as laid down in the sacred texts, including caste distinctions. "If [the king] infringed sacred custom too blatantly he incurred the hostility of the *brāhmans*, and often of the lower orders also." The Sanskrit epic, the *Mahābhārata*, authorized rebellion against any king who was tyrannical or failed to protect society's sacred structure. This was not mere theory. "More than one great dynasty, such as the Nandas, Mauryas and Sungas, fell as a result of *brāhmanic* intrigue."[11] The Brahmin, or priestly caste, stood at the top of the caste hierarchy, superior to the Kshatriya caste, which provided society's rulers. "By bowing three times before the Brahmin at his coronation, the king accepts his subordinate position, and his success depends on continued recognition of this fact." Still, Brahmins had no direct political authority. Even the royal chaplain or *purohita* was but one of the king's councilors.[12]

✦   Jesus embraced a transcendent authority while refusing earthly, political rule. "My kingdom is not of this world" (John 18:36), he declared, while also insisting on a distinction between the things of God and the things of Caesar (Matthew 22:21). A division between political and ecclesiastical authorities thus became entrenched, making competition between kings and bishops, emperors and popes, almost inevitable. Ambrose, bishop of Milan, attacked Emperor Theodosius for a massacre at Thessalonica in 390. Pope Gregory VII fought with the Holy Roman emperor, Henry IV, over the appointment of bishops in imperial territory between 1073 and 1085, with the pope insisting that lay authorities, including kings and emperors, had no right to invest anyone with a church office. The conflict was intense because church and state were both responsible for building a unified Christian society, yet "the boundaries between the state-like activities of the Church and those of secular rulers had never been clearly drawn."[13] For example, dating from the conversion of the Roman Emperor Constantine in 312, Roman and later Byzantine emperors convened church councils, while popes crowned the Holy Roman emperor and asserted the right to depose wayward secular rulers.

It is commonplace to fixate on how different these premodern religion-state arrangements are from each other. For example, the separation implied by Jesus' oft-quoted command about God and Caesar—"Render therefore to Caesar the things that are Caesar's and to God the things that are God's"—is frequently contrasted with the religion-state unity inherent in the practice of the Prophet Mohammed. Such differences are real. A focus on them therefore has its place.

However, the foregoing sketches of such varied relationships between religious and political authority over vast periods of history—Buddhist, Muslim, Hindu, and Christian—are impressive for another reason: They show how much these forms of relationship had in common. One striking commonality is that premodern relationships between religious and political actors tended to involve significant mutual dependence for the sake of overall social order and reliance on each other for the maintenance of rule. Political actors depended heavily on religious actors, and vice versa. This was true both materially and ideologically.

Materially, religious actors depended on political actors to collect revenue for them and to donate land to support religious institutions and activities. Buddhist monks, Christian churches, Hindu priests, and indigenous Chinese religions all depended to a large degree on government patronage to build houses of worship, provide land for monasteries, and establish systems of education. In addition, all of these religious actors also depended on political authorities to provide physical defense against external invasions and internal rebellions.

Typically, religious actors also depended on the ruler's sword to enforce orthodoxy and discipline—both within religious institutions and in society as a whole. After the conversion of Constantine to Christianity in 312, the Church relied on imperial authority and coercion to convene ecclesiastical councils (where the bishops of the Church gathered to settle questions of doctrine and other church affairs) and to punish heretics and schismatics. Constantine convened the Council of Nicaea in 321, the first great ecumenical council of the Church, and either a Western or Eastern emperor convened each of the subsequent six ecumenical councils. The imperial role was more than ceremonial. To help bring each council to a decisive conclusion, it was standard practice for the emperor to arrange for one of his high officials to "personally carr[y] round the creed the emperor had approved for everyone to sign if they wished to be spared the penalty of exile; which, needless to say, most did."[14] Furthermore, with the introduction of the Justinian Code, it became a formal duty of the emperor and other imperial officials to suppress heretical teaching (such as Arianism, a theological school of thought that challenged the link between God as father to Jesus by questioning the core concept of the Trinity, or the unity of the Father, Son, and Holy Spirit) and pagan worship.

Similarly, as mentioned above, it was among a Hindu king's most solemn duties to ensure that the caste hierarchy as laid down in the Hindu scriptures and the Laws of Manu be respected. And it was a requisite responsibility of Buddhist kings to enforce the discipline prescribed for monks in the Vinaya, the set of monastic rules orally passed down from the Buddha to his disciples.

With the widely accepted political responsibility for maintaining theological discipline usually came direct political involvement in religious appointments. Buddhist kings appointed the *sangha* hierarchy, including the chief monk, the *sangharaja*. Throughout Christian history, political officials at many levels played a significant role in the selection of bishops, archbishops, and even popes, a practice that sparked enormous competition and conflict between the papacy and numerous temporal rulers. The Byzantine emperor directly appointed the patriarch, the head of the Eastern Orthodox Church.

Power and benefits flowed in the other direction as well, from religious actors to political authorities. In almost all premodern societies, religious leaders supplied the political ruler with important advisors. Because religious elites—whether *ulema*, monks, bishops, or Brahmins—were often uniquely well versed in legal and historical texts, they were in an unparalleled position to give the ruler authoritative counsel on a wide range of issues. These issues went well beyond the domains of theology and morality to include economic and military matters. The church scholar Alcuin of York, for example, joined the court of Charlemagne in the late eighth century to become a leading advisor in several areas, including educational reform. The religious advisor might provide counsel on affairs of state, but often he played a specifically priestly role that, along with whatever transcendent and spiritual benefits it attracted, undoubtedly boosted the morale of the king and his retinue. The Hindu *purohita*, or royal chaplain, "wielded considerable influence in some cases through his role as the king's *guru* or spiritual preceptor." During military campaigns, he blessed the king's war elephants and horses and accompanied the king into battle, seeking to guarantee victory by his prayers, sacrifices, and incantations.[15] Of course, such access to political power benefited not only rulers but also the religious actors themselves, whose prestige and authority were enhanced by their proximity to the throne.

This mutual dependence, however, was far from symmetric. Political actors needed some material resources from religious actors. As we just noted, political rulers depended on the expert manpower religious elites were well positioned to provide. In some cases, the capacity of political actors to tax populations also depended on the cooperation of religious actors. Throughout the history of the Spanish Empire in the Americas, for example, the pope granted the king of Spain the right to collect church tithes and funnel the funds directly into the coffers of the Spanish crown, making up a large share of the imperial revenue. In general, however, the material dependence of religious actors on political actors was greater than that of political actors on religious actors. Without the material support of political actors, much of religion's institutional infrastructure—seminaries, monasteries, centers of worship—would be imperiled.

As the earlier sketches of premodern religion-state arrangements underscore, the ideological support political and religious actors gave to each other was at least as important as material support. Here, too, the mutual dependence of religious and political actors was often asymmetric. With respect to ideology, however, the asymmetry was usually the reverse of what it was for material support: Political actors usually depended more heavily on the ideological support that religious actors alone could provide than the other way around. As the great sociologist S. N. Eisenstadt found in his analysis of premodern religion-state relationships, "the religious organizations needed the protection and help of the political institutions for the establishment and maintenance of their positions, organizations, and wealth." However, "[t]he political institutions needed the basic legitimation and support which could be provided only by the religious elite." Religious actors representing the major religious traditions we are focusing on here—Christianity, Buddhism,

Hinduism, and Islam—did not depend on legitimation from governments because "none of these religions and religious organizations was founded or initiated by the monarchs." Instead, "all these religions had some independent historical beginnings."[16]

Religious and political actors overlapped in their authority to a degree that seems astonishing to us in the modern era. But we should also realize that, even prior to the modern world, religious and political authority remained separate and distinct.[17] "[I]n very few [ancient and medieval] empires did there exist even a partial fusion of some of the central political and religious roles," concluded Eisenstadt.[18] There were exceptions, of course—like the Prophet Mohammed, who assumed religious authority as well as all social and political authority, including all power to legislate, adjudicate disputes, and raise and command armies. But this is an extreme case even within Islamic history and practice. Mohammed's perfect fusion "was lost in the early centuries of Islam."[19]

There were two central ways that religious and political actors remained separate. First, they involved different people. As previously discussed, kings in premodern India were members of a different caste, the Kshatriya, than priests, who were Brahmins. Religious personnel in premodern Christianity and Buddhism were distinguished by special vows, clothing, discipline, and often lodging. Except in highly unusual circumstances, religious personnel could not assume direct political roles and positions, and vice versa. Even Muslim societies by the ninth and tenth centuries practiced a clear division of labor between religious figures, especially the interpreters of Islamic law, and essentially secular military and political figures—that is, between *ulema* and sultans.

Second, political and religious authorities performed separate tasks. It was unusual for religious actors to perform the main functions or responsibilities of political actors on a sustained basis, or vice versa. In the extraordinary circumstances following the collapse of the Roman Empire in the West (around 476), the Church did take on some political, administrative, and judicial functions. After all, "the Church alone had a centralized government, the Church alone had a bureaucracy, the Church alone kept records and followed legal precedents."[20] Despite its massive institutional advantages, however, the Church's political theology continued to insist on the idea that God gave "two swords," one spiritual and one temporal, for the right ordering of the world. Even "at the height of its power, [the Church] never took over all the functions of the state."[21]

The mutual dependence and mutual distinction characterizing the relationship between premodern religious and political actors helped to generate a third common feature of their relationship: mutual deference.

Religious actors and political actors could at times lock horns in ferocious conflict. History records instances of Buddhist monks, Brahmin priests, Hebrew prophets, Sunni sectarians, and Christian prelates propagandizing, conspiring, and sometimes struggling violently—and sometimes successfully—against princes, kings, queens, caliphs, sultans, and emperors. The powers that be periodically returned the favor, subjecting senior religious leaders to torture, assassination, imprisonment, exile, forcible removal from office, and judicial execution. Their institutions and personnel were usually distinct enough to make conflict possible, and their interests sometimes diverged enough to make it desirable or even necessary.

As a rule, however, the relationship between premodern religious and political actors was marked by significant mutual deference, respect, and cooperation. Religious actors accorded political rulers great deference for two major reasons. First, political rulers were almost always elevated religious figures in their own right. Whether as an incarnation of Indra or Vishnu (in Hinduism), the "shadow of God on earth" (in Islam), a future Buddha or Bodhisattva (in Buddhism), or God's "minister" and a vicar of Christ (in Christianity), the ruler was invested with his (and occasionally her) own divinely ordained authority. Since the ruler ruled by the will of God, it was believed, he commanded the presumptive fear, respect, and obedience of everyone, including religious authorities. Only under exceptional circumstances could this respect and obedience be legitimately withheld. Second, religious actors depended heavily on political actors for material support, as we have already noted, and they were generally inclined to treat their benefactors with respect.

For their part, political actors generally had compelling reasons to relate to religious actors in a spirit of deference and cooperation. Though Hindu kings—including the Hindu king of Nepal, until the abolition of the monarchy in 2008—were considered divine or quasi-divine, they prostrated themselves before Brahmin priests in the course of their coronation ceremonies partly to guarantee the priests' ancient privileges, including absolute brahminical immunity from execution, even by the king. Implicit in this royal guarantee was the king's recognition that his legitimacy derived from his playing an appointed role in the sacred order of society—and that it was Brahmins who largely determined how well he was playing this role.

Though virtually all premodern political actors enjoyed some intrinsic

divine authority, religious actors had enormous power to enhance or undermine the religious legitimacy of particular rulers. While political rulers could
subject particular religious actors to pressure or co-optation, in the long run
"they were continuously dependent on *some* religious organizations."[22] It was
usually possible for political actors to fool—or intimidate—some religious
actors some of the time. But it was mostly impossible to fool or intimidate all
of them all of the time. A king could destroy a "meddlesome" cleric, as King
Henry II of England arranged to kill the obstinate Archbishop of Canterbury
Thomas Becket in the twelfth century. But he could not destroy the entire
church without fatally undermining his own authority. Without the "mandate of Heaven," as conferred by one religious actor or another, there could
be no political authority.

The result of the mutual dependence, mutual distinction, and mutual deference of premodern religious and political actors was a prevailing pattern of
"friendly mergers." In the terms we introduced in the last chapter, religious
actors and political authorities the world over tended to be intertwined in
relationships that were both integrated and consensual.

Religious actors and political authorities were firmly integrated into
organic, holistic systems of authority. They were distinct from each other in
their authority and responsibilities and were seldom so intertwined as to be
indistinguishable. But this authority and these responsibilities lacked defined
boundaries. Furthermore, neither the political ruler nor the religious leader
was "sovereign" in the modern sense over his zone of authority. In fact, the
responsibilities of political and religious actors were often defined in ways
that *required* each set of actors to "trespass" on the other's "territory." In particular, the prevailing dependence of religious actors on political authorities
to provide material support, clerical appointments, and internal discipline
meant that premodern religious actors usually lacked significant autonomy.

At the same time, these arrangements tended to be consensual and friendly.
That is, religious actors and political authorities were institutionally and
ideologically interdependent in ways that both religious and political actors
considered necessary and legitimate. Their relationship was "friendly" not in
the sense that it was entirely free of conflict but in the sense that both sides
were ideologically invested in mutual cooperation. That is, both sides cooperated with each other under most circumstances for more than merely pragmatic reasons. They each accepted on principle the other's authority, properly
understood. And they each accepted, on principle, the duty and necessity of
working constructively with the other. The result was that premodern reli-

gious actors adhered to political theologies that as a rule cast them as loyal boosters of the powers that be.

EARLY MODERNITY: FROM FRIENDLY MERGER TO FRIENDLY TAKEOVER

Over the course of about three centuries, between roughly 1450 and 1750, the Christian West, the Muslim world, and parts of East Asia saw a quantum increase in the power of political rulers to control and regulate religious actors. We often associate the dawn of modernity with the idea of the "separation of church and state"—with the liberation of both church and state from domination and subjugation by the other. But the reality is quite different. In fact, during this period—what historians call the "early modern era"—the institutional connections between religion and government deepened in most parts of the world, forging even more tightly integrated relationships between religious and political authority. Over the course of this period, the balance of power shifted decisively in the direction of the state.

At this point, our story becomes largely (though not totally) centered on Europe—and will remain so until we arrive at the twentieth century. This is because the developments in religion and politics that took place in Europe following the Protestant Reformation (which began in 1517) came to shape the structure and conduct of politics all across the globe. The international system that eventually came to be codified in the United Nations Charter in 1945 is one whose basic structure and principles—territorial sovereign states, the principle of nonintervention, and the like—took shape in Europe at the Peace of Westphalia in 1648. It was then through the centuries-long colonization of Latin America, the Middle East, Africa, South Asia, and East Asia by European powers, followed by the granting of independence to these colonies, culminating after World War II, that the sovereign-states system spread to the entire globe. It was also through colonization and eventual independence that states around the world developed institutions of law and governance—including relationships between religion and state—that reflected European models. As we will see, one of the features of the global religious resurgence that began in the 1960s is that religious actors finally began to challenge what Europe had bequeathed to them.

Once this European states system was established and consolidated in the early modern period, the characteristically premodern "friendly merger" of political and religious actors tended to give way to a "friendly takeover" in which states intensified their domination of religious institutions.

The takeover was indeed friendly. An antireligious spirit seldom motivated the state. Moreover, religious actors often supported the takeover on the basis of sincerely held political theologies that accepted this sort of relationship. Political rulers and political philosophers of this period were not the antireligious Jacobins who in a future era would form the radical wing of the French Revolution; rather, they considered true religion the friend of good government and stable society. But they were convinced that political rulers needed to subject religious actors to systematic political regulation. Only under such "adult supervision," which governments were in a unique position to provide, could religious actors be trusted to play a constructive spiritual and social role.

Several trends contributed to political authorities' ascendance. The first was the rise of powerful, centralized states. This development began in the West some years before 1500, though it accelerated significantly after 1500. And in time it spread beyond the West, for example, to the Ottoman Empire. It involved a radical increase in the capacity, territorial jurisdiction, and centralization of power and authority in European states, which was demanded in part because of technological and tactical changes in the conduct of warfare.[23]

In contrast to the overlapping authorities that political scientist John Ruggie describes as characteristic of medieval Europe, in which temporal and religious authorities exercised prerogatives over the same territories, it was increasingly believed in the sixteenth and seventeenth centuries that within any given territory the establishment of a single political power was a necessary condition of peace, good order, and security. With sixteenth-century French political philosopher Jean Bodin, the term "sovereignty" was increasingly used to name this authority, and it was increasingly believed that sovereignty is indivisible. If a state lacks any aspect of sovereignty, it lacks sovereignty—period.

With their increased might, states became less inclined to exercise authority in cooperation with religious authorities—to share and divide their sovereignty, in other words—and more inclined to exercise authority over them. This was made easier by the fact that papal assertions of supreme authority over temporal rulers had begun to command less respect. By 1400, "the combination of an exalted theory of papal overlordship with a persistent practice of using the spiritual authority of the popes to serve local political ends sapped the prestige of the Roman see. . . ."[24] The high point of papal power of the eleventh and twelfth centuries was followed by a gradual increase in royal power across Europe.

Although the official political theologies prevalent in Christendom continued to speak of two powers, spiritual and temporal, representing the "things of God" and the "things of Caesar," working in harmony and balance in a unified Christian civilization, the de facto balance of power in England, France, Spain, and Sweden was tipping decidedly in Caesar's favor by the fifteenth century. Kings built increasingly strong states, amassed lands and revenue, and constructed distinct national identities. Less able to check the designs of kings, bishops—including the bishop of Rome, also known as the pope—increasingly found themselves pawns in political chess games. In France, for example, in 1438, King Charles VII issued the Pragmatic Sanction of Bourges, which established the "liberties" of the Gallican Church, restricting the pope's rights and in many cases making his jurisdiction subject to the will of the king. Though it was later revoked, the 1516 Concordat of Bologna between King Francis I of France and Pope Leo X recognized the power of the French crown to make appointments to high church offices, including the offices of archbishop and bishop. The Holy Roman emperor, too, along with national monarchs, exercised a growing role in the appointment of bishops.

Contributing to the expansion of state power was the rise of *raison d'état* and *politique* theories of statecraft, which argued that rulers should not allow religious and moral considerations to trump political necessity. Machiavelli regarded both the church and Christian morality as effeminate and enfeebling of a prosperous, powerful, and well-ordered republic. Though his writings do not contain direct philosophical or theological arguments against Christian theology or natural law, he was, as philosopher Jacques Maritain would later argue, the first philosopher in the Western tradition to counsel princes "not to be good" if circumstances required it.[25] Writing during a time of religious war, Hobbes prescribed that the state take an overriding interest in stability and security and that the church be kept out of politics altogether. Even churchman Cardinal Richelieu counseled French kings to follow the secularized morality of *raison d'état* and to act in a way that mostly eschewed the wishes of the Catholic Church.

Accelerating Europe's historical momentum toward the expansion of state power were fundamental challenges emanating from within the Church itself, culminating in the Protestant Reformation in 1517. So dramatic were the aims and repercussions of the Reformation that many historians have preferred to speak of a Protestant Revolution. Certainly, with respect to the relationship between religion and the state, Protestantism was revolutionary. In fact, it was Protestantism that above all made possible a "revolution in sovereignty" in sixteenth and seventeenth century Europe.[26]

Protestant political theology prescribed the seizure of the Church's remaining temporal powers and the end of the emperor's right to guard the Church's spiritual powers. All of these powers would be assumed by the prince, making him effectively sovereign. Predictably, this attack on the authority of church and empire resulted in a counterattack—the Counter-Reformation. Not so predictably, the Counter-Reformation had the effect of strengthening state authority over the church in both predominantly Catholic and predominantly Protestant countries.

In the face of Counter-Reformation Catholic missionary efforts and the activities of the new Jesuit order of priests in particular, but also even before this, Protestants willingly placed their sometimes embattled and splintering churches under the protective authority of princes. "The Prince," concluded German Reformed theologian Wolfgang Capito, "is a shepherd, a father, the visible head of the Church upon earth"—all the attributes normally given to the pope.[27] This pattern of state-church relations became known as "Erastianism," named for Thomas Erastus, an influential writer in the theological camp of Swiss reformer Ulrich Zwingli. Erastianism was the strong governance of church affairs by the state—much stronger governance than had been seen in Europe since before the High Middle Ages. Although each Protestant country contains its own story of flux, contestation, and unique arrangements, Erastianism became the rule in most of Protestant Europe. Erastian political theology sprang partly from the biblical focus of Protestant theology, which, for example, encouraged an unprecedented stress on the text of Romans 13:1–7: "Everyone must submit himself to the governing authorities." Elevated to new prominence, texts such as this seemed to demand "the subjection of the ecclesiastical sphere to the temporal."[28] In essence, this interpretation granted the state sovereignty over everyone and everything in its domains, including religion.

Even on the understanding of some Protestant theologians, this arrangement became a kind of caesaropapism, in which every Caesar assumed quasi-papal powers within his territory. "[I]nstead of a single Pope," wrote one loyal Protestant around 1560, "we today have a thousand, that is to say, as many as we have princes, magistrates and great lords, all of whom now exercise . . . ecclesiastical and civil functions, arming themselves with the sceptre, the sword and spiritual thunderbolts, in order to dictate to us even what doc-trines we must preach in our churches."[29]

In Catholic countries, the dynamic was oddly similar: the rapid spread of Protestantism on the continent drove Mother Church into the arms of more than one prince promising to defend Her. Because the Catholic Church needed greater political protection in the context of religious competition, the kings of Catholic states increased their leverage over popes and bishops. In France in particular, the Church bargained away a significant share of its autonomy in return for pledges from the French crown to defend its interests. In the arrangement known as "Gallicanism," codified in the 1594 "Liberties of the Gallican Church," though with precedents going back at least to the 1438 Pragmatic Sanction of Bourges, as we have seen, the king exercised an expansive authority over the Church in France. For example, the papal legate was forbidden to exercise his authority without the permission of the king (article 11); bishops were forbidden to travel to Rome without the permission of the king (article 13); and no Bull emanating from the Holy See could be published in French territory without the permission of the king (article 44).[30] Even outside France, despite the persistence of the Papal States (territories in Italy over which the pope was a temporal sovereign), states across Europe drastically diminished the temporal privileges previously enjoyed by bishops, such as holding offices, raising revenues, and ruling large tracts of land.

Yet another revolutionary development contributing to the rise of state power over the church was nationalism. There had often been a close link between religion and nationalism, and much recent scholarship argues that nationalism in Britain, France, Germany, Spain, Sweden, and elsewhere origi-nated in the sixteenth and seventeenth centuries and even earlier, thanks in large part to the role of religious factors.[31] It was no small part of the identity of France, for example, that she was considered "the eldest daughter of the Church," and that French kings were officially designated with the honorific *christianissimus* (most Christian). In this and other examples, nations derived a significant share of their identity and dignity from being a part of a greater spiritual whole.

After the Reformation, however, nations mobilized on behalf of a reli-gious community far less commonly than religious communities mobilized on behalf of their nation. More and more, in other words, religious com-munities were local and national, territorially and politically confined, and willing to see themselves as subordinate elements of larger national wholes. Far from any nation being subject to the proprietary claims of the Church, as implied in the traditional formula that "France is the eldest daughter of the Church," religion tended to become the property of the prince and the nation. This became particularly clear in the famous formulation of the 1555 Treaty of Augsburg, which ended the religious wars in Germany: *cuius regio, eius religio*—whose the region, his the religion. Especially when combined with growing princely authority, the rise of nationalism as a dominant basis of people's identity further subordinated the authority of the church to the authority of the state. Churches existed to serve nation-states, not the other way around.

The subjugation of religion and religious authorities to the state were further embodied in the Treaty of Westphalia in 1648, which ended the brutal religious wars that wracked Europe for thirty years.[32] This treaty consecrated the sovereign state, codified the principle of nonintervention and the inviolability of borders, and encouraged the secularization of political authority as it was exercised both within and across territorial boundaries. No longer was religion to be a prime mover of politics among states in the international system. If religion continued to have influence at all, it was a matter for individual rulers. Although the ideas of Westphalia have eroded over time, they have not been eliminated, especially in Europe.

Though our narrative has deliberately focused on Europe in the early modern period, it is noteworthy that Tokugawa Japan and the Ottoman Empire offer roughly coterminous examples of the state's growing authority over religious actors.

The Tokugawa or Edo period (1603–1868) saw the Japanese regime prohibit Catholicism and marshal Buddhism as an instrument of state power. It forced every Japanese household to "affiliate with specific Buddhist temples, thus creating a 'parochial system' hitherto unknown in the history of Japanese Buddhism. Government patronage, and the financial security that comes with it, enabled Buddhist schools to develop gigantic ecclesiastical superstructures." The government called on Buddhism to serve important political and social functions. "The significance of Buddhism during the Tokugawa period, that is, from the beginning of the seventeenth century to the mid-nineteenth century, was that it was not only an important arm of the feudal regime; it was also an effective framework for family and social cohesion." However, this intensified institutional integration between the government and Buddhist institutions brought with it the radical subordination of religion to the state—just like in Europe. Buddhist institutions "were robbed of nearly all spiritual freedom, influence, and initiative."[33]

The Ottoman Empire, too, increasingly subordinated religious to political authority after its conquest of Constantinople in 1453. When the Ottomans took control of Egypt in 1517, the Ottoman sultan obtained the title of caliph with all of its religious and political authority. The *ulema* performed state-appointed judicial functions, both interpreting *sharia* and deciding court cases. "The highest ranking mufti, the *shaykul-Islam*, was appointed by the sultan-caliph and exercised considerable authority over the affairs of the empire."[34] The *shaykul-Islam*'s statements "related not only to matters of religious policy, but also such major concerns of the state as declarations of war, relations with non-Muslim states, taxation, and innovations or inventions such as the printing press."[35]

However, neither the *shaykul-Islam* nor the *ulema* as a body enjoyed any institutional independence from the state. According to the authority on Turkish secularism Niyazi Berkes, "[t]he *ulama* order differed from the Christian clergy in its nature, function, and organization. The hierarchy which developed within that order bore no resemblance to the Catholic or Orthodox clerical hierarchy. They did not constitute a spiritual corps organized through a church." On the contrary, "[r]eligious matters were organized not through an autonomous church but by the state through the order of *ulama* which constituted an official and temporal body."[36] The Ottoman Empire's most important religious actors were part of the state, not separate from it. In fact, although Berkes draws a sharp contrast between the political weakness of the Ottoman *ulema* and the independence of the Christian clergy, we have already seen that numerous upheavals and developments in early modern Europe dramatically reduced the institutional independence and political power of Christian churches.

Premodern religious actors normally served as the loyal boosters of political authority, but they nonetheless enjoyed substantial ideological power to challenge and, if necessary, take away the legitimacy of political rulers. In contrast, modern religious actors were increasingly incorporated into the structures of government, and were called on to serve, in effect, as spiritual departments of the state. Consequently, compared to premodern religious actors, early modern religious actors combined some continuing ideological authority with a lower degree of institutional independence. During the early modern period, a deferential relationship, in which religious actors were accorded significant respect, shifted to a more instrumental relationship, in which religious actors increasingly became tools of state power.

LIBERTÉ, EGALITÉ, AND THE STATE'S HOSTILE TAKEOVER OF RELIGIOUS ACTORS

From the late eighteenth century to the late twentieth century, the subordination of religion to the state continued its dramatic global expansion—intellectually and politically, in theory and in practice. Emanating from the European experience, and, in large part, from its success in state-building, it became more widely accepted that the state should actively subordinate religious authority to political authority, religious institutions to political institutions, and religious claims to political claims—all in the interest of promoting the well-being of society as a whole. Though much of this secularization occurred within states, it was very much a transnational phenomenon, propelled by the global diffusion of ideas and international networks.

As radically as the early modern political secularism of Hugo Grotius, Jean Bodin, Thomas Hobbes, or John Locke broke from medieval integrationism, and as much as it sought to reduce the influence of churches as political players, it seldom mounted a direct or open assault on religion per se and, indeed, almost always expressed itself in biblical and orthodox terms. Intellectually, the decisive break with this pattern came with Jean-Jacques Rousseau's *Social Contract* in 1762; politically, it came with the French Revolution of 1789. For the first time, Rousseau and his Jacobin acolytes openly identified the church and Christianity as implacably hostile to any free and flourishing republic.[37] Thanks to their massive influence, this revolutionary approach to religion-state relations began to be implemented in more and more societies around the world. It was an approach of *conflictual integration,* in which states undertook the "hostile takeover" of religious actors.

Where Rousseau and his admirers taught that a strong and flourishing republic required a Spartan-style love of country above all things, the church taught heaven as the Christian's best and truest country. Where a unified republic required a love and devotion for all of one's fellow citizens, the church taught *extra ecclesiam nulla salus* ("outside the church there is no salvation") and thus created a spiritual and social chasm between Christian citizens and non-Christian citizens. Where a free republic elevated liberty of mind and spirit as the highest principle, the church elevated submission and humble obedience to God and his servants as the foundations of the Christian life. A church that remained beyond the control of the republican state and free to propagate its teachings without hindrance was therefore not merely a latent source of political instability but an active opponent of its core principles and purposes.[38]

The sense of an absolute conflict between the principles of the church and the kind of republic the French Revolution aspired to establish meant that a policy of separation between church and state was not sufficient. Instead, to be consistent, the republican state had to do no less than radically subordinate and transform the church. This campaign of "*déchristianisation*" consisted of a whole range of exotic innovations, including a new calendar based on the cycles of nature rather than the cycles of Christian salvation history, as well as a new set of religious rituals revolving around a Cult of the Supreme Being.[39] The policy also eliminated the church's right to perform marriages, its control over education, and its ownership of vast hectares of property. Even more seriously, the new regime brought the church more strongly under its supervisory control. While under the old regime the Gallican understanding between crown and pope involved a strong state role in the appointment of bishops and priests, the new regime took this further by requiring oaths of loyalty to the revolutionary republic and, in effect, ideological reeducation. Church personnel as well as ordinary Catholics who resisted these measures were subjected to violence, most notoriously in the Vendée civil war of 1793 to 1796, in which hundreds of thousands of Catholics were killed.[40]

Although some of these measures were turned back because of the restoration of the monarchy in France in 1814 and the resurrection of the Catholic Church, the revolutionary flag was raised high enough and long enough that radicals throughout Europe and its settler societies in the Americas rallied around it. What developed and took hold from the French Revolution was nothing less than a radical secularist template that positioned the church as Enemy Number One. Catholic countries throughout Europe and the Americas, therefore, saw the rise of wave after wave of anticlerical movements and parties in the nineteenth and twentieth centuries. Given such a history, it is reasonable to see the Revolution as providing the template for subsequent and often violent programs of radical political secularism, including those carried out by revolutionaries in twentieth-century Cambodia, China, Italy, Mexico, Russia, Spain, and Tunisia. The separation of church and state was no longer enough. The subordination and even abolition of religious institutions increasingly emerged as the new norm.

Sometimes these movements emerged with the help of French bayonets; in other cases they were spawned by the sheer example of the French Revolution's success in overthrowing the *ancien régime* and by the dissemination of its leading ideas. The writings of Thomas Paine, who lived in France in the early months of the Revolution (1789–90), had this kind of impact in the English-speaking world. The United Irish Movement and its violent 1798 insurrection, for example, were directly inspired by revolutionary example and ideas.[41] This diffusion and its consequences were by no means limited to Catholic countries. For the revolutionary Dutch Patriots, who were in exile in France in 1789, "the outbreak of the French Revolution, and universal ideology to which it gave rise, was an inspiring development."[42] French bayonets and the contagious ideological fervor that infected the Patriots combined to bring much of the program of the French Revolution—including its radical secularism—to the Low Countries in the form of the Batavian Republic in 1795. A major priority of the Batavian Revolution, in fact, was to abolish the Reformed Church's special political ties and privileges.[43]

The sense of an intractable conflict between the partisans of the church—especially, but not only, the Catholic Church—and the partisans of liberal progress deepened considerably in the second half of the nineteenth century. A key turning point was 1864. What had sometimes been an inchoate anticlerical attitude crystallized into a coherent political program in numerous countries after the publication in that year of Pope Pius IX's "Syllabus of Errors." As mentioned in Chapter One, the "Syllabus" condemned the doctrine that the pope "can and ought to reconcile himself with progress, with liberalism, and with modern civilization."[44] Pius IX did not define his terms very clearly, and much of his animus against "modern civilization" no doubt sprang from the fact that a modern state—Italy—was in the process of stripping him of lands he had controlled for a thousand years (the Papal States). Still, the widespread perception is what mattered for politics: "Europe saw the Pope condemn liberalism—whatever that was, the Pope condemned it."[45]

This pervasive perception precipitated a host of organized political campaigns designed to subject the Church to even greater state control and regulation. In Germany, Bismarck directed the parliament to limit the power of the Catholic Church in the *Kulturkampf* of the 1870s. In Belgium, the Liberal Party in the late 1870s implemented a program to restrict greatly the Catholic Church's role in education. The 1871 Paris Commune included the desecration of churches. In 1870s America, the Blaine Amendments, designed to prevent states from financially aiding "sectarian" (i.e., Catholic) schools, won legislative approval in dozens of states and only narrowly failed to pass the U.S. Congress.[46] Throughout Latin America, too, the Catholic Church saw its rights restricted during the 1860s and 1870s in Colombia, Guatemala,

El Salvador, and Nicaragua, and also in Bolivia, Brazil, Chile, Ecuador, Mexico, Peru, and Venezuela.[47] Later, in France, Émile Combes, Aristide Briand, and other radical republicans pushed through the 1905 Law of Separation of Church and State. While the law was less sweeping in its consequences than its framers intended, it nonetheless made a subordinationist political secularism an official, enduring, and nonnegotiable feature of France's political system and political culture—one that remains largely intact (though not beyond dispute) to this day.[48]

The year 1864 was significant for another reason: It was the year of the first meeting of the Communist International. There is little doubt that "Marxism was the most powerful philosophy of secularization in the nineteenth century."[49] In its beginnings, Communism was not an atheist philosophy: In the 1840s, Friedrich Engels, much to his puzzlement and frustration, met Christian Communists everywhere he went—in England, France, and Germany. Saint-Simon had advocated a kind of Christian socialism, and Ferdinand Lassalle, who was a more influential Communist theoretician than Marx until about 1870, expressly combined Christianity and Communism. But after Lassalle's death in 1864 and the publication of *Das Kapital* in 1867, Communism as a philosophy and as a transnational political movement increasingly incorporated a radical form of political secularism. At best, "religion is a man's private concern," as the 1875 Gotha Program put it; at worst, it was incompatible with a unified working-class movement. Either way, religion as an institution and an allegiance had to be systematically subordinated to political movements that sought the liberation of the proletariat from capitalist oppression. Particularly at a moment when the pope seemed to be losing his influence by declaring war on "progress," Communism spoke with a growing transnational moral authority—one that increasingly operated as an adversary of religion rather than an ally.

A host of other intellectual and political movements of the late eighteenth and nineteenth centuries that were otherwise mutually contradictory—Hegelian historicism, Bismarckian realism, Comtean positivism, Millian liberalism, American federalism, Spencerian progressivism, and Kantian rationalism—mostly agreed with Communists and radical Republicans on a set of propositions that, taken together, yielded powerful ideological support for a program of political secularism: that a great new age of reason, freedom, and progress was arriving, or would soon arrive; that this new age would be the final and culminating era of human history, a kind of secular eschaton or millennium;[50] that God, or Providence, or some divine or quasi-divine super-intending force, almost always understood in ways markedly different from orthodox Christian conceptions of God, was orchestrating world history in some essentially irresistible fashion so as to usher in this new and final age; and that an essential if not primary agent in the realization of this new age was the modern state.

This package of ideas justifies a view of the state that is in one sense not necessarily secular because it puts the state in the service of a world-historical mission imposed on it by a transcendent agent ("God," "Providence," "History"). But in another sense, it is radically secular because it grants the state a supreme ideological authority over sacred institutions and authorities—what we have been calling religious actors—that in the past would have enjoyed at least some political powers and privileges. In other words, churches and other specifically religious, confessional, and "sectarian" institutions were under an ideological obligation to accept a subordinate role vis-à-vis the state so that history could reach its intended destination.

These ideas about historical progress and the secular state also helped to generate robust concepts of nationalism and internationalism, which, in turn, further contributed to the advance of a political secularism that subordinated and instrumentalized religion in the nineteenth and twentieth centuries. Arguably, the greatest and most influential nationalist of the nineteenth century was Giuseppe Mazzini. Leader of the Young Italy movement and briefly dictator of the Roman Republic in 1849, Mazzini repudiated traditional Catholicism in favor of a religion of "universal humanity." He rejected the Fall and Original Sin, but believed that God was leading mankind ineluctably toward the "angelification" of the individual and the establishment of God's kingdom on earth. But God's kingdom, he believed, would eventuate in the destruction of the papacy and its replacement by a secular council of the nations, headquartered in Rome. This council would represent the authentic nations of the world—that is, those that possessed the irrefutable marks of nationality, including natural frontiers, distinct languages, and distinct cultures.[51] Echoing to some extent earlier thinkers like Rousseau, Giambattista Vico, and Johann Gottfried Herder, Mazzini believed that every nation had a distinct vocation or mission, and that the ultimate purpose of nations is to serve humanity and the international order as a whole. "For us the starting-point is Country; the object or aim is Collective Humanity."[52] Similar, quasi-religious elevations of the nation and nationalism achieved currency in France in the nineteenth century thanks to intellectuals Jules Michelet and Ernest Renan.[53] Such ideas greatly increased the ideological independence and authority of states vis-à-vis religious actors.

By 1882, Mazzini's disciple Renan was exulting, "We have driven metaphysical and theological abstractions out of politics."[54] In the same year, Nietzsche proclaimed much the same thing in more arresting terms: "God is dead. God remains dead. And we have killed him." In the voice of a deicidal "madman," the German philosopher declared that if God were dead, He had been murdered. And if He had been murdered, the deed had been done by a multitude of eager accomplices. "*We have killed him*—you and I," the madman cried.[55] We have driven God out of society, culture, and politics.

God occupied a place in *fin-de-siècle* Europe that was less prominent and more contested than at any time in European history. By the end of the eighteenth century, many in the West mobilized to jettison kings from their earthly thrones in an era of regicidal revolution; by the end of the nineteenth century, whether or not they read Nietzsche, a growing number of political thinkers and activists resembled Nietzsche's deicidal madman—they *wanted* to push God off his heavenly throne and build regimes that would sideline God forever. In Renan's formulation, they wanted to drive theology out of politics. Not all of them were so radical as to seek God's utter annihilation. That would come in the next century. But even relatively moderate political secularists were determined to secure either God's political subservience or God's political irrelevance. Between roughly 1870 and 1910, all across Western and Central Europe, anticlerical parties fought and won battles to reduce the role of religion in education and culture and to increase the state's regulation of it.[56] Behind these parties were a large and diverse family of radical secularist ideologies that arose to realize this aspiration: Republican, Marxist, Positivist, Liberal, Realist, Nationalist, Syndicalist, and Utilitarian. As much as they differed from each other, they shared a commitment to a form of political secularism that went well beyond "separation of church and state" or "render to Caesar the things that are Caesar's, and to God the things that are God's." Instead, this family of radical secularisms embraced the notion that, as far as social and political life is concerned, it is the place of Caesar to decide the place of God—and, if necessary, eliminate God's place in politics and society altogether.

The Hostile Takeover Consolidated: The Middle of the Twentieth Century

The political secularism that emerged and diffused throughout much of the West in the century after the French Revolution of 1789 became further radicalized and spread even more widely in the half-century after the Russian Revolution of 1917. States bent on containing the social and political influence of institutionalized religion adopted militant programs, seeking to eliminate the social and political influence of religion altogether, in some cases by destroying, subjugating, or eviscerating religious institutions and centers of religious authority. Meanwhile, states outside the West that had not yet been exposed to secularism in theory or practice became experiments in radical political secularization as elites from these non-Western locales adopted and promulgated these ideas at home. It is here that our story widens again from European to global.

The project of radical political secularism gained real political traction in 1917. In many corners of the globe, governments turned "their faces from God," writes political scientist Anthony Gill. "Not only did the constitutional council in Mexico effectively outlaw the Roman Catholic Church and other religious denominations but also a group of even more radical state builders [i.e., the Bolsheviks] seized power in a country halfway around the world."[57] Combined with the already established radicalism of French *laïcité* and the subsequent radicalism of Turkey's Kemalist revolution of the early 1920s, these revolutions succeeded in planting radical secularist experiments in the heart of the Catholic, Orthodox, and Muslim worlds within the first three decades of the twentieth century.

Revolutionary political activism of the Left and the Right was indeed the most consequential force for radical political secularization in the twentieth century.

Thanks to such revolutionary and totalitarian movements, religion came to be just one more victim in a raft of social and political upheaval. In the 1910s and 1920s, that part of the Russian Orthodox Church that was not wiped out became an arm of the Soviet state; the Catholic Church in Mexico was criminalized and deprived of its property and its right to engage in political activity; the Ottoman caliphate and *sharia* law were abolished in Turkey, much to the outrage of Muslims around the world, particularly in British India; in the 1930s and into the 1940s, the Nazis refused to permit the independence of religious bodies in preaching, education, and publication in Nazi-controlled countries and arrested or murdered thousands of religious leaders who resisted the National Socialist policy of subordinating religious institutions to the state; and in the late 1950s, the Lamaist theocracy in Tibet was systematically destroyed and the Dalai Lama ultimately forced into exile by Chinese Communists; [58] and perhaps the largest grassroots religious organization in the Muslim world, the Muslim Brotherhood, was decimated and driven underground by Egyptian authorities in the 1950s and 1960s.

These revolutionary forms of political secularism and their aggressive assaults on religion might seem like outliers. However, at the approximate midpoint of the twentieth century, in 1945, M. Searle Bates found in his exhaustive analysis of global religion-state relations that "recent intensifications of nationalism have fused with the increasing power and functions of the State to imperil and even to crush, in some lands, a liberty of religion formerly achieved." The result, he found, was that "[r]eligious liberty is today denied, deformed, or restricted for all or for part of the people in most of the countries of the world."[59] In fact, by our rough calculation, at least 50 percent of the world's population lived under political regimes that systematically restricted the right and capacity of religious organizations to influence society and politics at some point between 1917 and 1967.

As Bates notes, the surging nationalism associated with decolonization (1945–1970) was a major force for secularism. The nationalisms of great post-colonial leaders—Ataturk in Turkey, Senanayake in Sri Lanka, Nehru in India, Nasser in Egypt, Nkrumah in Ghana, Sukarno in Indonesia, and Kenyatta in Kenya—all generally appealed to notions of national or civilizational greatness in which religion was but one subordinate element. Often, their concepts of national identity deliberately bracketed or subordinated substantive religious contributions in the hope of unifying diverse ethnic and religious groups in the context of anticolonial struggles and postcolonial nation-building.[60] Sometimes nationalists in this period used religious appeals precisely to marginalize the social or political influence of traditional religion, as when Bourguiba of Tunisia, after publicly raising a glass of lemonade to his lips during Ramadan, proclaimed, "You 'are permitted' to drink during Ramadan, for the 'holy war,' that is, the effort to unite Islam, is first and foremost the battle of production. Conserve your strength so that you may work hard. . . ."[61] Because these leaders had slain all manner of colonial dragons and in some cases a domestic dragon or two, they enjoyed a charismatic authority that enabled them to secure some legitimacy for their sometimes audacious experiments in promoting nationalisms that marginalized religion.

Of course, to speak of these leaders as a group is not to imply that the secularist political agendas of, say, a Nehru and an Ataturk, or a Bourguiba and a Sukarno, were identical in all respects. Though Nehru, for example, secured a temporary ban of the Hindu-nationalist Rashtriya Swayamsevak Sangh (RSS) in the exceptional circumstances following Mahatma Gandhi's assassination in 1948, and though he personally bemoaned the influence of religion on Indian society,[62] he never undertook a wholesale Kemalist-style effort to drive organized religion out of Indian public life by coercive means. At the same time, though their tone and tactics differed, virtually every member of the first generation of postcolonial leaders articulated the hope that religious leaders and organizations would assume a smaller political role and exercise less political influence in their societies. They acted on this hope in different ways and with varying degrees of aggression, but it was a hope they all shared nonetheless.

These trends toward political secularism were closely related to the dominant dynamics of international politics. The calamity of World War I served to discredit throne-and-altar alliances between religion (especially Christianity, but also Islam in the Ottoman Empire) and the nation-state. The post-millennialist religious utopianism that helped to fuel liberal internationalism collapsed in the face of the failure of the League of Nations and the rise of violent totalitarianisms in the 1920s and 1930s, causing even religious thinkers to repudiate faith-based, idealistic, or moralistic approaches to international politics in favor of essentially secular doctrines like political realism.[63]

Furthermore, dominant global conflicts in this period tended to organize international politics into rival blocs defined in essentially secular terms: Republicans versus Nationalists in the Spanish Civil War; the Allies versus the Axis in World War II; the U.S. and the Western bloc versus the USSR and the Eastern bloc in the Cold War; European colonial powers versus anti-colonial movements such as the Indian National Congress and the Egyptian Free Officers as well as anticolonial ideologies such as Pan-Arabism or Pan-Africanism. Even those who tried to remain aloof from these conflicts often did so in the name of an alternative form of secular transnationalism, such as the Non-Aligned Movement launched by Nehru, Nasser, Nkrumah, Sukarno, and Tito at the Bandung Conference in 1955.

The "Bandung Generation" of Third World statesmen was hardly alone, however, in thinking that an essential ingredient of modern progress was the secularization of politics. Sometimes called the rationalization of authority, sometimes characterized as the absence of "praetorianism,"[64] the capacity of states to build up their own sources of authority and resist undue influence by religious and other actors was considered a hallmark of modern political development by an entire generation of postwar American social scientists and public intellectuals, including Gabriel Almond, Sidney Verba, Walt Whitman Rostow, David Apter, Daniel Lerner, Samuel P. Huntington, Arthur Schlesinger, Jr., Rupert Emerson, and Walter Lippmann.[65] Influenced by such ideas, American policymakers placed their bets on aggressively modernizing and secularizing leaders like the Shah of Iran and Ngo Din Diem of Vietnam.[66] Circa 1960, perhaps the only thing the United States State Department, the faculty of the Harvard Government Department, the Communist International, and the leaders of the Bandung Conference agreed on is that a society can be successful only insofar as its government and its citizenry keep religion from exercising a substantive influence on its politics.

THE RISE OF POLITICALLY ASSERTIVE RELIGION

By the late 1960s, everyone (a term we do not use lightly) believed that the widespread aspiration for political secularism—for a politics and public life free of substantive religious influences—was rapidly becoming reality in virtually all parts of the world. Writing about politics in Nasser's Egypt, Nkrumah's Ghana, Bourguiba's Tunisia, and Sihanouk's Cambodia, Jean Lacouture observed in 1970 that "religion is doing such a good job of strengthening political authority . . . that it is paving the way for its own deterioration."[67] Richard Mitchell, a sensitive analyst of religious politics in the Middle East, predicted in 1968 that "the essentially secular reform nationalism now in vogue in the Arab world will continue to operate to end the earlier appeal of [the Muslim Brotherhood]."[68] Most sweepingly, as quoted in Chapter One, eminent sociologist Peter Berger forecast in the same year that by the end of the century, religious believers would be reduced to small enclaves and remnants of a time past.[69] Secularization, it seemed, was not so much a speculative academic theory as an imminent global reality.

Despite political secularism's apparently unstoppable advances in the course of the twentieth century, however, it began to experience serious setbacks in the 1960s. This surprising new trend had several dimensions.

First, many of the most important agents of political secularism declined or disappeared. Nehru died in 1964, opening up space in the world's largest democracy for a more religious politics[70]; a series of coups thrust Indonesia's Sukarno from power in 1965, culminating in the liquidation of Indonesia's Communist Party (PKI) and the gradual rise of a more religion-based politics; Ghana's Nkrumah was overthrown in a coup in 1965–1966, thus ending the ideological hegemony of "Nkrumahism" and paving the way for Ghana's churches to assert a more independent political influence[71]; and the armies of Egpyt's Nasser were crushed by Israel in 1967, marking the beginning of the end of secular Pan-Arabism and clearing the way for Nasser's rival, King Faisal of Saudi Arabia, to create a new transnational movement defined by religion, the Organization of the Islamic Conference (OIC), which met for the first time in 1969.[72] At least as important, Nasser's defeat in 1967 and death in 1970 cleared the way for a variety of actors to forge—with growing success over time—a transnational, Pan-Islamic consciousness. At the same time, Communism, which had been a preeminent agent of global political secularization for a hundred years, was increasingly on the moral and strategic defensive thanks to the Sino-Soviet split, the widely unpopular Soviet invasion of Czechoslovakia in 1968, the publication of Solzhenitsyn's *The Gulag Archipelago* in 1973, and the Soviet invasion of Afghanistan in 1979. A movement that seemed to be in the vanguard of modern progress in the 1870s looked more like a declining and ideologically exhausted empire in the 1970s.

Second, many religious movements formerly sidelined or discredited by the global rise of political secularism began making a political comeback in the 1960s and '70s. The Roman Catholic Church received a fresh burst of social and political self-confidence through the Second Vatican Council (1962–1965), which led the Church to affirm democracy and religious freedom for all, not just Catholics, and to operate as a legitimate and autonomous actor in civil society rather than through often defensive "concordats" (or pacts) with individual governments. The charismatic, dynamic, and politically engaged papacy of John Paul II (1978–2005) increased this confidence all the more.[73] Hindu nationalism, the object of systematic attack and marginalization by the secular Congress Party (whose members were forbidden from belonging simultaneously to "communal" groups like the Rashtriya Swayamsevak Sangh (RSS)), played an increasingly assertive and influential role in politics, with its political wing, the Bharatiya Jana Sangh, winning 10 percent of the national vote in the 1967 general elections and helping to form the Janata coalition that resoundingly defeated Indira Gandhi's Congress in

1977, a party that had held power since independence.[74] The formation of an Islamic Republic in Iran in 1979 inspired Muslim movements around the world, Sunni and Shia alike, to believe that it was possible to Islamize politics and society.[75]

In general, one can discern a powerful qualitative shift in the orientation of religious organizations around the world in the second half of the twentieth century: In every major religious tradition, leaders and key movements abandoned an exclusive focus on spiritual or cultural activity and took up political activity as an integral component of their religious mission. The Muslim Brotherhood dropped the apoliticism of its founder Hassan al-Banna in favor of direct political engagement; RSS members in India began organizing political parties and other politically active organizations; the Catholic Church promoted far more robust clerical and lay activism in defense of human rights; conservative Protestants in the United States abandoned their long fundamentalist self-isolation and distaste for politics (lasting from the 1925 Scopes trial to the late 1940s) in favor of organized and sustained social and political activism through such bodies as the National Association of Evangelicals and World Vision[76]; and influential Buddhist leaders such as Walpola Rahula in Ceylon called for an end to quiescence on the part of monks and lay Buddhists and instead for a robust engagement with politics.[77]

But why did religious organizations demonstrate a growing desire and power to shape international politics after the late 1960s? Certainly, "retail" explanations—the death or overthrow of charismatic secular leaders, the declining legitimacy of Communism, the failure of secular states and ideologies to deliver rapid development—are part of the story. However, broader, "wholesale" explanations are required to clarify why religious actors made a political comeback across the international system, in such a wide variety of regions and religious traditions, and among both developed and developing countries.

The first such explanation is that some of the dominant political and social trends of the nineteenth and twentieth centuries failed to deliver the *coup de grâce* to religion most analysts anticipated. Modernization was expected to weaken the hold of religion on society as people became more free, rational, and cosmopolitan. Programs of political secularization were intended to cut religion off from the financial and symbolic support it received from the state, whereupon the social power of religious institutions was expected to weaken or collapse. However, such programs of institutional separation between state and religion, though often imposed on religious actors by aggressive secularists, did not necessarily end up weakening religion. Religious actors may have enjoyed fewer privileges, but they soon realized they enjoyed more freedom of maneuver.[78] And the urbanization, economic development, and growth of literacy brought by modernization often created a *petite bourgeoisie* with the inclination and resources to give religious actors the support and loyalty that the state had ceased to provide. In other words, modernization and secularization often combined to increase the autonomy and capacity of religious organizations to formulate their own political agendas and mobilize their own resources and followers.[79]

The second "wholesale" explanation is that the spread of democracy greatly increased the opportunity of religious actors to compete freely for political influence. At least some charismatic Third World leaders, such as Nasser, Bourguiba, Nkrumah, and Ataturk, were effective secularizers because they were latter-day Rousseauean lawgivers: They sat at the apex of authoritarian or only partially democratic systems, and they could impose their secularist decrees in the name of the "general will" without having to secure any genuine mandate from the people in competitive elections.

With the number of "free" and "partly free" countries jumping from 93 in 1975 to 147 in 2005,[80] religious groups and organizations around the world enjoy a greater opportunity to influence the political process by forming lobbies, fielding candidates, organizing political parties, and inviting politicians of all kinds to try to win their support. In countries that combine some modernization with little or no democratization, religious and other organizations experience dissonant dynamics: They may enjoy an increased capacity to formulate their own agenda and mobilize resources but little or no opportunity to promote that agenda in the formal political process, a mixture of conditions that is likely to generate violent militancy when combined with an integralist political theology. It is therefore little surprise that regions of the world that have experienced some modernization, little democratization, and the widespread diffusion of militant political theologies—the Arab Middle East and North Africa, above all—have produced radical religious movements such as Al Qaeda and Hezbollah.[81] (The factors that encourage religious actors to opt for violent militancy are explored in much further detail in Chapters Five and Six.)

A third explanation is that globalization increased the capacity of religious actors to project influence, mobilize resources, and attract followers across national boundaries, greatly enhancing their overall political position vis-à-vis nation-states. It was widely assumed that globalization would create a single global village, wiping away or at least blurring differences of religion, culture, and ethnicity.[82] But however much globalization has caused people to appreciate their common humanity, it has also caused some people to appreciate their religious particularity—how *different* their religion is from the religion (or lack of religion) espoused by the people they see on TV or the Internet. Moreover, the closing of otherwise vast distances of space and time has enabled particular groups of coreligionists not only to feel like spiritual brothers and sisters even across national boundaries but to act, react, and organize as coherent political agents.

Millions of Christians around the world, for example, circulate bulletins via the Internet and e-mail detailing how their fellow believers are persecuted in far-flung, obscure locales like Orissa in eastern India, Kaduna in Nigeria, and Sulawesi in Indonesia. And they act in remarkably coordinated fashion, forming transnational advocacy networks and coalitions that pressure governments and international organizations to stop the assaults on their faith.[83] Via cable television and the Internet, millions of Muslims around the world rapidly learned about how Mohammed was depicted and dishonored in cartoons published in Denmark, and soon Muslim governments, the OIC, and tens of thousands of ordinary Muslims lodged vehement protests as well as organized efforts in international bodies to proscribe religious "defamation."[84] The expansion and intensification of global immigration, communication, and transportation has made it possible for more and more religious communities to establish effective transnational networks and organizations. In short, not only do religious actors think globally but they also *act* globally. And thanks to the accelerating processes of globalization, they can increasingly muster resources, mobilize constituencies, and apply pressure on governments and international organizations in ways that other nonstate actors—and even many states—can only dream of.

The foregoing broad-brush portrait of the rise and decline of political secularism inevitably omits and distorts important events and trends. The period we describe as one long and dramatic ascent for radical political secularism, 1789 to roughly 1967, unquestionably saw the rise of some politically important religious movements, such as the rise of Christian Democracy in Western Europe after World War II, which succeeded at least to some extent in resisting the general trend.[85] Likewise, the period we describe as the reversal of political secularism, the late 1960s to the present, has seen some forms of political secularism remain fairly resilient, such as French *laïcité* or the Chinese government's powerful combination of Communism, capitalism, and Han nationalism. And our entire narrative would have to be differently crafted for the United States, which has remained persistently religious and saw powerful religious involvement in politics in its civil rights movement of the late 1950s and early 1960s. Even here, though, a sweeping "secular revolution" occurred in elite culture and politics in the late nineteenth and early twentieth centuries.[86]

Overall, however, we are confident that a basic qualitative shift in international politics has occurred. During most of the period between 1789 and 1967, political secularism put religious actors and ideologies on the defensive in much of the world. During most of the period between 1967 and the present, the situation has reversed, with politically engaged religious actors of all kinds, in every part of the world, putting secular regimes and ideologies on the defensive.

TRACKING RELIGION'S POLITICAL ASCENDANCY

The history of religion and politics that we have told is varied and complex. We have simplified—and probably oversimplified—a great deal. Even allowing for all the necessary caveats and qualifications, however, we think a reasonably clear and coherent trajectory emerges, one that has its roots in Europe and the evolution of the international state system that emanated from there.

Up until about 1789, religious actors and political authorities the world over tended to be tightly intertwined and mutually embedded in what in Chapter Two we called "integrated" religion-state arrangements. Furthermore, these arrangements tended to be "consensual." That is, religious actors and political authorities were institutionally and ideologically interdependent—depending on each other for material and ideological support—in ways that both religious and political actors considered necessary and legitimate. As in a "friendly merger" between corporations in the business world, religious actors were not only institutionally integrated with the state but held political theologies that, by and large, happily and voluntarily accepted this kind of arrangement. In the early modern period, from about 1500, the nature of the merger began to shift toward greater state dominance of religious actors. The "friendly merger" became more like a "friendly takeover" in many societies. But the essential features of the relationship—close integration and basic consent—remained in place.

Then, roughly between 1789 and well into the second half of the twentieth century, a very different pattern of conflictual integration became increasingly common. Here, political authorities further expanded their powers over religious actors, frequently turning them into subordinates and subdepartments of increasingly bureaucratized states rather than partners of roughly equal dignity and authority. Under the influence of French Republican ideology and, later, Marxism, many states began to consider religion an implicit threat to be contained. In response, many religious actors began to exchange passive political theologies for theologies of political mobilization and activism, such as Christian Democracy in Western Europe. Important exceptions to the ascendancy of conflictual integration certainly existed in this period—in the constitutional church-state separation in the United States, above all. Unquestionably, however, the dominant tendency in this period was for states to engage in the "hostile takeover" of religious actors.

Since World War II and particularly since the 1960s, however, the structural position of religious actors vis-à-vis political authorities has undergone yet another and in some ways more dramatic epochal shift. Religion-state arrangements have increasingly shifted away from integration toward various forms and degrees of institutional independence, in which religious actors enjoy at least some de facto or de jure freedom to act independently of state authorities and state ideologies. Sometimes through conflict and struggle and sometimes through mutual consent and constitutional change, religious actors have created expanding islands of autonomy. The growing institutional independence of religious actors means that they enjoy a political position that is not merely different in degree from their position in previous eras but different in kind. Less likely to be merged with the state and less likely to be taken over by the state, religious actors have increasingly become "peer competitors" with the state. This institutional shift has been fueled by the attitudinal and theological changes that have been evident in many religious traditions after 1789. In part reacting against revolutionary republicanism and in part transformed by its participatory and egalitarian spirit, religious actors across all the major religious traditions have abandoned political theologies of passive obedience in exchange for political theologies of involvement, mobilization, opposition, and resistance.

The historical shift toward religion's expanding autonomy has been hundreds of years in the making, and it is the key to understanding the current trajectory of religion's political influence. The political influence of religious actors is presently following an upward trajectory not fundamentally because religious belief, behavior, and belonging are on the rise, as suggested by such (very imperfect) indices as belief in God or church attendance. Rather, religion is enjoying a political ascendancy fundamentally because religious actors enjoy a qualitatively greater level of independence from political authorities than they enjoyed in the past—indeed, greater than they typically enjoyed in virtually any previous era of human history. And they increasingly adhere to qualitatively different political theologies that legitimate if not demand intense political engagement. In subsequent chapters, we explore the dramatic consequences of these shifts for numerous domains of world politics, including global democracy and democratization, extremism and terrorism, domestic conflicts and civil wars, and peace-building and reconciliation.

Chapter Four

RELIGION AND GLOBAL DEMOCRATIZATION

Religious actors are on a worldwide offensive. Today, many enjoy greater independence from state institutions than in previous eras of human history. Sometimes this autonomy is borne of conflict and struggle and remains unofficial and precarious; other times it is the result of widespread social consensus and enjoys legitimacy and permanence as official government policy. Either way, religious actors have carved out more space to construct independent identities, social agendas, and political goals. Sometimes as a cause and other times as a consequence of this enhanced political independence, they have also come to espouse activist political theologies—theologies that legitimate and even require greater engagement on the part of their followers.

These two factors go a long way toward explaining why the current century is "God's Century." Ever since the late 1960s and now well into the twenty-first century, nonstate religious actors have influenced world politics in unprecedented ways. No longer merely the creatures of princes, empires, and state bureaucracies, they help to set the regional and global political agenda. This is what we mean by resurgent religion.

Consider one example pulled from the headlines. A recent analysis of Middle East politics concluded that two of the region's erstwhile dominant players, Saudi Arabia and Egypt, are witnessing steep declines in influence. Why? The rise of Iran and Syria is part of the reason, but equally important is that these long-standing regional power-brokers are being "defied by influential nonstate groups like Hamas and Hizbollah." Indeed, the analysis goes on to point out that a major source of Iranian and Syrian leverage is *their strong ties to Hamas and Hezbollah.*[1]

More and more, religious actors take initiative, act with boldness, mobilize local and national populations, operate with extraordinary flexibility, and command transnational loyalty, global networks, and resources. In a growing number of contexts, religious leaders and organizations are acting, while states are being acted upon.

If religious actors are increasingly acting and on the offensive, this chapter begins to consider the all-important question: What are they acting *for*? What are their political agendas? And, with what kind of political consequences?

As crucial as it is to understand *that* religion's political influence is growing and that this resurgence flows from the expanding structural autonomy of religious actors and the increasing activism propelled by their political theologies, it is essential to grasp *what* religious actors are doing with this growing influence. How are they using it to shape politics within states and across states? And what factors explain why one set of religious actors might use their influence in one way, while another set of actors uses their influence in another? For example, what explains why the Russian Orthodox Church has used its growing influence in the era after the 1991 fall of the Soviet Union to legitimate xenophobic nationalism and the increasing authoritarianism of the Kremlin, rather than to promote democracy and human rights? Why have Muslim civil society organizations in Indonesia proven to be reliable and influential advocates of democracy, while Muslim organizations like Hamas and Hezbollah in the Middle East not only advocate but practice violent militancy and terrorism?

In this chapter, we look at the part that religion played in one of the most important global trends in the past generation: the global spread of democracy. Snapshots capture saffron-clad Burmese monks protesting their military dictatorship; Catholic nuns in the Philippines staring down the tanks of dictator Ferdinand Marcos; Turkish Muslims wearing Western suits and finally entering the corridors of power in Ankara; and, one month before the fall of the Berlin Wall in October 1989, East German Protestants singing at a candlelight demonstration in front of the Nikolaikirche in Leipzig.

Two crucial questions arise from these images:

✦ First, what are the different ways religious actors across the world relate to democracy? Are there prevailing patterns? Are some kinds of religious actors constructive? Are some kinds of religious actors destructive? Are some diffident? In other words, *how* do religious groups across the world interact with the ideals and institutions of political freedom?

✦ Second, what explains the different ways religious actors relate to democracy? What explains the prevailing patterns of interaction? In other words, *why* do different religious actors adopt different positions and postures in relation to democratic norms and procedures?

Before proceeding, it is important to stress that "democracy" means more than just elections. It has been said that some "democracies" are "illiberal" in the sense that they may hold meaningful elections yet disregard the civil and political rights of their people.[2] Past a certain point, we believe, such regimes do not deserve to be called democracies at all.

Real democracy requires more than free and fair elections and must also include the freedom to form and join organizations; freedom of expression; the right to vote; broad eligibility for public office; alternative sources of information; and a written constitution that respects fundamental liberties, including the rights of minorities. As political scientists Alfred Stepan and Juan Linz have emphasized, inherent in this set of minimum democratic conditions is not merely a set of political institutions but the existence of an independent civil society that "helps check the state and constantly generates [political] alternatives."[3] When society is unable to organize and speak for itself, there is no real democracy.

WHEN FAITH MEETS FREEDOM: WHAT'S AT STAKE

Why is it important to inquire into the relationship between democracy and resurgent religion? Four reasons stand out.

First, comprehending the relationship between resurgent religion and democracy is important for understanding the world's big strides toward democracy in recent history. One of the most consequential and hopeful global trends in the last quarter of the twentieth century was an authoritarian decline combined with a democratic ascendancy. To measure these trends, we use the widely respected scale of Freedom House, an organization that assesses and promotes human rights and democracy.[4] According to Freedom House, the number of "Free" countries doubled from 44 in 1972 to 89 in 2009, while the number of "Not Free" countries declined from 69 to 47 in the same period. Sixty percent of the world's 194 countries are now electoral democracies, compared to 46 percent in 1990. In a relatively short period of time, the "Free World" has gone from embattled bastion to global majority.

This global expansion raises a question: Did the expansion of religion's political influence documented in the previous chapter help or hinder global democratization? The question is particularly interesting and appropriate because the ascendance of religion and democracy occurred roughly in the same period in history. Democracy's global takeoff began around 1974. Religion's takeoff in terms of global political activism and influence began around the same time but somewhat earlier, in the late 1960s or early 1970s (the precise timing depends on what religious community one is talking about; in a handful of cases, such as in Sri Lanka, it began somewhat earlier, in the mid- to late 1950s). As a matter of historical understanding, is there any evidence that religion's political takeoff helps explain the timing and scope of democracy's global takeoff? In the previous chapter, we already suggested that in a number of contexts, the liberalization and democratization of political systems was one factor that helped give religious actors an unprecedented ability to organize and influence governments and societies around the world. Religious actors grew in political assertiveness and influence thanks in part to a global decline in authoritarian repression.

For example, Charles Kurzman and Ijlal Naqvi exhaustively analyzed countries whose populations are at least 30 percent Muslim and found—consistent with our argument about the timing of religion's global political resurgence—that Islamic parties in such contexts became a growing force between 1968 and 2008. In fact, their analysis examines all of the elections that have occurred in such countries since the 1960s and uncovers a quantifiable pattern. Whereas the proportion of elections involving Islamic parties was only 28 percent in the 1960s, it grew to 35 percent in the first nine years of the twenty-first century. In addition, consistent with our argument about the conditions contributing to the religious resurgence, they found that where there was more democracy, Islamic parties were *even more likely* to be present. Among the most democratic countries with large Muslim populations, 48 percent of elections included Islamic parties, while only 28 percent of elections featured Islamic parties in less democratic countries.[5]

In other words, as we suggested in Chapter One, the enhanced political assertiveness religious actors enjoyed was a direct consequence of the global decline in authoritarian repression and a concomitant increase in political competition. Exemplifying this pattern is Egypt, where Anwar Sadat liberalized the government's policy toward some religious leaders and organizations shortly after succeeding Nasser as president, releasing the leaders of the Muslim Brotherhood from prison and allowing them a greater voice in society. Though Sadat hoped to use these religious leaders to compensate for the ideological vacuum left by the collapse of Nasser's pan-Arab nationalism as well as to counter the pro-Soviet left, especially on university campuses, the Muslim Brothers rapidly capitalized on their new freedom by influencing mosques, creating a social service network, and reactivating the mass support base they had built before they fell victim to systematic state repression and disruption in the 1950s.[6]

The question we address here: As many political systems and societies around the world became more open in the 1970s, what was the basic position of religious actors in relation to processes of expanding political freedom?

Any number of positions was possible. We mention four.

One possibility is that religious actors took advantage of this expanding freedom to propagate their teachings and increase their social influence but did little to expand political freedom themselves. We could call this the "free rider" possibility.

A second possibility is that once the freedom train left the station, religious actors not only got on board but tried to help push the train farther and faster. In other words, they may not have been a primary or initial agent of democratization, but they took some steps to support it and deepen it once it got going. We could call this the "supporting actor" possibility.

A third possibility is that religious actors were in the vanguard of democracy promotion. Either by themselves or in concert with other groups, they were among the first social actors to vigorously advocate and promote democratic rule. We could call this the "leading role" possibility.

A fourth and final possibility is that religious actors took steps to slow, dilute, or stop progress toward democracy, either through their active support of authoritarian regimes and movements or through their active opposition to the establishment of democratic institutions. This can be called the "reactionary resistance" possibility.

Understanding how the world's major religious actors related to democracy—whether as free riders, supporting actors, leading actors, or reactionary resisters—is crucial for understanding the democracy wave itself. If democracy expanded with the active support, cooperation, and even leadership of religious actors, this would help to explain why democracy successfully took root in so many of the world's societies.

Yet, if the position of many of the world's major religious actors was largely one of indifference or resistance to democracy, then democracy would not be so universal and exportable after all. Indeed, a closer look at the democracy data shows that global expansion has stalled. The percentage of the world's countries Freedom House classes as "electoral democracies" has remained stuck at around 60 percent for nearly fifteen years and in fact declined by four points—from 64 percent to 60 percent—between 2005 and 2009. Could it be that the kind of freedom democracy requires—including individual rights, equality for women, and respect for religious minorities—is more than many traditional religions and cultures are prepared to tolerate?

Second, understanding how religion and democracy interacted in recent years is crucial for characterizing the political resurgence of religion. Much scholarly and popular analysis, resurrecting the spirit of the secularization thesis, has cast resurgent or revivalist religion as "fundamentalist." A major rationale for this label is the belief that assertive or "strong" religion inevitably conflicts with the modern world. In particular, many argue that what modern religious revivalists share is a militant opposition to the freedom, pluralism, and democratic spirit that are thought to be characteristic of modern society.[7] This alleged antimodernist and antidemocratic tendency of religion is thought to justify the wide use of "fundamentalism" as an analytical category applicable to any and all religious leaders and groups apparently uncomfortable with modern liberal freedom, whether the so-called Christian Right in the United States, Hindu-nationalist movements in India, or extremist forms of Islamism in the Muslim world. Such "fundamentalist" groups react against liberal freedom, it is thought, either by establishing closed religious subcultures that regulate the lives of their members in an oppressive fashion, or by imposing faith-based legal and cultural systems on entire societies.

If our investigation reveals that the world's major religious actors have been largely indifferent or resistant to democratization, this would indeed suggest that these actors have "fundamentalist" tendencies and that "fundamentalism" is the right way to characterize much of the global religious resurgence. If, however, a wide range of revivalist religious actors not only tolerated the expansion of liberal freedom but actively promoted it, "fundamentalist" would be a misleading rubric. At stake is what motivates and drives religious actors in recent world history.

Third, understanding the relationship between religion and democracy would yield enormous insight into the nature and trajectory of global politics as a whole. As we have noted, world politics over the last forty years has seen two powerful waves sweep across it: a wave of democracy and a wave of religious activism.

If many major religious actors are "free riders" or engaged in "reactionary resistance" against democracy, then it follows that the global current of democratization is being set off course by a global crosscurrent of what may be best described as fundamentalism. And some of the recurring instability in world politics might then be explained as a consequence of a continuous collision between these actors and democracy. Furthermore, resurgent religion might be another explanation for the fact that the last decade or so has seen the global progress of democracy slow to a standstill. Perhaps early on, religious actors exploited political openness to expand their own power but in later years used their influence to slow the pace and scope of democratic consolidation—a pattern, for example, that seems to characterize the political behavior of the Russian Orthodox Church since the fall of Communism.

Yet, what if it turns out that many or most religious actors were "supporting actors" or even played a "leading role" in advancing democracy? Perhaps religion and democracy are natural allies, waiting for the right conditions to surge ahead together, each reinforcing the other. If true, global democratization may have stalled in recent years in part because determined authoritarian regimes have blocked or stymied the prodemocratic activism of religious actors.

Fourth, understanding the relationship between religion and democracy is crucial for addressing urgent and contemporary policy debates surrounding the promotion of democracy around the world. If the religious surge in global politics inhibited democratization, then a secular public space may be a precondition of true democracy after all—much as French Republicans and the partisans of Kemal Ataturk's Turkish Revolution have long argued. This would suggest that the best way for contemporary governments to pave the way for democracy is to sharply limit the influence of faith-based actors on political life. As Middle East analyst and historian Martin Kramer has claimed about the Muslim world, a political system can safely invite the full-fledged participation of religious actors only when a strong state—a "secular guardian"—can compel them to maintain a moderate course shorn of any radical tendencies.[8]

By this logic, the Egyptian regime of President Hosni Mubarak, which has long banned the Muslim Brotherhood as a formal organization and continues to bar its official participation in mainstream politics, may be on the right track. In late 2009, in fact, the Mubarak regime "launched a fresh campaign against the banned Muslim Brotherhood . . . arbitrarily arresting hundreds of members, from young bloggers to senior leaders."[9] These moves are designed to keep the Muslim Brotherhood out of politics and public life and restrict it to "private" activities such as social service delivery.

However, if the religious surge facilitated democratization, at least under some conditions, then public spaces can be opened up to religious influences not only without endangering democracy but with the expectation of advancing it. If this logic is correct, religious organizations should be given maximum room to operate in political society in order to channel the opinions of otherwise voiceless people and to check otherwise unchecked governments (except, of course, where the religious organizations in question are so violent and extremist that they are intrinsically inimical to democratic norms and practice). Religious actors would be integral components of what is considered a core feature of democracy: the existence of a "robust and critical" civil society able to check the state.

THE LANDSCAPE: RELIGIOUS ACTORS AND GLOBAL DEMOCRATIZATION

So does the interaction between religious actors and democratization over the last forty or so years reveal any striking pattern or "big picture"? Have faith and freedom mostly cooperated? Or mostly collided?

To answer these questions first consider all the world's countries that have enjoyed some substantial democratization between 1972 and 2009. A country deemed to have undergone "substantial democratization" needs to have met *at least one* of the three following criteria:

✦ *Its aggregate Freedom House political freedom rating has improved by at least 3 points.* For example, in 1972 Burkina Faso had a Political Rights score of 7 and a Civil Liberties score of 5, giving it an aggregate political freedom rating of 12. By 2009 its Political Rights score was 5 and Civil Liberties score 3, giving it an aggregate rating of 8, meaning that its overall political freedom rating improved by 4 points between 1972 and 2009. Burkina Faso, then, experienced substantial democratization in this period (even if it remains far from a shining beacon of Jeffersonian democracy).

✦ *Its Freedom House category shifted either from "Not Free" to "Partly Free" or from "Partly Free" to "Free."* For example, during the semiauthoritarian "Emergency" imposed on Indian society by Prime Minister Indira Gandhi in 1975, Freedom House categorized India as "Partly Free," giving its Political Rights a score of 2 and its Civil Liberties a score of 5. By 1977, after the

Emergency, India shifted back to "Free" and continues to hold that rating today, with its Political Rights most recently scored at 2 and Civil Liberties at 3. This, too, counts as an instance of substantial democratization—an important qualitative shift—even though the quantitative improvement in India's aggregate political freedom amounted to only 2 points (from 7 to 5).

✦ *A territory undergoes a "double transition" to political independence as well as to some measure of political freedom following independence.* A transition to sovereignty is itself considered substantial democratization in our analysis. It makes little sense, after all, to speak of "democratization" in the case of a country such as Uzbekistan, which, though it achieved independence with the breakup of the Soviet Union, is now a perfect tyranny with a maximally undemocratic aggregate Freedom House rating of 14—7 for Political Rights and 7 for Civil Liberties. Even if it sees no improvement in its aggregate political freedom rating or no formal shift from a less free to a more free Freedom House category, it is reasonable to judge that substantial democratization has occurred if a territory not only achieves sovereignty but ultimately earns a "Free" or "Partly Free" designation from Freedom House. (However, if the recently independent country in question suffered a substantial democratic reversal, with its aggregate political freedom rating swinging at least 3 points in an undemocratic direction by 2009, we do not count it as a case of substantial democratization.)

This approach to defining "substantial democratization" admittedly privileges democratic progress over democratic perfection. This is not to diminish the value and importance of consolidated democracy. We noted above that democracy by its nature requires a wide range of freedoms, institutions, and procedures that go well beyond elections. But given our interest in analyzing the global movement toward political freedom, and how religious dynamics interacted with this broad movement, we want to look at all countries that moved a substantial distance toward full democracy—even if many of them did not reach the finish line.[10] This approach also squares better with the messiness of political reality. As critics of democratic transition theory have underscored, democratization is not necessarily a process with a single foreordained end point. Regardless of where regimes ended up on the democratic continuum, we wanted to assess religion's relationship to all serious democratic progress, or what some may prefer to term "liberalization." No democracy is perfectly consolidated, after all.

Table 4.1

CASES OF SUBSTANTIAL DEMOCRATIZATION
BY REGION, 1972–2009

	WORLD	AFRICA	AMERICAS	ASIA	EUROPE
Cases of Substantial *Democratization*	78	24	15	15	24

With "substantial democratization" so defined, the world has seen 78 cases of substantial democratization between 1972 and 2009. That means more than 40 percent of the world's nearly 200 countries have made serious democratic progress since the 1970s. There has indeed been a massive global march toward political freedom.

As Table 4.1 shows, this great march of democratization has covered the globe. Every region—Africa, the Americas, Asia, Europe—has seen a good number of countries experience substantial democratic progress. Africa and Europe have each seen two dozen countries move in a democratic direction. That is about half the countries in each of those regions. The Americas and Asia have each seen 15 countries make substantial strides toward political freedom. That translates into about a third of Asia's countries and almost half of the countries in the Americas. In other words, global democratization has redrawn the political map of every part of the world.

Importantly, this political transformation includes Muslim-majority countries. Some analysts have described the Muslim world as relatively inhospitable to democracy, and with some justification.[11] However, numerous Muslim-majority countries, such as Bangladesh, Bosnia-Herzegovina, Indonesia, Mali, Niger, Senegal, and Turkey, have made serious democratic gains in the last forty years.[12] In fact, of the 78 countries that have experienced substantial democratization between 1972 and 2009, 17—more than 20 percent—have Muslim majorities or Muslim pluralities.[13]

Though systematic analysis demonstrates that the Middle East and North Africa have proven relatively resistant to democratization, the world's democratic wave made some inroads even in the Arab Middle East. Iraq is one Middle Eastern country that has made measurable democratic progress in

Table 4.2

DEMOCRATIZING COUNTRIES WHERE
RELIGIOUS ACTORS PLAYED A DEMOCRATIZING ROLE,
1972–2009

	WORLD	AFRICA	AMERICAS	ASIA	EUROPE
Total Number of Cases of Substantial Democratization	78	24	15	15	24
Number of Democratizing Countries Where Religious Actors Played a Democratizing Role	48	13	11	10	14
Democratizing Countries Where Religious Actors Played a Democratizing Role (By Region)		Benin Burundi Congo-B* Ghana Kenya Liberia Malawi Mali Mozambique Namibia Nigeria South Africa Zambia	Bolivia Brazil Chile El Salvador Haiti Guatemala Mexico Nicaragua Paraguay Peru Uruguay	India Indonesia Iraq Kuwait Pakistan Philippines South Korea Taiwan Timor-Leste Turkey	Bosnia-Herzegovina Croatia Czech Republic Germany Kosovo Lithuania Poland Portugal Romania Serbia Slovakia Slovenia Spain Ukraine

* Congo-B is the Republic of the Congo, also sometimes known as Congo-Brazzaville (for its capital city, Brazzaville), and is to be distinguished from the Democratic Republic of the Congo or Congo-Kinshasa (for its capital city, Kinshasa).

recent years and is one of the 78 cases of democratization noted in Table 4.1. Of course, Iraq is unique. Saddam Hussein's dictatorship was brought down by a multinational force led by the United States and the United Kingdom in 2003. But the country's arduous construction of democratic procedures and institutions—still far from complete—is due largely to the efforts of a wide range of Iraqi groups, including religious actors. And this progress has moved Iraq's combined Freedom House score 3 points in a democratic direction since 2003. Also among the 78 cases is Kuwait, which shifted from "Not Free" to "Partly Free" between 1972 and 2009 and currently enjoys a combined Freedom House score of 8. Another case, albeit an ambiguous one, is Jordan. While Jordan also made enough progress to move from "Not Free" to "Partly Free" in the classification of Freedom House during the 1980s and achieved a combined Freedom House score as low as 6 by 1992, it subsequently backslid. Like many countries that marched toward freedom in the heady years after the fall of the Berlin Wall in 1989, its political trajectory in the intervening period has been a zigzag rather than a straight line. Though its Freedom House score was as low as 8 in 2000, it is now 11. Its serious democratic regress means that it does not count as a case of "net democratization" between 1972 and 2009. Still, these cases demonstrate that the global wave of democratization has not left the Muslim world—including the Arab Middle East—untouched.

How religious actors made a difference in the cases of Iraq and Jordan will be discussed later in this chapter. But along with the case of Kuwait, they clearly show that the global wave of democratization has swept into the Muslim world—and the Arab Middle East.

So how did religious actors relate to this massive march toward freedom? The short answer is that the democratizing role of religious actors between 1972 and 2009 was massive. As Table 4.2 indicates, religious actors played a democratizing role in 48 of the 78 countries that witnessed substantial democratization in this period. In other words, in well over half of democratizing countries at least some religious actors were a prodemocratic force.

A few clarifications are immediately in order. First, this stage of our analysis enumerates only *countries* in which at least one religious actor contributed to democratization, not the prodemocratic religious actors themselves. (In the next section, we turn to an analysis of prodemocratic religious actors.) In several of these 48 countries, such as Kenya, South Africa, and South Korea, *multiple* religious actors from diverse religious traditions undertook prodemocratic activity; in other countries, such as Lithuania and Poland, only one religious actor did so.

Second, the claim that religious actors worked to promote democracy in this vast number of democratizing countries does not mean that they were necessarily the single most decisive factor in generating democratic political change. Our assessment is not based on the ultimate political impact of religious activism, either on its own or in comparison with other factors that scholars believe to have contributed to democratization in a given country—such as level of economic development, for instance. Nor does it necessarily mean that *all* religious actors in these countries acted to advance political freedom. As we explore in more detail below, religious actors were divided into prodemocratic and antidemocratic camps in some countries.

What our claim does begin to answer is the first major question we posed earlier: How have religious groups interacted with the ideals and institutions of political freedom? The crux of our claim hinges not on the ultimate political impact of religious actors, but on their basic political disposition and activism. Have they been aloof as "free riders" or hostile as "reactionary resisters"? Or have religious actors been "leading" or "supporting" actors? Where a religious actor has undertaken some substantial, documented activity on behalf of democracy and democratization, we classify that actor as having played a democratizing role.

Specifically, what determines our classification of religious actors as "democratizing" is whether they undertook at least one of the five following forms of political activity in an organized and sustained manner:

1. *Protest or organized opposition to an authoritarian government.* An example of a public version is the demonstrations for democracy in Burma led by Buddhist monks in 2007.

2. *A religious ceremony or program that bears antiauthoritarian implications.* A defining example here is the open-air masses that Pope John Paul II conducted for hundreds of thousands of Poles over the course of three pilgrimages to Communist Poland beginning in 1979. Poles clearly understood that the human rights references in the pope's homilies were directed at them and their autocratic overseers.

3. *Coordination and cooperation with international or transnational actors to weaken an authoritarian government or strengthen a transitional democratic government.* Here again, John Paul II is an example. Mobilizing the transnational authority structure of the Catholic Church, he traveled to sites of authoritarian rule around the world to bolster national Catholic churches and challenge dictators.

4. *Active encouragement or support of domestic opposition groups and actors.* Turkey's Islamic Justice and Development Party, for instance, formed a coalition with other parties and important groups in order to make its way into power in 2002.
5. *Mediation or brokering of negotiations between political actors to facilitate the transition to a more stable and more democratic order.* Numerous examples of this can be found in Chapter Seven, which looks at the mediation of peace agreements. In many cases, peace agreements also involved transitions to democracy.[14]

Applying these criteria, then, yields the results in Table 4.2. Remarkably, in about 62 percent of the world's democratizing countries, at least some religious actors actively aligned themselves with democratization. Here, religious actors were not neutral about the fate of democracy—and were certainly neither "free riders" nor "reactionary resisters"—but worked actively in its favor.

Furthermore, as Table 4.2 indicates, the democratizing activity of religious actors was as pervasive as it was massive. More than half of the democratizing countries *in each major region of the world* saw religious actors play a prodemocratic role. In the Americas, religious actors played a democratizing role in about 73 percent of cases of democratization—11 out of 15 countries. In Asia, the proportion was 67 percent—10 of 15 cases. Prodemocracy monks and mullahs, priests and patriarchs, were everywhere—North and South, East and West, developed world and developing world.

If the sheer quantity of prodemocracy religious activism was impressive, so was its quality. As Table 4.3 shows, religious actors played a *leading* prodemocratic role in 30 of the 48 cases in which religious actors played some democratizing role. That is, compared to other social actors, whether business leaders, political parties, or human rights activists, religious leaders and organizations were in the forefront of opposing authoritarian regimes or encouraging the formation of more democratic ones (or both). This does not necessarily mean that religious actors were *the* most important leaders of democratization movements. But if a religious actor played a leading role, it does mean that it was among the most prominent promoters of democracy in any given society.

Whether in politics or the theater, discerning if an actor should be classified as "leading" or "supporting" is not always easy. But one good indicator is the timing of their appearance in the drama—did they make their entrance in

Table 4.3

TYPE OF DEMOCRATIZING ROLE RELIGIOUS ACTORS PLAYED
IN DEMOCRATIZING COUNTRIES, 1972–2009

	WORLD	AFRICA	AMERICAS	ASIA	EUROPE
Total Democratizing Countries	78	24	15	15	24
Number of Democratizing Countries Where Religious Actors Played a LEADING Democratizing Role	30	9	7	8	6
Number of Democratizing Countries Where Religious Actors Played a SUPPORTING Democratizing Role	18	4	4	2	8
Democratized Countries Where Religious Actors Played a Democratizing Role (by region)	Benin (L)* Burundi (S) Congo-B† (S) Ghana (L) Kenya (L) Liberia (L) Malawi (L) Mali (S) Mozambique (L) Namibia (L) Nigeria (S) South Africa (L) Zambia (L)	Bolivia (S) Brazil (L) Chile (L) El Salvador (L) Haiti (L) Guatemala (L) Mexico (S) Nicaragua (L) Paraguay (S) Peru (S) Uruguay (L)	India (L) Indonesia (L) Iraq (L) Kuwait (L) Pakistan (S) Philippines (L) South Korea (L) Taiwan (S) Timor-Leste (L) Turkey (L)	Bosnia-Herzegovina (S) Croatia (L) Czech Republic (S) Germany (S) Kosovo (S) Lithuania (L) Poland (L) Portugal (S) Romania (L) Serbia (L) Slovakia (S) Slovenia (S) Spain (L) Ukraine (S)

* (L) or (S) after the name of each country indicates whether the democratizing religious actor(s) in that country played a leading (L) or supporting (S) democratic role.

† Congo-B is the Republic of the Congo, also sometimes known as Congo-Brazzaville (for its capital city, Brazzaville), and is to be distinguished from the Democratic Republic of the Congo or Congo-Kinshasa (for its capital city, Kinshasa).

Act I, or did they stay offstage until Act II or III? Leading actors tend to appear early and not wait behind the scenes until the later acts. Another indicator is their relationship to the central action of the story—did they help initiate or shape some of its defining dynamic, or were they mostly its passive receptors, foils, or victims? Leading actors shape the flow and outcome of the action. A final indicator is sheer volume—how often and how much did we hear from them? Did they have many lines or only a few? Leading actors typically appear onstage early, frequently, and volubly. A supporting actor, for his or her part, might do one or two of these things—appear early in the drama *or* help shape the defining action of the story *or* mount a constant and voluble dramatic presence. But it is characteristic of a leading actor to do all of the above—i.e., to appear early, often, *and* with dramatic consequence.

As Table 4.3 demonstrates, no part of the world failed to see numerous religious actors playing just this kind of leading role on behalf of democratic change. In fact, these leading prodemocratic religious actors were actively involved in nearly 40 percent of all global cases of democratization from 1972 through 2009 (30 of 78). In Asia, religious actors played a leading pro-democratic role in more than half of all democratization cases: 8 of 15. There, Muslim leaders like Grand Ayatollah Ali al-Sistani in Iraq and the late Abdurrahman Wahid in Indonesia have been prominent opponents of religious radicalism and narrow sectarianism and pressed for forms of Islam supportive of democracy and religious reconciliation.

Consider the leading pro-democratic role of Sistani, Iraq's most influential Shiite cleric. When L. Paul Bremer, head of the post-invasion provisional authority in Iraq, proposed a plan to draft a new constitution through an unelected council chosen largely by the U.S., Sistani issued a blunt *fatwa* in June 2003, declaring that such a council could not be trusted to "create a constitution conforming with the greater interests of the Iraqi people and expressing the national identity, whose basis is Islam." He unwaveringly demanded immediate popular elections, setting the stage for a protracted conflict with Bremer, who "didn't want a Shiite cleric dictating the terms of Iraq's political future," in the words of one U.S. official. Ultimately, the force of Sistani's authority accelerated the handover to an interim Iraqi government as well as the staging of democratic elections, held in January 2005, which chose an assembly to oversee the writing of Iraq's constitution. The Ayatollah's prodemocratic activism did not stop there. He has urged women to make full use of the political franchise—comparing women who vote to Zaynab, the sister of the martyred imam Husayn, whom Shiites revere as Muhammad's legitimate successor—and has mobilized his followers to oppose the radical cleric Muqtada al-Sadr. Recently, Sistani issued statements condemning vote-buying as *haram* (forbidden by Islam) and urging Iraqi citizens to defy terror-ist threats and vote in the March 2010 national elections. All this justifies one Iraqi scholar's assessment of Sistani and his associates as "Iraq's most consis-tent and effective advocates of elections and parliamentary representation."[15]

In Africa, the Catholic and Presbyterian churches played a decisive role in galvanizing opposition to the authoritarian rule of Hastings Banda in Malawi, and the Anglican Church was a leading source of opposition to apartheid in South Africa as well as the authoritarian regime of Daniel arap Moi in Kenya. Throughout Latin America, the Catholic Church was a prominent and influential agent of democratization, playing a leading role in Brazil, Chile, El Salvador, Guatemala, Nicaragua, and even in relatively secular Uruguay. In Europe, Catholic and Protestant leaders and groups undermined numer-ous Communist regimes with the encouragement and often direct inter-vention of Pope John Paul II, while Orthodox churches and leaders such as Archbishop Pavle, patriarch of the Serbian Orthodox Church, worked in the post-Communist period to oppose antidemocratic nationalist regimes, such as that of Slobodan Milošević.

In all these cases, religious actors played an important role in Acts I, II, and III of the democratization drama. They often fired the first decisive shot at an authoritarian government, as did the Catholic Church in Malawi, with its Lenten Pastoral Letter of March 1992—the first public criticism of Banda's increasingly brutal dictatorship. In the course of Act II—the middle and fre-quently long and uncertain phase of democratization—these religious actors were often instrumental in organizing and sustaining democratic opposition movements and maintaining pressure on authoritarian or quasi-authoritarian regimes, as was true of a succession of Islamist parties in Turkey from the 1970s up through today. And these religious actors often played a crucial role in the final stage of democratization, Act III, as did the Catholic Church in Mozambique, mediating between the prodemocratic opposition and authori-tarian loyalists and helping to secure a stable democratic settlement.

So the bottom line is clear. In most of the cases where democracy was on the march between 1972 and 2009, freedom had a friend in religion. Fur-thermore, in most of the cases where religion was freedom's ally, it was a principal combatant. It did not merely cheer from the sidelines but fought in the front lines.

This finding challenges the view of the secularization thesis—particularly in its latest "neo-atheist" version—that militant religion and illiberal politics are conjoined twins. In many of the instances where religious actors have been militant in recent decades, they have militated for political freedom, with their inevitable opponent being one variety or another of authoritarianism. Left-wing authoritarian regimes, right-wing authoritarian regimes, and authoritarian regimes perhaps best classified as postcolonial messianic regimes—in which political authority was vested in a figure or party that had been instrumental in a struggle against a colonial empire—all bore the brunt of prodemocratic religious militancy.

Yet this finding about how religious actors related to democratization in recent decades raises numerous questions. If religious actors were on the side of freedom in 48 of the world's 78 cases of democratization since 1972, what about the remaining 30 cases? Why did religious actors in those other cases fail to rally to the cause of freedom in a clear, deliberate, and sustained way? What separates the democratizers from the nondemocratizers?

And what about the 47 countries categorized as "Not Free" by Freedom House—almost a quarter of the world's 200 or so nation-states—that have failed to make substantial democratic gains? Does *their* lack of substantial democratic progress have anything to do with religious actors? Are antidemocratic religious actors partly responsible for helping to keep the "Not Free World" unfree? Does the democratic deficit in these countries persist *despite* the democratizing efforts of religious actors?

Taken together, these questions press us to go beyond our description of how religious actors have participated in global democratization. They demand an explanation of *why* the relationship between religion and democratization is so complex and variable when all the relevant global cases are considered.

EXPLAINING WHEN FAITH SERVES FREEDOM

Let us first consider those religious actors that squarely positioned themselves on the side of democracy and democratization, whether in a supporting or leading role. Exactly what kinds of religious actors played a democratizing role in the 48 global cases of democratization described above? We have already observed that prodemocratic religious actors were dispersed across the world's major geographic regions. Another way to characterize them is in terms of their basic religious identity and tradition. What religious traditions

Table 4.4

RELIGIOUS ACTORS THAT PLAYED A DEMOCRATIZING ROLE IN GLOBAL CASES OF DEMOCRATIZATION, 1972–2009

NUMBER OF DEMOCRATIZED COUNTRIES WHERE RELIGIOUS ACTORS PLAYED A DEMOCRATIZING ROLE

TYPE OF RELIGIOUS ACTOR	In the World	In Africa	In the Americas	In Asia	In Europe
Catholic	36 (22 L / 14 S)	Benin (L) Burundi (S) Congo-B (S) Ghana (L) Kenya (L) Liberia (L) Malawi (L) Mozambique (L) Namibia (S) Nigeria (S) South Africa (L) Zambia (L)	Bolivia (S) Brazil (L) Chile (L) El Salvador (L) Guatemala (L) Haiti (L) Mexico (S) Nicaragua (L) Paraguay (S) Peru (S) Uruguay (L)	Philippines (L) South Korea (L) Timor-Leste (L)	Croatia (L) Czech Republic (S) Kosovo (S) Lithuania (L) Poland (L) Portugal (S) Slovakia (S) Slovenia (S) Spain (L) Ukraine (S)
Hindu	1 (1L)	0	0	India (L)	0
Muslim	12 (5 L / 7 S)	Kenya (S) Mali (S) Nigeria (S)*	0	India (L) Indonesia (L) Iraq (L) Kuwait (L) Pakistan (S) Turkey (L)	Bosnia-Herzegovina (S) Kosovo (S) Serbia (S)
Orthodox	4 (1 L / 3 S)	0	0	0	Bosnia-Herzegovina (S) Kosovo (S) Serbia (L) Ukraine (S)
Protestant	19 (8 L / 11 S)	Congo-B (S) Ghana (L) Kenya (L) Liberia (S) Malawi (L) Mozambique (S) Namibia (L) Nigeria (S) South Africa (L) Zambia (L)	Brazil (S) Chile (S) Nicaragua (S) Peru (S)	Philippines (S) South Korea (L) Taiwan (S)	Germany (S) Romania (L)

* A country is listed more than once when more than one kind of religious actor played a democratizing role in that country. For example, because Catholic, Muslim, and Protestant actors played a democratizing role in Nigeria, Nigeria is listed under each of those three categories of democratizing religious actor.

did these prodemocratic actors represent, and in what proportions? Did these prodemocratic religious actors tend to be concentrated in one religious tradition, or were they distributed fairly evenly across the major world religions? Some have suggested that Protestantism in particular or Western Christianity in general serves as a special or even unique incubator of democracy. Protestantism was indeed an important shaper of modern democracy when it appeared in Europe and America during the sixteenth through eighteenth centuries. Is this the case today? The basic answers to these questions are presented in Table 4.4.

As Table 4.4 shows, among democratizing religious actors no single religion or religious tradition has enjoyed a monopoly on prodemocratic activism. In the past generation's wave of democratization, at least one prodemocratic actor has emerged from almost every one of the world's major religious traditions.

For example, self-consciously Hindu actors in India were in the forefront of protesting and resisting Indira Gandhi's authoritarian "Emergency" suspension of democracy between 1975 and 1977—in part because such actors, especially leaders of the Jana Sangh Hindu-nationalist political party that preceded today's Bharatiya Janata Party (BJP), were its disproportionate victims.[16] Actors in the Orthodox Christian Church played a notable role in support of democracy in four European countries—not only in Serbia under the leadership of Patriarch Pavle but also in Bosnia-Herzegovina, Kosovo, and Ukraine. As we have already noted, Muslim actors played important prodemocratic roles in Iraq and Indonesia. In total, we found, Muslim actors played a leading or supporting democratizing role in some 12 countries in Africa, Asia, and Europe. Protestant actors played a democratizing role in every region of the world, actively promoting democracy in a total of 19 countries. Catholic actors played a prodemocratic role in an impressive 36 countries, particularly in Africa, the Americas, and Europe, but also in three countries in Asia.

The other basic fact that emerges from the religious distribution of prodemocratic activism, however, is that it is far from even. Although almost every religious tradition has seen at least some prodemocratic activism, the fact is that religious actors from the Catholic tradition accounted for an overwhelming proportion of religious activism on behalf of democracy between 1972 and 2009. In three-quarters of the cases where religious actors played a role in democratization—36 of 48 countries—at least one of the prodemocratic religious actors was Catholic.[17] In 18 of 48 cases, the *only* religious actors that played a leading or supporting democratizing role were Catholic actors.

To put the Catholic contribution in stark terms, if one were to subtract the contribution of Catholic leaders and organizations, religious actors would have played a role in far fewer cases of global democratization—about 30 of 78. Absent an array of Catholic clerics, lay activists, and groups, ranging from Pope John Paul II to archbishops such as Oscar Romero in El Salvador and Michael Francis in Liberia to human rights groups such as the Vicariate of Solidarity in Chile, efforts to advance democracy and human rights would have been far weaker, particularly in Africa and the Americas. This is true in part because of the quality and level of Catholic involvement. As Table 4.4 indicates, in 22 of the 36 countries where Catholic actors played a serious democratizing role, the role they played was a leading one. Only within the category of Catholic prodemocratic actors, in fact, did a majority play a leading democratizing role; among actors from the Muslim, Protestant, and Orthodox traditions, the majority played a supporting one.

In the absence of this robust prodemocratic Catholic activism, it is likely that fewer countries would have enjoyed substantial, sustained, and stable democratic progress. It has been hard enough to sustain nascent democracy across the globe even with the involvement of prodemocratic Catholic actors. Without them, democratic gains would have been even more precarious.

Any satisfactory explanation of why some religious actors have been prodemocratic and others indifferent or hostile to democracy must begin by addressing the range of behavior we have just described. Such an explanatory account would have to reckon with the fact that actors from a wide range of religious traditions—Catholic, Hindu, Muslim, Orthodox and Protestant—have actively supported recent cases of democratization. Any explanation would therefore have to go beyond what is sometimes called "cultural essentialism." In this kind of view, which is espoused by international development analyst Lawrence Harrison, for example, the simple truth is that "some cultures do better than others": some cultures and religions—especially Protestant and Confucian ones—lay more solid foundations for economic and political development than other cultures.[18]

Whatever its merits, this view cannot explain why religious actors from traditions that Harrison terms "progress-resistant"—such as Islam and Orthodoxy—have nevertheless acted as agents of democratic progress. It also cannot explain why some actors from more "progress-prone" religious traditions failed to promote democratic progress. For example, why did the Anglican Church fail to promote democracy in Uganda but serve as a leading proponent of democratization in neighboring Kenya? Why did the Catholic

Church fail to promote democracy in Argentina but undertake prodemocratic activity in neighboring Chile and Brazil?

At the same time, a satisfactory explanatory account would have to account for the high proportion of Catholic and to a lesser extent Protestant actors involved in global democratization. What characteristics did these types of actors tend to have that fewer actors in other religious traditions possessed? What qualities put so many of these actors in a position to engage in democratizing activity? And yet, given the existence of prodemocratic religious actors outside the Catholic and Protestant traditions, it is clear that whatever characteristics helped make Catholic and Protestant prodemocratic actors so prevalent could not have been their exclusive franchise. There was political salvation—or at least democratization—outside the church.

The lopsided distribution of democratic religious actors is no doubt partly due to the uneven nature of global religious demography itself. The world's religious communities are uneven both in terms of their absolute populations and their global dispersions. The Roman Catholic Church not only has about a billion global adherents—more than any other world religion—but it has large communities in dozens of countries. Hinduism's adherents, by contrast, are concentrated overwhelmingly in India and Nepal, with much smaller communities in a handful of other countries. With this grossly uneven demographic distribution, it is not surprising that there is a grossly uneven democratizing distribution, with Catholic actors playing a role in many more cases of global democratization than Hindu actors.

But religious demography was and is not political destiny. Islam's global population is greater than Protestantism's—1.5 billion versus about 800 million (at the present writing). And Islam's global dispersion is comparable, with large Muslim communities spread across Africa, Asia, and southeastern Europe. Yet Protestant actors were involved in more cases of democratization than Muslim actors. Conversely, religious actors played a leading role in some political transitions even in countries where they represented a relatively small proportion of the overall population. The Catholic Church in Liberia, led by Archbishop Michael Francis, relentlessly protested the authoritarian regimes of Samuel Doe and later Charles Taylor, and was indispensable in stimulating international awareness and action, even though the Catholic share of Liberia's population is only about 3 percent. Neither demography nor culture alone, then, provides a satisfying account of why some religious actors were prodemocratic and some were indifferent or hostile to democracy.

Before we try to offer a more satisfying explanation of prodemocratic religious actors, however, we need to do two things: make sure we are not overlooking any other prodemocratic actors, and take a look at the antidemocratic ones.

We observed a few pages ago that "almost" every major religious tradition is represented by at least one prodemocratic actor. One religious tradition that is not so represented and is not included at all in Table 4.4 is Judaism. In fact, the world's only Jewish-majority state, Israel, did not become a democracy or make democratic progress during the period analyzed here (1972–2009) for the simple reason that Israel has been a liberal electoral democracy ever since its founding in 1948, and Freedom House has never categorized it as anything other than "Free" (with a fairly stable combined rating of 3 or 4 since 1977). Furthermore, the overwhelming majority of the world's 14 million Jews who live outside Israel, about 9 million, live in Western countries (mostly in the United States and France) that have been stable, consolidated democracies throughout the period in question. Due to the nature of Jewish demography, in other words, there is little organized Jewish presence and few Jewish actors in those regions of the world—Africa, Asia, the Americas, and Eastern and Central Europe—that have democratized in recent years. Judaism has lacked the demographic opportunity, in other words, to mount serious prodemocratic activism in politically volatile and dynamic parts of the world.

Another religious tradition conspicuously absent from Table 4.4 is Buddhism. The absence of Buddhist actors from the roster of recent prodemocratic activism is more difficult to explain than the absence of Judaism. Buddhism's absence is not due to a small global population highly concentrated in already democratized countries. Buddhism has a large global population with a significant organized presence and numerous Buddhist actors in many countries. Furthermore, some countries with large Buddhist populations made at least some democratic progress between 1972 and 2009, particularly South Korea and Taiwan. How did Buddhist actors relate to these cases of democratization?

Close inspection suggests that Buddhist actors failed to play leading or supporting roles in the political dynamics that generated democratic progress in South Korea or Taiwan. In Taiwan, even though Christians are only about 5 percent of the population and Buddhists more than 30 percent, André Laliberté notes that it was the Presbyterian Church that "stood at the forefront of the struggle for democratization in the 1970s and 1980s." In contrast, "Buddhists did not play a comparable role in the process of transition to democracy in Taiwan," and Buddhist groups were slow to develop a similar democratic theology and level of political activism.[19] Much the same story could be told about South Korea, where Catholic and Presbyterian churches played a leading role in pressing for democratic political change in the 1970s and 1980s, during all of the major acts of the democratization drama, while Buddhist actors remained relatively quiescent.[20]

This is not to say that Buddhist organizations are antidemocratic or contributed nothing to democratic consolidation in these cases. Consider the consolidation of Taiwan's democracy after the democratic transition of the mid-1990s (during which, according to Freedom House, Taiwan shifted from Partly Free and an aggregate score (combining political and civil liberties) of 8, in 1993, to Free and an aggregate score of 4, by 1996. According to sociologist Richard Madsen, democratization fostered a flowering of Buddhist organizations in the 1990s, which, in turn, contributed to the vitalization of civil society and a deepening of democracy. But even in Madsen's account, Buddhist actors contributed to democratic consolidation less through any leading or supporting role in Taiwan's political transformation than through social and humanitarian efforts that indirectly supported democracy by fostering egalitarianism, tolerance, and civic cooperation.[21]

Yet, is it really the case that the world's recent political history contains no examples of Buddhist leaders, movements, or organizations engaging in direct and significant democratizing activity? In fact, a moment's reflection brings to mind a number of Buddhist actors that have struggled—and struggle to this day—for democracy, self-determination, and human rights. Think of the Dalai Lama and his high-profile advocacy of greater political freedom and self-determination for Tibet. Or consider the thousands of Theravada Buddhist monks that formed the vanguard of the "Saffron Revolution" in Burma in August and September 2007.

The countries in which these religious actors have engaged in democratizing activity—China and Burma—have conspicuously failed to make substantial democratic progress. The problem has been with the highly repressive regimes they have challenged; not due to the religious actors themselves. They have engaged in a variety of deliberate, organized, and sustained political activities to advance democracy. And in the case of the monks in Burma and the Dalai Lama from Tibet, they have played a leading prodemocratic role.

In fact, wider analysis reveals 22 countries that have failed to see substantial

Table 4.5

RELIGIOUS ACTORS THAT ATTEMPTED A DEMOCRATIZING ROLE IN CASES OF FAILED DEMOCRATIZATION OR DEMOCRATIZATION, 1972–2009

DEMOCRATIZED COUNTRIES WHERE RELIGIOUS ACTORS PLAYED A DEMOCRATIZING ROLE

TYPE OF RELIGIOUS ACTOR	In the World	In Africa	In the Americas	In Asia	In Europe
Buddhist	3	0	0	Burma China / Tibet Vietnam*	0
Catholic	11	Angola* Congo-Kinshasa* Madagascar* Zimbabwe	Colombia Cuba* Honduras* Venezuela	China Malaysia Vietnam*	0
Hindu	2	0	0	Fiji Malaysia	0
Muslim	11	Algeria* Cote d'Ivoire* Egypt* Tunisia	0	China / Xinjiang Iran Jordan* Malaysia Syria* Tajikistan Uzbekistan	0
Orthodox	1	Egypt*	0	0	0
Protestant	4	Madagascar* Zimbabwe	0	China Vietnam*	0
Total Countries/ Religious Actors	22/32	8/11	4/4	10/17	0

* Indicates countries that failed to make substantial democratic progress as defined in the text of this chapter but nonetheless made *some* measurable democratic progress between 1972 and 2009—i.e., an improvement in their combined Freedom House Political Rights and Civil Liberties scores of at least one point. Countries not so designated saw either no change, or deterioration, in their Freedom House scores.

democratic progress but have nonetheless been witness to high levels of pro-democratic religious activism. Table 4.5 presents these cases, many of which are well known, such as the Muslim Brotherhood's advocacy of greater political competition in Egypt or protests against political and religious repression by unregistered Protestant and Catholic churches in China. Not so well known are other cases, such as the organized resistance of Hindu actors to ethnoreligious authoritarianism in Muslim-majority Malaysia and Christian-majority Fiji.

Here again we see a wide range of prodemocratic religious actors—across all major geographic regions and, in this case, all major religious traditions (except Judaism, for the reasons elaborated earlier). Among these 22 coun-

---

Table 4.6

UNDEMOCRATIC COUNTRIES IN WHICH RELIGIOUS ACTORS PLAYED A COUNTERDEMOCRATIZING ROLE, 1972–2009

UNDEMOCRATIC COUNTRY	TYPE OF RELIGIOUS ACTOR COUNTERING DEMOCRACY
1. Afghanistan	Muslim
2. Algeria	Muslim
3. Fiji	Protestant
4. Iran	Muslim
5. Lebanon	Muslim and Catholic (Maronite)
6. Malaysia	Muslim
7. Saudi Arabia	Muslim
8. Sri Lanka	Buddhist
9. Sudan	Muslim
10. Russia	Orthodox

Table 4.7

DEMOCRATIZING COUNTRIES IN WHICH RELIGIOUS ACTORS PLAYED A COUNTERDEMOCRATIZING ROLE, 1972–2009

	IN THE WORLD	IN AFRICA	IN THE AMERICAS	IN ASIA	IN EUROPE
Total Democratizing Countries	78	24	15	15	24
Number of Democratizing Countries Where Religious Actors Played a LEADING Antidemocratic Role	19	5	4	5	5
Number of Democratizing Countries Where Religious Actors Played a SUPPORTING Antidemocratic Role	10	1	0	1	8
Democratizing Countries Where Religious Actors Played an Antidemocratic Role (By Region)		Kenya (L)* Liberia (L) Mali (L) South Africa (L) Uganda (S) Zambia (L)	Argentina (L) Chile (L) Guatemala (L) Nicaragua (L)	Bangladesh (L) India (L) Iraq (L) Pakistan (L) South Korea (L) Taiwan (S)	Bosnia-Herzegovina (S) Bulgaria (S) Croatia (L) Czech Republic (S) Estonia (S) Germany (S) Greece (S) Hungary (S) Portugal (L) Romania (S) Slovakia (L) Spain (L) Ukraine (L)

* (L) or (S) after the name of each country indicates whether the antidemocratic religious actor(s) in that country played a leading (i.e., actively) antidemocratic or a supporting (i.e., passively) antidemocratic role.

tries, involving 32 religious actors, in fact, we see a somewhat less lopsided concentration of religious actors than we saw with the 48 countries where prodemocratic religious actors were involved in democratization.

Finally, we must consider the antidemocratic religious actors that directly opposed democracy and democratization. First, we consider those undemocratic countries in which major religious actors have helped to keep the forces of democratization at bay. As of this writing in 2010, Iran's clerical regime continues to organize the trials and executions of prodemocratic activists on the grounds that they are guilty of *moharebeh*, or waging war against God. Iran is not alone: there are ten countries in which antidemocratic religious actors have actively obstructed democratic progress and have helped to strengthen authoritarian regimes, trends, or movements. Table 4.6 lists these cases.

Second, we consider those countries that made democratic progress *despite the antidemocratic activism of some religious actors*. Table 4.7 presents these cases, in which religious actors played two different types of antidemocratic role. Religious actors played a leading antidemocratic role where they were enthusiastic and ideologically committed supporters of authoritarianism, and where they actively lent the authoritarian regime in question symbolic and/or material support. Religious actors played a supporting antidemocratic role where they passively followed the lead of other actors, especially political actors; functioned as largely nonideological supporters of the powers that be, including the state; and where they lent the authoritarian regime relatively minimal symbolic or material support. We have identified some 29 countries in which antidemocratic religious actors attempted—but largely failed—to stop, slow, or limit democratization.

TOWARD AN EXPLANATION

Two central factors best explain the political stances and activities of religious actors: the relationship between religion and state, and political theology. Religious actors are far more likely to be prodemocratic when they enjoy some institutional independence from the state and from dominant centers of political power to which the state might be captive (such as dominant ethnic groups), and when they have a democratic political theology. Where religious actors lack either or both of these qualities—one institutional and one ideological—they are likely to fall well short of prodemocratic activism. In some cases, they will be politically agnostic, indifferent, and quiescent; in other cases they may be so institutionally or ideologically invested in an authoritarian "old regime" that they are positively hostile to democratic ideas and activism. In extreme cases, such as the Taliban in Afghanistan or the clerical Guardian Council in Iran, where there is such a high degree of fusion between religious actors and the machinery of state power that the two become virtually indistinguishable, they may inflict severe violence and repression on dissenters (who are considered both apostates and traitors).

Those religious actors that support democratization by and large enjoy that type of relationship with state authority that we have termed "conflictual independence" (the upper-right-hand corner of Figure 2.2). What this means is that they live under an authoritarian regime that strives to deny them their freedom but that they have fought back against this regime successfully enough to retain significant independence to conduct their own affairs—worship, education, control of their leadership—as well as to mount resistance against the regime. Their condition is one that commentator George Weigel has called "moral extraterritoriality"—a protected island of free activity in a sea of harsh control. They are independent, but conflictually so. Both the Catholic Church in Poland during Communist rule between the late 1940s and 1989 and major Muslim movements under the dictatorship of Suharto in Indonesia from 1967 to 1998 are examples of religious actors that were both conflictually independent as well as potent forces in bringing down authoritarian regimes.

By contrast, religious actors that are "conflictually integrated" (the lower-right-hand corner of Figure 2.2) are those who live under an authoritarian regime that has suppressed them so effectively, often brutally, that they are hardly independent at all and thus unable to mount any serious democratizing resistance. The Russian, Bulgarian, and Romanian Orthodox churches under Communist regimes during the Cold War are examples. Different still are religious actors that are "consensually integrated" with their state, meaning that they enjoy a privileged relationship that gives them little incentive to resist and little distance from the regime with which to resist. Finally, there are consensually independent relationships between religion and state, which in most cases involve the very liberal democratic constitutional arrangements to which democratizing religious actors aspire. Here, autonomy has been won. In terms of basic freedom, religious actors have little left to fight for: they are free to carry on their business of worship and education, and to work for justice and spread their faith. Conflictual independence, then, is the condition that enables religious actors to strive for the democracy that they do not yet enjoy.

What motivates religious actors in these circumstances to strive for democracy? It is their ideas or theology. To say that a religious actor carries a democratic political theology is to say that this actor holds doctrines that favor democratic ideas and institutions on theological grounds. Most religious actors that favor democracy have come to do so relatively late in the history of their tradition. Elections, freedom of assembly, the separation of powers cannot be found in the Bible, the Quran, the Torah, and the Vedas, though some of these founding texts, and surely some more than others, contain ideas favorable to democracy. It is rather in particular historical circumstances that religious actors' doctrines of democracy develop—for example, colonial America in the case of some Protestant churches; the global political environment after the Second World War in the case of Catholicism; and in the case of certain Turkish Islamic movements, the growth of a middle class in Turkey in the late twentieth century. Once these doctrines develop, they motivate action.

What is the evidence for the influence of the relationship between religion and state and political theology upon religious actors' democratic activity?

The Catholic Wave

Political scientist Samuel P. Huntington observed that the Third Wave of democratization—his term for the expansion of global democracy in the period between 1974 and 1991—was "overwhelmingly a Catholic Wave."[22] Our data corroborate Huntington's conclusion for the much longer period between 1972 and 2009. Again, the Church served as a lead or supporting actor in 36 of 48 cases—exactly three-quarters. From a historical perspective, this is a striking finding. As Chapter Three showed, the nineteenth and early twentieth centuries were a time when the Catholic Church was stridently at odds with Europe's democracies. How, then, did the Catholic Church come to be the motor of global democratic change?

What propelled the Catholic Wave was a momentous shift in political theology that took place in the Second Vatican Council in Rome, where, from 1962 to 1965, the Church's bishops gathered from all over the globe to discuss the Church's relationship to the modern world. One of the achievements of the Council was to proclaim human rights, peace, and economic development with an authority, force, and philosophical and theological foundation that the Church had not previously applied to these concepts. Most strikingly, the Church came to endorse religious freedom—the right of people to choose and to practice their own religious faith—as a human right. Why had it not proclaimed such a right earlier? There are two reasons. First, nascent European democracies put forth a model of religious freedom that involved suppressing the Catholic Church. Their influence was the French Revolution, which proclaimed individual rights but sought to kill off the organizational structure of the Church, which it associated with a corrupt aristocracy and monarchy. Practicing such conflictual integration, European democracy was itself less than liberal. Second, for its part the Catholic Church retained a medieval political theology that held that, ideally, the Catholic faith was to be established as the official religion in any given realm and that members of other religions had no absolute right to practice their faith. By 1965, though, several factors brought the Church to embrace religious freedom explicitly: its experience of flourishing in the United States, whose constitution guarantees religious freedom; a new friendliness to the Church in Western European democracies after World War II; and the development of philosophical and theological foundations for religious freedom among Catholic philosophers.

Enabled by the unusually tight authority structure of a global network of bishops united around the pope, the new political theology spread to national Catholic churches around the world—a prime example of the power of religion to wield transnational influence in the modern world. The seed of the new political theology, however, did not fall onto fertile soil everywhere. Some national churches came to promote democracy with great vigor while others remained resistant. The promoters were those who both embraced the new political theology most thoroughly (and in a few cases had already embraced it prior to the Council) and enjoyed or managed to establish independence from their state institutions.

Four broad patterns bear out these influences. The first consists of national Catholic churches that had already established conflictual independence from state institutions prior to the Council. Of these, it was the churches in which liberal democratic thought became most deeply and widely lodged among both clerics and laypeople that came to oppose dictatorships most assertively. The model here is Poland, which had a long history of defending its institutional independence against Prussian, Russian, and Austro-Hungarian monarchs during Poland's occupation between 1795 and 1918 and then under Communism after the Second World War. After Vatican II, the Polish Church came to advocate explicitly for human rights and democracy, especially after one of its native bishops became Pope John Paul II. A similar pattern—first independence, then adoption of liberal democratic political theology, then opposition to dictatorship—can be found in Catholic churches in Lithuania,

Ukraine, and South Korea. It can also be found in several Latin American countries, almost all of whose Catholic churches had become disestablished, and thus independent, by 1925. When dictatorships swept over the region in the 1960s and 1970s, once again those national churches in which democratic ideas had been most fully embraced came to demand democracy most strongly: Bolivia, Brazil, Chile, Ecuador, Guatemala, Nicaragua, and Peru.

A second pattern consists of national Catholic churches which, at the time of the Second Vatican Council, enjoyed a symbiotic relationship with dictators who supported these churches and benefited from the spiritual legitimacy that these churches provided: consensual integration. But then, as a result of the Council's teachings, the bishops of these churches withdrew from these relationships and assumed a posture of opposition: conflictual independence. In these cases, changes in political theology preceded and propelled changes in the relationship between religion and state. Fitting this pattern are the Spanish Catholic Church, which had enjoyed a tight relationship with Generalissimo Francisco Franco until the late 1960s, as well as Catholic churches in Portugal and the Philippines.

In a third pattern, a national Catholic Church's independence from its state and its liberal democratic political theology emerged at the same time and led to the Church's active agitation for democracy. This was a common pattern among African Catholic churches, including ones in Congo, Ghana, Kenya, Malawi, Mozambique, South Africa, Zambia, and Zimbabwe.

A final pattern reflects the fact that the Catholic Church's backing for democracy during the past generation has been far from universal. It consists of cases in which the Church either failed to oppose or else actually supported authoritarian regimes. The Catholic Church in both the Czech Republic and Hungary, for instance, opposed Communist dictatorships far less vigorously than did Catholic churches in Poland and Lithuania, while in Africa, Catholic churches in Angola, Uganda, and Rwanda were weak forces for freedom in comparison to their counterparts elsewhere. The Catholic Church in Paraguay was feeble in its protest in comparison to the churches in Brazil and Chile, while the Argentine Catholic Church remained allied with the military dictatorship that carried out the Dirty War of 1976 to 1983. Each of these churches failed to establish independence from its regime and had absorbed democratic political theology far less than other Catholic churches in the same neighborhood that were much more aggressive in standing up to the local autocrat.

The Eastern Orthodox Church

Eastern Orthodox churches hardly contributed at all to the fall of a junta in Greece in 1974, to the collapse of Communist regimes in Romania and Bulgaria in 1989, or to democratization in Ukraine or Russia when Communism fell there in 1991. True, in the late 1990s and 2000s, Orthodox churches contributed positively to democracy in Bosnia-Herzegovina, Kosovo, Serbia, and the Orange Revolution of Ukraine, but in all of these cases except for Serbia, they were supporting rather than lead actors.

What explains the weakness of Orthodox churches as democratizers in comparison to the broad pattern of support for democracy in the post–Vatican II Catholic Church? Ever since the Great Schism of 1054 separated the Eastern Orthodox churches from Latin Christendom and the authority of the pope, Orthodox churches have practiced an acquiescent "symphonic" relationship with political authority, whether this authority takes the form of the medieval Byzantine emperor, Muslim rulers in the Ottoman Empire following the fall of Constantinople in 1453, nineteenth-century monarchs, or Communist dictators. Divided along national lines since the nineteenth century, Orthodox churches have lacked the transnational authority structure and global reach of the Catholic Church. Nor did they experience the common embrace of democratic political theology that the Second Vatican Council brought about. It was not until the 1990s that democratic thinking made its way into a few Orthodox churches, especially those of the former Yugoslavia, which then came to make a modest contribution to democracy.

Protestantism

Protestant churches preceded the Catholic Church by some three hundred years in developing political theologies that favored features of democracy like religious freedom and the independence of church and state. But not all of them. Even at that time, it was the small churches of the "radical reformation" that favored religious liberty and the separation of political and religious authority in England, the Netherlands, and America, in contrast to Lutheran and Anglican churches which held a doctrine of Erastianism (the systematic control of the church by the state we discussed in Chapter Three) that favored the state's role as a protector and even a partial governor of the church.

Today's Protestant churches remain diverse in their political theology, in their relationship to their respective states, as well as in their size and internal structure. They range from large transnational "mainline" churches, including Anglican, Baptist, Methodist, and Presbyterian churches, to thousands of independent churches, many of them Pentecostal, that meet in storefronts and ramshackle buildings in cities and villages throughout Latin America, Africa, and Asia. They vary, too, in their support for democracy. Lutheran churches in East Germany, Latvia, and Estonia, having incorporated Erastian enmeshment with the state into both their thought and their practice, contributed very little to the downfall of Communism at the end of the Cold War. Exceptional were grassroots members of the East German church, who espoused human rights, kept a distance from the regime, and were integral in organizing the protest rallies of fall 1989. The candlelight protests at the Nikolaikirche in Leipzig on October 9, 1989, conducted nonviolently in the face of brutal police beatings, remains one of the great episodes that led to the fall of the Berlin Wall. Elsewhere in the world, it is those Protestant churches that have maintained the heritage of that strand of the Reformation that stressed independence from the state and doctrines of individual freedom and self-governance that have proven the most powerful democratizers. The churches in the South African Council of Churches, which opposed the apartheid state, the Kenyan Anglican Church, and the Taiwanese Presbyterian Church are among those who fit the description.[23] By contrast, the Dutch Reformed Church of South Africa and some Protestant churches in Guatemala and Rwanda remained consensually integrated with their respective states and scantly supported democracy.[24] A final category of Protestant churches consists of ones that may have been independent from their authoritarian state but whose theology of personal salvation largely shunned political action, as was true of some Pentecostals in Brazil, Chile, Kenya, and South Korea.

Islam

Since September 11, 2001, no religion's compatibility with democracy has been disputed more than that of Islam. Skeptics find obstacles to democracy in Islam's lack of an intellectual basis for constitutionalism, human rights, and democracy; its proneness to fundamentalism; its stress on revelation over popular opinion and legislative deliberation; its treatment of women; and its lack of economic and political development. Defenders rejoin that Islam includes a multiplicity of voices, sources of law, and schools of political thought; a historical tradition of respecting minorities, especially Jews and Christians, who are considered "people of the book"; and concepts that favor democracy including *shurah* (consultation), *ijma* (consensus), and *ijtihad* (independent interpretive judgment). Our inquiry here, though, is not into

Islamic thought but into the relationship of Islam to politics, as it is practiced and voiced. What does the record show?

A bird's-eye view suggests a dearth of democracy. In 47 countries, Muslims make up a majority of the population. Only three of these, Indonesia, Mali, and Senegal, are ranked fully "Free" by Freedom House. Even Indonesia's status must be qualified by its place on the high end of countries that restrict religious freedom and witness social hostilities toward religious minorities, as a recent report by the Pew Forum on Religion & Public Life shows.[25] In a statistical analysis of global Islam, political scientist Steven Fish demonstrates a strong relationship between Islam and authoritarianism, one that holds even when other relevant factors such as economic development and ethnic uniformity are thrown into the equation.[26] The pattern is even starker in the Arab portion of the Islamic world—the Middle East, mostly—which altogether lacks an electoral democracy or "Free" country.[27] Nor has Islam played a strong role in the global democratization of the past generation. Between 1981 and 2001, not a single Muslim country jumped into the group of "Free" countries, while two Muslim countries departed from the "Partly Free" group and ten moved into the "Not Free" cluster.[28] Still, as our data above show, Muslim actors played a prodemocratic role in 12 countries where some democratic progress occurred (as distinguished from a full democratic transition to "Free" status). Yet this in a religion that includes 1.5 billion adherents, or a quarter of the world's population. There seems little doubt that the Muslim world is an underperformer with respect to democratization.

Authoritarianism, however, is not the whole story of Islam. Although only three Muslim-majority states are free, about a quarter of them are electoral democracies, meaning that even if they fail to guarantee important human rights, they hold genuinely contested elections. Indeed, if the focus is electoral democracies, there is evidence that things have improved. Between the early 1990s and 2005, political scientist Vali Nasr has shown that a "rise of Muslim democracy" has occurred in countries like Bangladesh, Indonesia, Malaysia, Pakistan, and Turkey, where parties with Islamic identities have come to contest elections and, even more crucially, stand for election a second time rather than hold on to power.[29] Democratic Islamic movements have also emerged in states like Jordan and Egypt. Judging by population rather than countries, roughly half of the world's Muslims now live under democratic constitutions. Indonesia, the country with the world's largest Muslim population, is a democracy. And if we combine the 12 democratizing countries in which Muslim actors played a prodemocratic role (noted above) with the 11 countries in which Muslim actors promoted democracy where democratization stalled or reversed, the picture looks brighter still.

Although Islam contains a deficit of democracy, it is not a complete dearth. Behind the deficit is the wide prevalence within Islam of integrated institutions and of a political theology that advocates such institutions. Political scientist Jonathan Fox indeed finds that the level of "government involvement in religion"—something much like integration—in Islam is at least twice that of all other world religions.[30]

But if authoritarianism and integration are common in Islam, Islam is not always the reason for the authoritarianism or the integration. Two broad patterns of integrated institutions can be found in Islam. Regimes that make up the first pattern are in fact hardly religious, but highly secular. Governance is based on Western-inspired ideals of nationalism, economic growth, the modernization of traditional forms of family life and gender relations, in some cases socialism, and, not least, the sharp restriction of religious authority. On the basis of these ideas, such regimes typically form an alliance with a moderate faction of Islam that it designates as official. It provides this official faction or institution with legal and economic support even while keeping a close eye on its activities (consensual integration), while simultaneously marginalizing and suppressing conservative and radical Islamic movements (conflictual integration). This pattern in fact includes the vast majority of Islamic authoritarian governments in the twentieth century. A model for this pattern is Kemal Ataturk's Turkish Republic. It also includes a number of Muslim states that emerged from colonial independence after World War II, including Algeria, Egypt, Suharto's Indonesia, Iran under the Shah, Saddam Hussein's Ba'athist Iraq, Jordan, Kuwait, Libya, Morocco, Syria, Bourguiba's Tunisia, Turkey, and Yemen, as well as several of the Central Asian republics that won independence when the Soviet Union fell in 1991. What this first pattern reveals is that authoritarianism in Islam is as much the result of the French Revolution as the Iranian Revolution.

The Iranian Revolution, however, is indeed the standard-bearer for a second pattern of authoritarianism in Islam. This one consists of regimes that are based on a political theology of Radical Islamic Revivalism, which, as we describe in Chapter Two, promotes a strong and traditional form of *sharia*, or Islamic law. Once in power, Islamic Revivalists fashion integrated regimes that both promote and regulate their preferred interpretation of faith while suppressing dissenting views and religious minorities. On the basis of their political theology, integrated regimes are formed. Outside Iran, such regimes have also reigned in Afghanistan under the Taliban, in 12 out of 36 states in contemporary Nigeria, in Saudi Arabia, where Radical Revivalists are closely allied with the monarchy, and in Sudan.

Still another pattern consists of those democratic regimes and movements that do exist in Islam. These, too, bear out the importance of ideas and institutions. In both Mali and Senegal, Islamic movements with strong commitments to democratic governance and the rights of religious minorities help to sustain a regime that upholds these values. In Indonesia, the Nahdlatul Ulama (NU) movement, which carries a commitment to the separation of religious and political authority and a culture of religious pluralism that is at least six centuries old, became a crucial partner in the coalition of movements that brought down the dictatorship of Haji Mohamed Suharto and encouraged multiparty elections in 1999. Most dramatic, though, is the Islamic movement in Turkey, which arose to challenge the very prototype of an Islamic secular authoritarian regime. As mentioned in Chapter Two, the Islamic Justice and Development Party became the dominant coalition partner in the Turkish government in 2002 after decades of being suppressed by the military arm of the secular Kemalist regime, with whom it had a conflictually differentiated relationship. The party's political theology springs from the Nurcu and Nakşibendi movements, which fused Sufi spirituality with democratic ideals. Its governance has brought greater democratic competition to Turkey, though the country is still wanting in certain dimensions of democracy: for example, freedom for minority religious groups as well as majority religious institutions, such as mosques (which are tightly controlled by Turkey's Ministry of Religious Affairs).

Other movements within Islam are partially democratic insofar as they favor electoral politics but are illiberal insofar as they seek restrictive laws that are based on *sharia* and that allow little freedom for religious minorities. Examples are the Jamaat-e-Islami in Pakistan, the Muslim Brotherhood in Egypt, the Islamic Party of Malaysia, and Hamas in the Palestinian Authority. These parties each espouse a political theology that endorses this combination of views while supporting and participating in their respective state's electoral politics.

Hinduism

In India, Hinduism of the sort championed by Mahatma Gandhi and the Congress Party helped to found a democracy based on religious freedom in

1947 and later resisted the emergency rule of Indira Gandhi in the mid-1970s. In recent decades, though, a far more integrationist brand of Hinduism has sought to curtail India's otherwise consensually independent institutions. After the Hindu-nationalist Bharatiya Janata Party gained the prime minister-ship in 1998 and control of several state governments around the same time, it sponsored laws designed to advance Hindu culture and to restrict conversions to Christianity and Islam and has even been complicit in pogroms against religious minorities. Though Hindu-nationalist actors operate in a consen-sually independent framework and they embrace electoral democracy, their political theology drives them to seek an integrationist regime that would establish a privileged relationship between the state and Hindu institutions and culture and diminish the democratic freedoms of religious minorities. In Nepal, which is 96 percent Hindu, organized religious movements played little role in the country's recent transition from a kingdom to a democratic republic. Hindus in fact protested the declaration of Nepal as a secular repub-lic in which Hinduism would no longer be the official religion.

Buddhism

Buddhist movements in the world today practice both independent and inte-grated relationships with their governments. In Sri Lanka and Thailand can be found a consensual integration in which the *sangha*, or community of monks, offers its support and advice to the government, which in turn sup-ports the *sangha* legally and financially. The governments of Burma, Laos, and Vietnam, by contrast, practice a conflictual integration involving tight control over the governance and doings of the *sangha*. The political theology of the *sangha* in integrated settings is either one of passivity toward politics or else one of religious nationalism much like Hinduism in India. Over the past fifty years, a different form of political theology, Engaged Buddhism, has developed that fuses ancient Buddhist concepts of peace and tolerance with modern Western ideas such as human rights, democracy, nonviolence, and environmentalism. Movements built on these ideas have striven to influence the policies of governments in Cambodia, Japan, Korea, Taiwan, Thailand, Vietnam, and Burma, sometimes succeeding in moving them toward con-sensual independence, while sometimes encountering fierce opposition. Like other religions, Buddhism hosts a diversity of political theologies and rela-tionships with political authorities.

CONCLUSION

To answer the questions that we posed at the beginning of this chapter, religious actors formed a crucial part of the drama of global democratization during the past generation—sometimes as lead actors, sometimes as supporting actors, sometimes as free riders, and sometimes as reactionary resisters. Religious democratizers have been found most numerously in the Catholic tradition but also come from every major religion on the planet. Every religious tradition also contains actors who have been passive, impotent, or resistant to democratization. Overall, however, the preponderant disposition of religious actors in relation to democratization has been one of supportive engagement. Religious actors have resisted democratization in some 39 countries (29 of which experienced democratic progress anyway, while 10 remained undemocratic). But they have promoted democratization in some 70 countries (48 of which underwent some democratization, while 22 failed to do so).

What distinguishes these different types of political activism is the presence of a liberal democratic political theology and of a conflictually independent relationship with dictatorships and other forms of undemocratic authority. These traits characterized the Catholic Church in Poland, the Islamic movement in Indonesia, Shiite clerics such as Sistani in Iraq, and the protesters at the Nikolaikirche in Leipzig, but not the Catholic Church in Argentina, the ayatollahs in Iran, or the Orthodox Church in Cold War Bulgaria.

In Chapters Five and Six, we will see a mirroring dynamic by which those religious actors who are most integrated with their states and who carry a political theology that itself calls for integrated political institutions are the most prone to terrorism and to fighting civil wars. We first look at terrorism.

Chapter Five

THE "GLOCAL" DIMENSIONS OF RELIGIOUS TERRORISM

O N MARCH 10, 2009, FIVE PRISONERS AT THE GUANTÁNAMO Bay detention facility issued a statement in which they responded with pride to allegations that they were to blame for the conspiracy surrounding the attacks of September 11, 2001. The accused thanked God that they were "terrorists to the bone,"[1] and described the charges leveled against them as "badges of honor."[2] In the six-page court filing, Khaled Sheikh Mohammed and the other defendants sought to justify the attacks as a righteous response to U.S. actions in Muslim societies. Their actions, they said, were legitimated by Islam: "We fight you over defending Muslims, their land, their holy sites, and their religion as a whole."[3]

It is indisputable that religion and belief matter today. In October 2001, Al Qaeda leader Osama bin Laden declared his belief "that terrorism against 'infidels' will assure one 'a supreme place in heaven.' "[4] September 11 was "a seminal event,"[5] in the words of the eminent French philosopher René Girard, which would prove to have global consequences for religious violence. On November 2, 2004, Mohammed Bouyeri killed the controversial Dutch film-maker Theo van Gogh "because of what he believed and what he said."[6] Van Gogh was critical of radical Islam, most notably in his August 2004 film *Submission*. Bouyeri was charged as a member of the Islamic Hofstad Network and was judged to have had a religious motivation in carrying out his attack. "What moved me to do what I did was purely my faith," he told a Dutch court in July 2005. "I was motivated by the law that commands me to cut off the head of anyone who insults Allah and his prophet."[7] As a result, the van Gogh murder was deemed an act of terrorism.[8]

Why does religious terrorism deserve more attention than secular terrorism? Two reasons stand out. First, religiously motivated terrorism is more deadly.[9] Salafi-jihadist groups who espouse a radical form of Sunni Islam such as Al Qaeda, for example, have been responsible for most of the suicide terrorism missions from 1981 to 2007. Their attacks have resulted in the largest proportion of terrorist deaths, accounting for one-third of all terrorist fatalities for the period, killing an average of 17 people per attack and wounding an additional 39. (In contrast, groups espousing secular ideologies, such as Marxists and nationalist-separatists, perpetrated about 15 percent of terrorist attacks, killing on average 3 to 4 people and wounding another 8 to 16 per attack).[10]

The second is religious terrorism's relation to the worldwide trends of globalization, democratization, and modernization. As we noted in earlier chapters, these trends accelerated in the 1970s. As they did so, spreading across the globe, they provided a major stimulus to religiously inspired terrorism. Clearly, technological modernization—in communications and weaponry—has enhanced the capacity and lethality of all terrorist groups, including religious ones. Less obviously, but just as genuinely, the global spread of democracy has increased the expectation of peoples everywhere that they should determine their political destiny, yet the growing dissonance between the global expansion of freedom and the local intensification of oppression in some regions—most notably in the Middle East and North Africa—renders violent militancy a plausible (if not the only realistic) path to liberation. Militancy becomes all the more plausible—as well as pious and heroic—where the Islamic-revivalist political theologies we met in Chapter Two are prevalent. Finally, though state actors had a reasonable opportunity to quell religious terrorist movements while they were confined within national borders, many of these movements have escaped these borders and become regional or global thanks to globalization. Religious terrorism is a "glocal" phenomenon in which global dynamics and local issues are interlinked. Whereas most religious terrorism was conducted locally, today there exists a vast network of local groups with global ties that share ideas, resources, and personnel to wage their terrorist campaigns. Because all these trends are likely to persist, if not intensify, in the coming years, we will continue to see demonstrations of religious terrorism like those we saw on September 11, 2001.

The bottom line is that religious terrorism is an urgent matter.

Yet political scientists frequently miss the religious dimensions of terrorist violence. And those who have recognized religion's importance often treat it superficially. Why? A leading international relations scholar, Robert Keohane, explained that "the attacks of September 11 reveal that all mainstream theories of world politics are relentlessly secular with respect to motivation. They ignore the impact of religion, despite the fact that world-shaking political movements have so often been fueled by religious fervor."[11] Keohane was right: In the post–September 11 world, we *must* bear in mind the beliefs and motivations that fuel religious violence. His candid plea for deeper scholarship on religious violence is an open invitation to all analysts and observers of world politics to overcome their "relentlessly secular" understanding of what drives the dominant actors and events in the field.

While 9/11 was an extraordinarily influential event, it was only one example of an increase in religious terrorism over the past generation. This widespread phenomenon is the subject of the present chapter. Under what conditions are states more or less likely to suffer from religiously based terrorism? Under what conditions are religious actors likely to commit terrorist acts? Our central contentions are that religious terrorism is most likely to occur when there is an integrated relationship between the state and a particular religion or religious actor (usually a majority religion or socially dominant religious actor) *and* when this integrated relationship systematically excludes and alienates another religious actor that embraces a political theology demanding its own integrated relationship with the state. However, we also argue that religious terrorism is likely whenever a religious actor with an integrationist political theology is deeply dissatisfied with the political status quo—as when a partially integrated political system has not integrated far enough or fast enough to satisfy the religious actor's aspirations, or when a political system flouts the actor's sense of religious correctness by making political and religious authority mutually independent. We further make the case that those states that fail to address the grievances and expectations of religious actors within their borders contribute to the globalization of terrorism. What was a largely localized phenomenon in the 1970s and 1980s has now become globalized. The cases of Saudi Arabia and Afghanistan, explored later in the chapter, illustrate this link.

To see how the integration of religion and state begets religious violence, consider a case we noted in Chapter Two—India's Hindu nationalists, who seek a close, tightly woven relationship with the state. In our terminology, India remains consensually independent. At the national level, religious and political authority are substantially and legally independent of each other, the state does not privilege or promote one religion or religious actor above others, and the Constitution officially makes the Indian Republic "secular." Yet Hindu nationalists seek to move the country toward a form of consensual *integration*, in which the state actively promotes India as a Hindu nation and takes measures to restrict other religions like Islam and Christianity. A number of parties and movements support the Hindu cause, above all, the Bharatiya Janata Party (BJP), which, after mounting steady electoral gains over three decades, became the lead party in a coalition government from 1998 to 2004. This movement toward integration, albeit consensual among Hindu nationalists, excludes other religious groups, leading to violent conflict.

To many, the recent emergence of Hindu nationalism clearly contradicts the spirit of India's consensually independent arrangement. "Although the Hindus would numerically dominate," journalist Robert D. Kaplan describes, "they could not ignore or trample the rights of tens of millions of Muslims. Indeed, the 'greatest good' necessitated that the conscience of the new nation and the ruling Congress Party be avowedly secular."[12]

Today, Hindu-Muslim tensions are perhaps most visible in the northwestern state of Gujarat. In April 2009, a historian based there declared the conflict to be "worse than at any time since the partition."[13] For Gujarat this negative trend in religiously based violence began on February 27, 2002, when a group of Muslims set a train full of Hindu passengers ablaze after reportedly being taunted by them. Fifty-eight were killed. In the ensuing riots, however, it was mostly Muslims who were targeted by Hindu militants, who reportedly carried out "ritualistic killings" and raped 400 Muslim women.[14] In the end, virtually all 2,000 who lost their lives were Muslim. Fully supporting the Hindu militants was the government of Gujarat, one of the most intensely Hindu nationalist in all of India.

Why does the integration of religion and state cultivate religious terrorism? The problem is this: With respect to the religious that the state favors, integration is consensual. Yet the very same arrangement is conflictual for religious actors to whom the state does not grant the privileges enjoyed by the favored religious actor. Where an integrated system exists, one or more groups are bound to be unhappy with that status quo. In some cases, the unsatisfied group is secularist, while in other cases this group is of a different religious tradition than the privileged actor. Because integration privileges individual actors and groups, it undermines democracy, which is not supposed to privilege anyone. And it leads to violence.

Political theology is important as well. Doctrines that justify religious terrorism legitimize large-scale violence. As terrorism expert Bruce Hoffman has observed, such doctrines constitute an important difference between religious and other types of terror: "Whereas secular terrorists generally consider indiscriminate violence to be immoral and counterproductive, religious terrorists regard such violence not only as morally justified but as a necessary expedient for the attainment of their goals."[15] It is when the doctrines of a religious actor prescribe a close integration between itself and the state that the religious actor is prone to violence. It will go to great lengths to seek such an integrated relationship. Today, for instance, the majority of terrorism in the world is inspired by Salafism, an Islamic doctrine that prescribes tight integration between religion and state.

The rest of the chapter undertakes to defend our two central claims, the first about relationships between religious and political authority, the second about political theology. In the next section we take a more careful look at exactly what religious terrorism is. Then comes a profile and history of religious terrorism, followed by an examination of five countries. We see that the relationship between religion and state exercises a great deal of influence on how successful that state is in quelling terrorism. While the first case, Northern Ireland, is an example of a state dealing with terrorism effectively by allowing a good deal of independence, the second, India, demonstrates how a state can shift from a good situation to a bad one as it favors one tradition over others. In contrast, Sri Lanka, Israel, and Saudi Arabia are countries where the state has not managed to rein in terrorism. Our fifth case, Saudi Arabia, shows how a political environment provided the breeding ground for what would become today's "global jihad" movement. Finally, the chapter concludes with a discussion of the implications of our findings for both theory and policy, in particular, for the war in Afghanistan.

TERRORISM AND RELIGIOUS TERRORISM— A MATTER OF DEFINITION

Terrorism evokes images of chaos, destruction, fear, and bloodshed. The explosion of bombs in city centers, the use of explosive devices on busy urban roads, and the self-destruction of committed individuals in the act of suicide terrorism have become commonplace around the globe. In some instances, this violence involves the planting of bombs; in others, it is men and women sacrificing themselves. This variety makes it difficult to find a common definition of terrorism. In his own survey of the literature, Hoffman finds 109 definitions.[16] In our view, two important and related features pertain to all terrorism: First, it is done in the service of some political objective, such as to undermine the legitimacy of a political elite or regime or to overthrow the existing political order. Terrorists in the Palestinian territories clearly seek to delegitimatize the state of Israel, either to bring about its end altogether, to create an autonomous Palestinian state, or both. Purely symbolic violence would not qualify as terrorism. There must exist an objective beyond the spectacular destruction associated with the violence. The second key element is fear. Although terrorists frequently attack government targets such as police stations and military bases, their usual modus operandi is to strike indiscriminately at populations that include civilians. The reason is that physical destruction is only part of what terrorists seek. They also aim to instill fear among the general population in the hope that the system will crack and revolution will occur.

This definition of terrorism respects but broadens the definitions that have won wide consensus among political analysts. It agrees with the claim of the National Consortium for the Study of Terrorism and Responses to Terrorism (START) that terrorism is "[t]he threatened or actual use of illegal force and violence by a non-state actor to attain a political, economic, religious or social goal through fear, coercion or intimidation."[17] Helpfully, this description includes multiple motivations. Religion is rarely the lone impetus for terrorism. And, as Bruce Hoffman notes, terrorism as we understand the concept today "is fundamentally and inherently political."[18] Through acts of violence, terrorists aim to demonstrate the weakness of target governments and scare populations, all in an effort to transform politics.

The most important way in which we wish to broaden the definition of terrorism is to include informal violence—systematic targeting of particular ethnic, religious, or other groups that is not organized by a state, army, or network, including riots, pogroms, other waves of killing and destruction, as well as what is usually called terrorism. In recent decades, informal violence has been on the rise, with terrorism at its epicenter. It is not spontaneous but rather quite organized.[19]

Omitting informal violence from terrorism, as databases often do, cannot be justified. In eastern India, the state of Orissa has seen a pattern of violence perpetrated by Hindu actors against Christian homes, churches, businesses, and entire villages. The violence appears to have come first from the Hindu side, but systematic attacks from both sides are now common.[20] Such acts of terrorism give rise to a spiral of violence and are likely to go uncounted.

Similar dynamics are in play in Nigeria between organized Christian and Muslim gangs. In recent years, religious violence, a sort that differs from the country's historic ethnic and tribal violence, has broken out widely.[21] Often, a single event sparks extensive and destructive rioting.[22]

In Indonesia, religious violence involves Muslim-Christian and Hindu-Muslim conflicts. Whereas the former type is a more recent development, the latter sort has endured for more than a century.[23] Beginning in 1994, a new wave of violence swept over Indonesia, some of which focused its destruction on Christian and ethnic Chinese Indonesians, their property, and their churches. And following September 11, 2001, attacks in the country were increasingly viewed as religious in nature and motivation, coming especially from the Sunni Islamic group Jemaah Islamiyah.[24] Indonesia, however, has experienced less publicized types of violence as well. From 1995 to 2004, collective violence in only four Indonesian provinces resulted in an annual average of 500 lynching deaths.[25]

A definition that fails to count informal religious violence as religious terrorism might well be a neater one but would omit a crucial form of religious violence around the globe today. And what good is a definition if it hinders our grasp of a problem in the real world?

A PROFILE AND HISTORY OF RELIGIOUS TERRORISM

Before the nineteenth century, religion motivated virtually all terrorist activity.[26] In 1968 it motivated none of the world's existing eleven terrorist groups.[27] The difference was secularization, which gave rise to terrorist groups motivated not only by nationalist and political ideologies but also by a host of unpredictable and unknown factors.[28] Even the religious terrorism that exists today rarely involves religion alone; social, political, economic, and environmental factors are often in play as well.[29]

Since 1968, religious terrorism has risen and become more global.[30] When religious terrorism came onto the scene, it was linked in part to Iran's Islamic Revolution of 1979. By the end of the 1980s, however, the same type of violence had expanded beyond Muslim-majority societies and had affected all major faith traditions.[31] Religious motivation is responsible for the largest proportion of terrorist attacks with known perpetrators from 1998 to 2004. Although all faith traditions have seen terrorists emerge from their midst, in this recent period Muslims have accounted for the overwhelming majority of attacks: 98 percent involved Islamic ideas as a motivation for violence.[32] Modern religious terrorism follows closely the historical story line that we advance in this book insofar as global trends of modernization, democratization, and globalization have not only enhanced the domestic tensions, forces, and capabilities that give rise to religious terrorism, but have also caused religious terrorism to spread into the global arena and to become an even greater threat.

A dramatic subplot in the rise of religious terrorism is the rise of suicide terrorism. These figures, too, have been steadily increasing since 1981, with the largest spike occurring after 2001.[33] As suicide attacks by secular groups have fallen off, the rate of religious suicide missions has increased. The modern phenomenon of religiously inspired suicide terrorism began in Lebanon, where the tactic was used by Hezbollah, a Shiite Muslim organization that formed in 1982. Although Hezbollah—the "Party of God"—did much to popularize suicide missions and the notion of martyrdom, the tradition of martyrdom has been prominent throughout Shiite history. Beginning with the death of Imam Hussein in the seventh century C.E., martyrdom has continued to play a role in modern Muslim contexts, including in Iran's seminal Islamic Revolution of 1979 and more recent movements of political Islam.[34] Since 1994, suicide missions have experienced a "global proliferation," increasing markedly after 2001 and escalating again in 2005.[35] Corresponding to this increase is also an increase in the death toll wrought by these religiously based terrorist attacks.

Another theme to emerge from the statistics on religious terrorism is the dominance of one particular school of thought: Salafi-jihadism, described as "the guiding ideology of Al Qaeda."[36] The data show that Salafi-jihadist suicide missions rose sharply from 2001 to 2007, followed distantly in numbers by missions motivated by other ideologies. Putting these trends together, the increase in deaths resulting from suicide attacks is probably linked to the heightened presence of Salafi-jihadist thought among responsible groups.

INTEGRATION, POLITICAL THEOLOGY, AND RELIGIOUS TERRORISM

What is the relationship between religious actors, terrorism, and the state? Under what conditions are we likely to see religious terrorism used in pursuit of a political end? Earlier we argued that two variables are key: (1) the independence of religious and political authority; and (2) political theology, religious actors' doctrines about politics. Shifts in either of these factors will cause a state to become vulnerable to religious terrorism. If one religious actor is privileged by the state in a consensually integrated arrangement and other religious actors tolerate that elevated status, then that state is unlikely to experience religious terrorism. On the other hand, if one or more of the other religious actors oppose the arrangement, then it faces a higher risk of religious terrorism. How high depends on the political theology of the nonprivileged religious actor(s). The rest of this section highlights different configurations and illustrates them with a number of examples.

Religious ideas that are conducive to terrorism will result in violence. Although this seems like a simple truism, the link between ideas and violence is not always straightforward. Religion and its place in public or even private life is sometimes the object over which the enemies are fighting. In other cases, religion might simply supply the identity of a faction in a conflict but not the issue over which the fighting occurs. Additionally, just as with nationalism, religion is used at times as a means to attain political ends. In such cases, religious terrorist organizations recruit members by appealing to religious sentiments but in reality may have nonreligious goals as their focus. Hoffman writes that religious groups have the ability to "transform abstract political ideologies and objectives into a religious imperative."[37] Nevertheless, whereas the motivations of terrorists can range from extremely religious to political, most tend to pursue a mixture of religious and political ends.[38] Islamic religious ideas, in particular, are too often a scapegoat for terrorism. While it is true that religious terrorism is disproportionately found in Islam, a focus on ideas alone obscures the role that state-religion relationships in the Muslim world play in fomenting religious terrorism and even in incubating the political theologies that support terrorism. We might conjecture that other religious actors—Christian, Jewish, Hindu, or otherwise—would respond similarly if subjected to sustained suppression. In fact, conjecture is unnecessary given the recent, real-world examples of Christian-supported terrorism by the Irish Republican Army opposing British rule in Northern Ireland; Jewish-Zionist terrorism by groups such as Irgun opposing British rule in Palestine; and active Hindu and Christian involvement in the recently defeated Tamil Tiger terrorist group opposing Sinhalese-Buddhist domination in Sri Lanka. The examples could be multiplied.

This is not to deny that a political theology that proclaims a goal of close integration between religion and state can spring up on its own, apart from interacting with the state. In a state that tends to uphold a relationship of independence with its resident religious actors, tension could develop if a group's political theology conflicts with the outlook of the state. In such cases, the religious actor might push for a shift in the status quo. And, most importantly, if the political theology of the actor supports the use of violence, then that state could very well face a higher risk of religious terrorism. Again, the Hindu-nationalist movement represents a clear example. India is a democratic republic that practices consensual independence with its religious actors, and in this democratic context Hindu nationalism has won increasing influence through the ballot box thanks to the success of the BJP at the national and state levels. Yet the limits of Hindu-nationalist progress—including the failure to build a temple for Ram in Ayodhya in northern India—have left the most extreme members of the so-called *"sangh parivar,"* or family of Hindutva-oriented organizations, feeling disappointed, alienated, and betrayed. Based on an elaborate and long-held political theology that legitimates violence in the defense of the Hindu cause, these groups—including the RSS and VHP, whom we have encountered in previous chapters—have not hesitated to inflict massive informal violence on Muslims in Gujarat and Christians in Orissa to quicken the fulfillment of their goal of a "Hindu Rashtra," or Hindu polity across the subcontinent.

Consider another example: terrorism in the United States. Its strong tradition of consensual independence between religion and state suggests that religious terrorists will always be a marginal force. But religious terrorism has developed in the American context on account of groups who hold a violent political theology—the Christian white supremacist movement, for instance. Although the April 1995 bombing of the Alfred P. Murrah Federal Office Building in Oklahoma City was perhaps the most visible contemporary consequence of this movement, so-called Christian militias seem to abound. Such militia groups have grown and spread in recent years, but "their pedigree can be traced back to the Posse Comitatus (Latin for 'power of the country') movement founded during the 1970s and its 1980s offshoot—with which Timothy McVeigh is also believed to have had ties—the Arizona Patriots."[39] The Christian Patriots, like the extremist Aryan Nations umbrella organization, push for the "cleansing" of the United States and advocate "mass death and destruction."[40]

In the United States as elsewhere, religious actors who resort to terrorism and other extreme acts of violence have often experienced some type of alienation. Jessica Stern, an expert on terrorism, makes this case, citing the example of how a "gentle but frustrated" pastor, Kerry Noble, became involved with an Arkansas-based Christian cult named the Covenant, the

Sword, and the Arm of the Lord (CSA). Through the influence of that organization, Noble became "a terrorist prepared to countenance 'war' against the cult's enemies—blacks, Jews, 'mud people,' and the U.S. government."[41]

In the modern Republic of Turkey we find a different scenario—a regime that seeks to impose integration of a secular kind. In a country that is 99.8 percent religiously Muslim and approximately 20 percent ethnically Kurdish, Turkey has experienced conflict and terrorism from groups who opposed the political status quo. The Turkish government has designated twelve organizations terrorist, five of which have a fundamentalist orientation and in some cases favor the reestablishment of the Caliphate.[42] One of the most active and brutal religious terrorist organizations is Turkish Hezbollah, a Kurdish Sunni party that carries an Islamist orientation, has few ties to Shiite Iran, Lebanon's Hezbollah, or even the broader Kurdish community, and opposes both the Turkish state and the Kurdistan Workers' Party (the PKK).[43] Known for brutality, torture, and indiscriminate violence (some in Turkey call it the "party of slaughter"), its ultimate aim is to overthrow the secular order in Turkey and establish a strict Islamic state in its place.

As described in previous chapters, the Turkish government was founded in 1923 by Mustafa Kemal Ataturk on the ideals of nationalism, economic development, and secularism and has always regulated sharply the speech, practice, leadership, and even dress of Turkey's Muslims. It is only because an Islamic political movement has risen up to challenge the dominance of the Kemalist regime and is powerful enough to avoid being stamped out that religion and state in Turkey can be said to be independent. But it is a conflictual independence: Whenever the Islamic party has posed a serious threat to electoral victory, Turkey's army and judiciary have stepped in to quash it, as they have done decennially in 1960, 1971, 1980, and, in a "soft" coup, in 1997. Yet, like a phoenix, the Islamic party has consistently returned, reconstituting itself under a new name and finally winning control of Parliament and the prime ministership in 2002. But this party, the Justice and Development Party (or AKP), is a more secular Islamic party than previous incarnations: In the face of unease regarding AKP control, upon taking office, Prime Minister Recep Tayyip Erdoğan "disavowed this Islamist past and pledged allegiance to Turkey's pro-secular, western orientation"—a move that some argue rendered Turkey more vulnerable to terrorism from Islamic sources.[44] While the AKP's public message of moderation might embolden more extreme Islamist groups such as Turkish Hezbollah to take action, others fear that the AKP might itself be the downfall of Turkish secularism.[45] It continues to live under the Damocletian sword of judicial and military intervention because both the courts and the army are prepared to step in—again—if they consider the AKP too dangerous to Turkish secularism.

Integrated states or religious actors who seek integration, then, are the chief sources of religious terrorism. Briefly stated, if a religious actor that is *not* privileged by the state holds a political theology that runs counter to the interests of the state, then that religious actor will likely seek a change in the status quo. If the political theology of that actor supports the use of violence, the state is likely to face a higher risk of religious terrorism. Integrated states are more likely to beget violence because they leave little room for real democracy. Unless dissatisfaction can be expressed through the openness that freedom of speech, press, and assembly provide, an actor could believe reasonably that aggressive means are the only kind likely to effect change. It is a classic situation of the bullet versus the ballot, where repression of religion as a result of the integrationist policies of the state has left religious actors feeling oppressed and resentful. Because the state is less willing to compromise, so, too, are the religious actors.

In contemporary Russia, we see a different state of affairs. Russia is experiencing an increase in religious violence as it shifts from independence to integration. Under Soviet Communism, the state harshly suppressed the Orthodox Church—a classic case of conflictual integration. However, after the Soviet Union collapsed in 1991, a fairly high level of religious freedom prevailed in Russia. But since then, the Orthodox Church has, with the help of the state, fortified its dominant status. This privileging is consensual among the mainstream population; the elevated status of the church has become institutionalized; and the religious freedom of non-Orthodox Christians has been curtailed. Other Christians, Muslims, and Buddhists have taken notice. Muslims are dissatisfied with the restriction of worship to "official," registered mosques, the 3,537 (as of 2004) of which do not come close to accommodating Russia's Muslim population, which is estimated somewhere between 14 million and 21 million (or 10 to 15 percent of the total Russian population).[46] Muslims' resentment is exacerbated by the facile branding of non-state-sanctioned religious practice as fundamentalist, extremist, and tied to the global jihadist movement. Russia's Muslims "are denounced as Wahhabis, followers of the puritanical sect from Saudi Arabia, a word that has become Russian shorthand for any Islamic militant."[47] Resentments give way to action, at times leading to violence. The Caucasus is one region in which local Muslims are becoming alienated from what they see as a Christian-dominated state.

In the southern republic of Karachayevo-Cherkessia, for instance, both Islam and Islamic militancy have become more widespread.[48] As one Muslim man from that republic told the *New York Times*: "They will pressure me enough, and then I will blow somebody's head off."[49] The dynamic whereby religion-state integration encourages religious terrorism does not get more vivid.

Pakistan provides yet another striking case of a state that integrates a religion, in this case consensually, yet contains a significant minority of non-adherents to the privileged faith. Within this officially Islamic state, Sunni-Shiite violence often breaks out due to perceptions that one group wields too much power in national governance.[50] Pakistan's population is 95 percent Muslim, with a 75 percent Sunni majority and a 20 percent Shiite minority.[51] As a result of sectarian tension, terrorist violence has been carried out by Sunni organizations such as Sipah-e-Sahaba Pakistan (SSP) and Shiite groups such as Sipah-e-Muhammad (The Army of Muhammad). In existence since 1985, SSP aims to decrease Shiite influence in Pakistan and increase the Sunni character of the state apparatus. Sipah-e-Muhammad, for its part, primarily seeks to protect minority Shiites from Sunni violence and attacks.[52]

For Pakistan, dealing with terrorism is difficult for one palpable reason—namely that the Pakistani government, or at least a powerful part of it, actively supports terrorist groups and missions—such as Lashkar-e-Taiba and its present front organization, Jamaat-ud-Dawa—that strike India and Indian-controlled Kashmir. As C. Christine Fair and Karthik Vaidyanathan have argued, the Pakistani government will not be able to eradicate the type of terrorism it does not want (groups resembling Sipah-e-Sahaba, for example) as long as it tolerates another, more desirable brand of terrorism: "The problem principally arises from Pakistan's persistent belief that it can contain some forms of militancy (for example, Taliban and Al Qaeda remnants and sectarian groups) while sustaining those groups that claim to operate in Kashmir."[53]

Ambiguous relationships between states and religious actors generate problems of their own. In a number of West European states, for instance, levels of religious belief and practice may be low and relationships between religion and state may be consensually independent in practice, but some governments continue to privilege Christian churches with various forms of symbolic and financial support. It has been said, for example, that France operates in a framework of imperfect secularism. That is, rather than upholding complete independence between the state and religious actors, the French government enforces secularism with Catholic undertones. In 1905, France officially separated church and state via a doctrine of *laïcité* that granted its citizens religious freedom but also involved a combination of government support and government control of religion that smacks of consensual integrationism.[54] In part, this involves a privileging of the country's Catholic heritage. As political scientist Jocelyne Cesari notes, seven of France's eleven national holidays correspond with religious celebrations of the Catholic Church.[55] At the same time, *laïcité* involves strong oversight of Catholic education. But it is France's religious minorities that are particularly disadvantaged by this ambiguous religion-state arrangement. They bear the brunt of secularism's restrictions and gestures of disapproval, while receiving few of the benefits of France's de facto accommodations of religion. The total ban on *burqa*-style veils (full-length gowns covering the face and entire body) approved almost unanimously by France's lower house of parliament in July 2010 and the March 2004 law banning "conspicuous" religious symbols in public schools are primarily a response to the growing presence of Islam in French society and the perceived threat that public displays of (Muslim) religious belief pose to *laïcité*.[56] Largely missing from this discussion is an acknowledgment that French notions of secularism are hardly applied evenly to all religions. If this point is not given its due, the rift between the state (and its privileged majority) and a growing population of minority religious actors will likely deepen. For example, distinguished historian Joan Wallach Scott argues that the ban on the *burqa*—overwhelmingly popular in France—would not only result in "further isolation of those Muslims who want some recognition for their religious practices in France" but also "exacerbate tensions, increase discrimination, and convince even those who seek integration into the countries in which they live and work—and are often citizens—that the deck is stacked against them."[57] France thus represents a case where the state upholds a relatively consensual form of independence, while increasingly alienated minority religious actors experience it as conflictual integration. If our analysis is correct, France may well see more religious unrest—and possibly religious terrorism—in its future.

We have already seen homegrown terrorists tragically strike in Madrid in 2004, Amsterdam in 2004, and London in 2005. Consider Britain for a moment and its inability to acknowledge the ways in which its own religion and state relationship has privileged Christianity. Archbishop of Canterbury Rowan Williams was criticized roundly by his fellow Britons for trying to revise such arrangements by arguing in favor of allowing British Muslims to govern themselves in some areas of life through *sharia* law and courts.[58]

His proposal was rejected for two reasons: Either the population had potentially failed to recognize the fact of integration—that is, the privileging of the Anglican Church—or they feared *sharia* law. Neither alternative could be comforting to moderate (i.e., the majority of) Muslims in Britain and elsewhere, who were watching these events closely. Similar dynamics are operating throughout Europe. Consequently, many European Muslim communities now see their relationship with the state in a conflictual light. The central question, then, is how European states will respond before religiously based terrorism grows further.

Religious Terrorism and the State

The relationship between religious terrorism and the state is complex and depends on the perceptions of the actors and whether they view the situation in a conflictual or consensual light. The next section considers a mix of five cases, highlighting how the independence or integration of religious and political authority, whether consensual or conflictual, has impacted the fact or level of terrorism in that state. We start with Northern Ireland, a success case of sorts, and then move on to India, Sri Lanka, Israel, and finish with Saudi Arabia, a case that has resulted in the global diffusion of religiously based terrorism.

Where It Went Right: Northern Ireland

Northern Ireland is the only case we examine where a state has dealt with terrorism in a relatively effective and lasting way. Here the actors who undertook terrorism (as part of a mix of strategies that also included military and police targets)—the Irish Republican Army (IRA) and Protestant paramilitary groups—were ultimately incorporated into Northern Ireland's political structure under a power-sharing agreement.[59] Since the Good Friday Accords of April 1998, peace in Northern Ireland has been durable despite some efforts by spoilers to undermine it. The IRA has reportedly disarmed as of 2005 and appears to be committed to pursuing its goals of a united Ireland through peaceful means.[60]

At first sight, it may seem that the Northern Ireland case does not fit our argument well. The relationship between religion and state had been one of consensual independence dating back at least to the Government of Ireland Act of 1920, which gave all Northern Irish citizens religious freedom and allowed all churches, Protestant and Catholic, their full privileges, including the power to appoint bishops and other leaders. To be sure, Catholics in Ireland remember a long history of the British government strongly suppressing the Catholic Church, dating back to King Henry VIII's seizure of supremacy over the Catholic Church in England. But as of the mid-nineteenth century, the days of state suppression were largely over. Even the Protestant Church of Ireland—the branch of the Anglican Church in Ireland—had been disestablished since 1871.

The primary grievances of Northern Ireland's minority Catholic community in the twentieth century were not indeed conflictual integration on the part of the government. Rather, they resulted from the discrimination that they felt at the hands of the majority Protestant population in housing, employment, and other social and economic matters, as well as the denial of their aspiration that Northern Ireland be united with the Republic of Ireland so that the entire island would form a single Irish—and Catholic—state. Their faith mattered insofar as it defined them as a community, but it did not yield a distinctive political theology apart from a demand for self-determination. Further, Northern Irish Catholics were far from united in harboring these grievances, including the Catholic Church, which was enduringly ambivalent toward the violent struggle. A more distinctive political theology could be found on the other side in the Reverend Ian Paisley and his followers in the Democratic Unionist Party, who viewed the Catholic Church and its attendant political aspirations as being illicit according to a true interpretation of the Bible. But Paisley's was only one faction among Protestants, who were united far more by their desire to remain politically united with Great Britain.

Still, there is a sense in which Northern Ireland's consensually integrated relationship between religion and state made a difference: by permitting a peace agreement to evolve. Early in "the Troubles," the period of violence spanning from the late 1960s to the Good Friday Agreement of 1998, the British government's repression fueled terrorism in a manner evocative of conflictual integration:

The tragic events of November 1972, which came to be known as Bloody Sunday, led to a considerable surge of support and recruitment for the IRA. They were suddenly viewed by many in Northern Ireland and in other countries as legitimate defenders of the Catholic communities. This led to a cycle of action-repression-reaction in Northern Ireland—similar to that which we have seen between the Israeli security forces and terrorist groups in the Palestinian Territories—which produced an escalation of violence during the first half of the 1970s.[61]

Later, when the IRA shifted slightly to support less violent tactics, the political status quo also shifted to one of greater accommodation. This is a case, then, where both key players made a decision to move in the same direction. Whether or not this sort of consensus is a necessary part of reaching a relatively stable peace, it certainly seems to help. Northern Ireland has now entered a new phase of accommodation and reconciliation with the 1998 signing and implementation of the Good Friday Agreement. Shortly after the agreement was achieved, the general sentiment was one of cooperation: "Northern Ireland is attempting to overcome its own history, in which pessimism and bitterness and hatred have shaped the character of many of the residents on the small island."[62] Episodes of terrorist violence continue but are quite sporadic. More importantly, when they do occur, the populations on both sides have come to see them as criminal acts, not political ones.[63] In this experience lies an important lesson for governments that want to reduce terrorism: If a state responds to aggression with its own excessive use of force, the terrorist group it is attempting to suppress will likely be strengthened.

What difference did consensual independence make in contributing to the positive dynamic of peace? Could the Good Friday Agreement still have come about had there been an integrated arrangement in Northern Ireland that favored the Protestant government of Great Britain and Northern Ireland? We can hypothesize that such an arrangement would have deepened Catholic grievances radically. The question is impossible to answer definitively through the case of Northern Ireland itself. Because its twentieth-century history was consistently one of consensual independence, it is impossible to prove how the conflict would have evolved in its absence. It is rather in contrast to other cases that we see the effects of consensual independence being absent. As we will see, these cases lead us to believe that had Northern Ireland had an integrated regime, then it is more likely that Good Friday 1998 would have been a day of continued repression and counterviolence than one of hope for peace.

Where It Is Going Wrong: India
The relationship between religious and political authority in India is extraordinarily complex and dynamic. Though India is a consensually independent

liberal democracy with religious freedom, it does not practice complete separation between the state and religion. In its practice of secularism, the state actively supports religion and maintains close ties with all of India's religious communities, while granting them substantial freedom in self-governance. The Indian government, for example, subsidizes the participation of Indian Muslims in the *hajj* and supports the maintenance of Hindu temples, yet does not control Muslim or Hindu organizations or appoint their leaders. However, as we have noted, India has seen a powerful religious and political movement—Hindu nationalism—undertake ambitious efforts to shift the country toward an integration in which the state privileges Hinduism as the basis of Indian culture and identity and demotes other religions to a decidedly inferior status.

The movement toward a more openly professed integration gained momentum with the rise of the BJP and its first national electoral victory in 1998. As it grew in strength, the BJP brought the ideology of Hindu nationalism—or Hindutva—to center stage. Although the BJP (and the rest of its National Democratic Alliance) has been the opposition party since 2004, the climate in India has grown steadily more conflictual. The rise of the BJP has been called "a triumph for Hindu nationalism, for an awakening and resurgent Hindu identity, and, at the same time, condemned as a threat to the secular state and to the rights and security of religious minorities."[64] The BJP controls the governments of a half-dozen Indian states, including Madhya Pradesh, Chhattisgarh, Gujarat, and Karnataka, where it has implemented changes in educational, cultural, and religious policy to reflect Hindu-nationalist ideology. Most recently, as we noted in Chapter One, the BJP-controlled Karnataka assembly passed a cow-protection bill in July 2010 that effectively incorporates Hindu views of the cow's sacred status into state law by criminalizing the slaughter of cows; the possession, transportation, use, or sale of beef; and even the *advocacy* of beef consumption. Though India is about 80 percent Hindu (with Muslim, Christian, and Sikh religious minorities constituting 13.4 percent, 2.3 percent, and 1.9 percent, respectively, according to the official census), most Indian Hindus do not support the BJP or the Hindu-nationalist agenda in its entirety, which accounts for the party's poor showing in the last two national elections. Yet the movement has secured enough of a foothold in Indian politics and political discourse—particularly in states in the broad, Hindi-speaking middle of India, known as the "cow belt"—to be a source of profound disquiet, especially for religious minorities.

Today, religious terrorism comes from both Muslim and Hindu sources.[65]

As early as 1996, the BJP's message of Hindu nationalism began to stir feelings of unease among India's Muslim population. As one member of the Jamaat-e-Islami Party stated, "They say one nation, one people, one culture, which is repugnant to the very Constitution of our Country."[66] More recently, Islamic terrorism has intensified in India as a domestic problem with international consequences. In November 2008, Lashkar-e-Taiba—a Muslim group advocating Islamic rule that has ties to Pakistan and Osama bin Laden—perpetrated attacks against the city of Mumbai. The days-long ordeal took the lives of more than 160 people. With the persistence of favor for Hinduism, we can expect more religious terrorism.

Where It Went Wrong: Sri Lanka, Israel, and Saudi Arabia

SRI LANKA

In Sri Lanka, tension has arisen from the state's privileging of Buddhists over non-Buddhists. Hostilities between Sri Lanka's mostly Hindu Tamil ethnic minority and its mostly Buddhist Sinhalese ethnic majority have been attributed partly to British favoritism toward the Tamil minority during the colonial period. Following independence in 1948, the Buddhist Sinhalese took power and enacted policies that ultimately marginalized the Tamil community in terms of religion, culture, and language.[67] Following years of perceived mistreatment, Tamil opposition to the Sinhalese government culminated in the formation of the Liberation Tigers of Tamil Eelam (LTTE), or the Tamil Tigers, in the mid-1970s. A separatist guerrilla group, the LTTE aimed to create an independent Tamil state called Eelam in northeast Sri Lanka. Its view was relatively simple: With the Sinhalese in power, it was not possible for the Tamils to be fully emancipated; thus, the Tamils advocated self-determination rather than any overtly religious goal. Though the Tigers have often been characterized as a secular, Marxist group, they developed a religiously charged martyrology around their fallen military heroes and suicide bombers, turning them into Hindu deities and saints. They maintained close ties with Hindu and Christian groups and have used religious symbolism to counter the hegemonic Sinhalese-Buddhist state. Similar to Northern Ireland and the IRA, religion shaped the identity and sense of grievance of a nationalist movement. But the Tamil Tigers also made Tamil nationalism a religious cause, investing it with sacred and eternal significance through the deliberate invocation of Hindu rituals and symbols.[68]

1956 was a pivotal year in the politics of Sri Lanka (then Ceylon). Coinciding with the 2,500th anniversary of the Buddha's passing into nirvana, Sri Lanka saw a wave of activists—often with saffron-robed monks at the forefront—demand that the secular-leaning, Anglophone political elite accord greater respect to the religious and cultural heritage of the Sinhalese-Buddhist majority. Elections the same year resulted in a government dominated by Sinhalese nationalists, who quickly passed a law declaring Sinhalese to be the only official language of Sri Lanka. Although a provision was added in 1958 to recognize the Tamil minority and its language, dissatisfaction remained.[69] The uncompromising linguistic and religious nationalism of Prime Minister Sirimavo Bandaranaike (widow of Solomon Bandaranaike, who spearheaded the country's "Buddhist Revolution" in 1956) gained ground in the 1960s and 1970s. This movement culminated in the 1972 Constitution, which officially accorded Buddhism "the foremost place" among the country's religions. Ultimately, the historical privileging of the Buddhist majority brought about a relationship with the state that was consensually integrated for Buddhists but conflictually integrated for Hindu and Christian Tamils (almost no Tamils are Buddhists).

Sri Lanka is another striking example of a dynamic we have already discussed: An increasingly integrationist regime creates a kind of "cultural claustrophobia," in which religious minorities feel trapped in a shrinking space that does not permit adequate autonomy or self-expression. In Sri Lanka's case, the minorities felt doubly trapped, both because of their ethno-linguistic identity and because of their religion. In this atmosphere of vulnerability, a group emerged—the Tamil Tigers—whose ideology and ambitions were as totalist and uncompromising as those of Sinhalese-Buddhist nationalists. The Tigers sought not merely a place at the political table but to subject up to half of Sri Lankan territory to the unchallenged sway of their brand of Tamil nationalism—a nationalism that was clearly enfolded within a Hindu framework. This quasi-religious nationalism lent the Tamil Tigers an integrationist political theology of their own, which sought an absolute and totalitarian fusion of polity, ethnicity, and deity. Given our framework, it is not surprising that such a vision, so radically opposed to (but also in some ways mirroring) the Sinhalese-dominated Sri Lankan polity, should have generated the sustained and systematic use of terrorism over so many years, until the outright defeat and destruction of the Tigers in May 2009.

However, Sri Lanka's characteristic patterns of religion-state integration and Sinhalese-Buddhist domination remain firmly in place. Consequently, its religious and ethnic minorities continue to harbor a host of deep-seated concerns and grievances that—so far—show little sign of being concretely addressed. It is therefore too early to conclude that the country has left its history of ethno-religious violence securely behind.

ISRAEL

In certain important respects, Israel is a democracy with religious freedom, manifesting consensual independence between religion and state. Yet its privileging of the Jewish faith pushes it toward the realm of consensual integration. Radical Jews and a large body of Palestinian Muslims reject both of the above characterizations and perceive Israel to be a conflictually integrated state. Many of them also harbor political theologies that have prompted them to carry out religious terrorism in order to further their own agendas. Both groups have responded in kind to Israel's national goals: First, that the Jewish nation, in order to survive, must have a state. Second, that the Jewish state must maintain a Jewish majority, for a Jewish minority could risk further persecution. And third, that the majority Jewish state must be democratic in order to keep control of national security in the hands of the Jews. Both radical Jewish and Muslim religious actors are dissatisfied with the status quo.

Prime Minister Yitzhak Rabin was assassinated in 1995 by Yigal Amir, a right-wing Jewish radical with an Orthodox background. Not wanting to compromise any Jewish territory, Amir turned to extreme measures to prevent peace from succeeding. Amir killed Rabin to punish the Israeli leader for signing the Oslo Accords of 1993. In a similar vein, the Jewish terrorist organizations Kach and Kahane Chai in 2005 allegedly opposed Prime Minister Ariel Sharon's plan to withdraw from the Gaza Strip. Both groups aim to expel Arabs from Israel—a goal that would be impossible under the current Israeli state as outlined above. Perhaps the most destruction caused by the groups was in February 1994, however, when Kach supporter Baruch Goldstein attacked the Ibrahimi Mosque in Hebron, killing 29 and wounding many more.

As the jihadist movement to liberate Muslim lands has gained legitimacy and become more globalized, it, too, has contributed to religious terrorism in Israel and Palestine. Its ideology emphasizes that Muslims long have been humiliated at the hands of Western and colonial powers, a belief that resonates strongly with long-suffering Palestinians. In Israel, a number of religious actors are responsible for Islamic terrorism, but this type of violence is most often represented by the group Hamas. Dedicated to forming a Palestinian state,

Hamas calls on all Muslims to engage in jihad to liberate that territory from Jewish hands and for the destruction of Israel itself. Over time, the Palestinian struggle for statehood has traveled the trajectory from secular nationalist to the radical political theology of Hamas. With such a theological imperative profoundly shaping the Palestinian side, and with the continuing strength of Jewish insistence on a theologically grounded claim to the Holy Land as well as a growing integration between the Israeli state and Orthodox Judaism, a satisfactory resolution to the long-standing ordeal hardly seems possible.

SAUDI ARABIA

Saudi Arabia is yet another case in which a repressive regime of religion-state integration generates a terrorist response under certain conditions. In this respect, Saudi Arabia is not alone; Algeria, Egypt, Pakistan, Sri Lanka, and the Philippines also demonstrate the core argument that integrated regimes can lead to terrorism.[70] Saudi Arabia, however, exemplifies something more. It demonstrates how local religion-state relationships can yield massive global consequences. In the case of Saudi Arabia, local dynamics provided the seedbed for the emergence of global jihadist terrorism. How did this happen?

In the Saudi case, Islamist opposition groups in disagreement with the brand of Islam supported by the government have sought to "bring about a comprehensive transformation in the kingdom's socioeconomic and political life."[71] This conflictual relationship between the state and religious actors can be traced back to November 20, 1979. On that day, Juhayman al-'Utaybi's Ikhwan group took control of the Grand Mosque in Mecca.

A precursor to the Ikhwan had developed in the 1960s under the name al-Jama'a al-Salafiyya al-Muhtasiba (JSM).[72] The JSM began as a group concentrating solely on reforming the religious and moral status quo, and its conservative stances led the group to reject much of modern society.[73] Following an ideological split with some members of the organization in 1977, Juhayman and what was left of the group began referring to themselves simply as the *ikhwan*, or the "brothers." Juhayman taught that the Saudi government as an institution was un-Islamic and illegitimate.

The group led by Juhayman on November 20, 1979, numbered approximately 300. They locked themselves in the mosque compound, holding hostage thousands of worshipers. Waiting for the coming of the Mahdi, or "the Islamic equivalent of the Messiah,"[74] the Ikhwan rebels had chosen to begin their task on the first day of the Islamic calendar's fifteenth century. They remained in the mosque until December 4, 1979, when Saudi officials were able to regain control of the mosque.

Two weeks after the start of the siege, the Saudi government suppressed the uprising in a quick and violent manner that did much to fuel the growth of Islamist groups. It could have been otherwise: "The seizure of the Grand Mosque—the first large-scale operation by an international jihadi movement in modern times—was shrugged off as a local incident, an anachronistic throwback to Arabia's Bedouin past," writes journalist Yaroslav Trofimov.[75] Since that time, the case has been made that the siege at Mecca and its aftermath ultimately led to the formation of Al Qaeda and the global jihad movement.[76]

In the 1980s, the jihadist movement developed as a third type of Islamism in Saudi Arabia alongside the earlier Sahwa, or Islamic awakening, and the rejectionist school of the JSM. This new jihadist strain differed in two significant respects from previous intellectual traditions: its militancy and its interest in radical political reform. Importantly, this movement set its sights on international political change, not merely reformation within the Saudi state. As Thomas Hegghammer and Stéphane Lacroix note, the Saudi government's efforts to quash domestic Islamist movements at an early stage ultimately backfired:

> The Mecca event shook the regime, which was concentrating its political control on leftist groups and never expected its foes to come from religious circles. It decided, however, that only a reinforcement of the powers of the religious establishment and its control on Saudi society would prevent such unrest from happening again. Ironically, it was the other main Islamist current, the more institutionally integrated Sahwa, which benefited from these new policies and grew stronger throughout the 1980s until it openly confronted the regime in the early 1990s.[77]

Ultimately, Saudi Arabia not only failed to accommodate a diversity of religious challenges to its legitimacy but responded to these challenges by reinforcing its integrationist relationship with a single, narrow brand of Islam represented by a single religious actor. Saudi Arabia's increasingly repressive integrationism, combined with the increasingly militant political theologies of its religious dissenters, left no room for mutual accommodation. Since the kingdom afforded no space for its militant dissenters to exist, much less operate, and since the political theology of these dissenters gave them a much wider set of ambitions, they went global, with an ever-expanding field of operations that encompassed Afghanistan, Sudan, Kenya, Tanzania, and—in time—New York and Washington.

Summing Up the Cases

One useful lesson of this study is the ability to predict which transitions within states are the most likely to yield religious terrorism. Integration, it seems, generates troublesome results. In a state where integration dominates, there is little room for autonomy, which means that a religious actor will be more likely to turn to violence than to social or political mechanisms when seeking change. Independence is key in avoiding religious terrorism, as it allows for the free exercise of thought and the exchange of ideas. That is to say, it affords religious actors room to change the system without resorting to violence and terrorism.

OVERCOMING RELIGIOUS TERRORISM

Religious terrorism is special. Groups espousing religious ideals are stubborn; stopping them is thus more difficult than stopping other terrorists. Since 1968, whereas 62 percent of terrorist organizations have been terminated, only 32 percent of religious terrorist organizations have ceased to exist.[78] Religious terrorist groups are unique in that not one such organization has come to an end through outright defeat since 1968 (though, as we have noted, the defeat of the ethno-religious Tamil Tigers is at least a partial exception to this pattern).[79] A 2008 study by the RAND Corporation finds that among all 648 terrorist groups in its data set, 7 percent end through military force, 10 percent through victory, 40 percent through policing, and 43 percent through processes of politicization.[80] Of the 648 groups, 41 percent have ended, 38 percent remain active, and 21 percent ended because their members joined other terrorist organizations.[81] Regarding the 45 religious terrorist groups that have ended, 26 (or 57.78 percent) splintered, 13 (or 28.89 percent) succumbed to policing efforts, 3 (or 6.67 percent) fell to military force, and 3 (6.67 percent) shifted toward political activity.[82]

To end religious terrorism, two options are available: Either circumvent such violence before it starts or end it after it begins. These are both straightforward approaches, and yet the data show that we are not making enough progress on either front. On one hand, religious terrorism is on the rise. On the other, no good solution has been found to defeat it.

Responding to religious terrorism and other forms of religious extremism will require engaging not only in damage control and containment but also in preventive measures. An approach that prevents religious terrorism from becoming an attractive option in the first place has much to recommend it. As political scientist Mia Bloom suggests, "The key is to reduce the Palestinian motivations for suicide bombing rather than their capabilities to carry them out." Attacking religious terrorists' motivations at their core will require attention to religion in addition to other sociopolitical factors that can prove to be influential in complex ways. Whereas the political theology of a religious group and its members can be studied, such study necessitates a broad view of the many factors that lead to violence. As terrorism analyst Jessica Stern writes, religious terrorism today is more complicated and less easy to deal with directly than previous forms of terrorist action:

> The terrorism we currently face is not only a response to political grievances, as was common in the 1960s and 1970s, and which might, in principle, be remediable. It is a response to the "God-shaped hole" in modern culture about which Sartre wrote, and to values like tolerance and equal rights for women that are supremely irritating to those who feel left behind by modernity.[83]

Responses to strains of religious terrorism will therefore be multilayered, containing both short- and long-term solutions.

Concluding Thoughts: Afghanistan

In recent decades, Afghanistan has been a key player in the growth of globalized religious violence. It is a country where terrorism has been homegrown and has paved the way to religious civil war—the subject of the next chapter.

Before Al Qaeda was formed, there was Abdullah Azzam, the so-called "imam of jihad." For our topic, Azzam's intellectual legacy is of immense importance. As a graduate of the renowned Al-Azhar University in Cairo, Azzam became a well-known and respected expert on ideas related to jihad. He did not go so far as to articulate the idea of a "global jihad," but it does appear that he paved the way for others to do so after his assassination in 1989. Thomas Hegghammer helpfully observes the major differences between Azzam and his successors. Compared to Al Qaeda leaders Osama bin Laden and Ayman Zawahiri, he was more moderate. Although he did support the notion of the external jihad, "he was never in favor of carrying out strikes on the territory of the faraway enemy" but instead envisaged "a strategy closer to guerilla warfare than to terrorism. And despite his pan-Islamist, inter-nationalist perspective, he never called for a 'global insurrection' against the enemies of Islam."[84] Significantly, then, Azzam focused his teachings on domestic resistance within the state of Afghanistan, which he saw as a first and necessary step in the fight.[85]

Despite Azzam's focus on bringing about a legitimate Islamic government in Afghanistan, his ideas led to a theological shift that would have global ram-ifications. Through his modern application of jihad, he promoted an integra-tionist political theology that arose directly in response to a political context in which a Soviet-backed regime threatened the coercive integration and sub-jugation of Islam. Indeed, this case provides us with one of many examples in which shifts toward integration are brought on by a political context. Can we argue, then, that with the right politics in place, we can avoid integrationist movements with the maximalist goal of fusing religion and state? Of course, as Hindu-nationalist violence in India and Christian supremacist violence in the United States both demonstrate, consensually independent regimes that afford space for religious diversity are no surefire guarantee against the emergence of integrationist movements prepared to use terrorist methods. But integrationist regimes—and the reactive integrationist movements and theologies they sometimes foster—make such terrorism far more probable, deadly, and determined.

Due to the conditions present in Afghanistan, Azzam's ideas eventually led to the spread of religious terrorism through propaganda and transnational networks well beyond that country's borders.[86] As we will see in the next chapter, the theological shift that fostered religious terrorism in Afghanistan would also contribute to the country's civil war.

Chapter Six

RELIGIOUS CIVIL WARS: NASTY, BRUTISH, AND LONG

ACTS OF RELIGIOUS TERRORISM USUALLY AIM AT SINGLE, focused targets—a mosque in Iraq, a café in Jerusalem, a resort in Bali, skyscrapers in New York—and kill smaller numbers of people than full-scale wars. Civil wars, by contrast, involve large populations in prolonged bloodshed that typically takes tens of thousands, and sometimes millions, of lives, destroys social fabrics, and spills beyond a country's borders to infect a broader region. The two sorts of violence cannot be completely separated. Sometimes terrorism occurs within or even leads to civil war—as in Afghanistan.

Whereas religiously based acts of terror did not play a large role in the Afghan conflict at first, they became an integral part of that civil war over time. Religious terrorism did not simply arise naturally from Afghan soil; rather it was taken up by religious people who very much believed that it would help them to advance their political objectives. Religious terrorism then became part and parcel of the civil war, contributing to a death toll of 1.5-to-2 million civilians—one of the deadliest any society has ever sustained in a civil war—as well as to the country's general instability.

Exactly when did terrorism become a problem for Afghanistan? Groups including "Muslim guerrillas" perpetrated one attack in 1973 on Afghan soil and three more in 1979, as the civil war began in earnest.[1] After that, Afghanistan experienced a lull in terrorist violence. But significant attacks began again in March 1988 and have continued with fervor ever since. What is more, terrorism in Afghanistan has had a distinctly religious tinge. For instance, of 143 attacks carried out in 2003 and 2004, 77 of these had a known perpetrator, and in each of these cases the responsible group embraced religion as a central motivation.[2]

The occurrence of 83 attacks in 2003 and only 60 incidents in 2004 suggested that terrorism was on the wane. However, "the Taliban-led insurgency remained strong and resilient in the South and East"[3] in 2007 and has continued to pose a grave threat to Afghanistan since that time.[4]

In an address to the United Nations General Assembly on September 25, 2007, Afghan President Hamid Karzai argued for the necessity of tackling Afghan terrorism with an eye to global considerations:

> May I emphasize, ladies and gentlemen, that we were the prime victim of terrorism and terrorism was never, nor is it today, a home-grown phenomenon in Afghanistan. Therefore, this threat can only be overcome if addressed appropriately across its regional international dimensions. . . .[5]

Karzai is correct. Afghanistan exemplifies a pattern in which a local civil war becomes intertwined with regional and global dynamics.[6] As religion exercised a growing power in international affairs, Afghanistan was not immune. As its civil war raged, regional and global ideas entered its borders and contributed to the war's continuation.

Religion was not an important element in the Afghan civil war initially, but as in so many other cases, it eventually grew to be a significant factor. The beginning of the Afghanistan civil war is traced to a 1978 socialist uprising. What was called the Saur Revolution "introduced Marxist-oriented radical reforms in Afghanistan that led to disruptive changes in the social, economic, and political structures of a predominantly feudo-tribal society."[7] The Soviet Union invaded Afghanistan in 1979 in order to bolster the Communist regime that it had helped to install there. Because Muslim movements considered the regime profoundly contrary to the tenets of their religion, they took up arms against the Soviets. The *mujahideen* eventually defeated the Soviets and drove them out of Afghanistan in 1989. When these fighters experienced internal rifts, the more powerful Taliban, waiting in the wings, emerged as another resistance group in 1994 and took power in 1996 with the objective of enforcing a fundamentalist conception of Islamic law in Afghanistan.

Through all of these events, dating back to 1973, a consistent integration between political and religious authority has persisted in Afghanistan—that is, a condition in which the government either closely allies with one religious faction and marginalizes the rest or in which the government subdues all religious actors, as is characteristic of Marxist and Communist regimes. The difficulty of this conflict stems in part from the fact that it has gone through several forms of integration, in which different factors were central. It has successively involved a Marxist revolution, a clash over religious and ethnic differences, and a simple question of power.

Religion's role in Afghanistan's politics has been fortified by global forces. Although Zalmay Khalilzad wrote in 1995 that the Afghan civil war arose only partly from questions of ideology,[8] in 1999, Rasul Bakhsh Rais noted the extent to which the conflict had been internationalized based largely on ties of identity and ideology between Afghanistan and other states in the region, especially Pakistan. According to Rais, it was these factors that allowed the war to spread beyond its borders: "The situation in Afghanistan is more complex than before. Various groups in Afghanistan share ethnic and religious bonds with similar groups in the neighboring states, which invites a natural interest in their well-being."[9] For instance, the Shiite state of Iran made an effort to support the Shiites in Afghanistan both politically and militarily in the hopes that they would become a powerful force in the post-Soviet context.[10] This interest was particularly strong in light of the Taliban's opposition to Shiite Islam.

What have been the consequences of the Afghan civil war? Perhaps most notably, the rise of the Taliban, which has been called "one of the war's by-products."[11] Espousing the strictest interpretation of Sharia law, the Taliban governed from 1996 to 2001, during which it prohibited "pork, pig, pig oil, anything made from human hair, satellite dishes, cinematography, and equipment that produces the joy of music, pool tables, chess, masks, alcohol, tapes, computers, VCRs, television, anything that propagates sex and is full of music, wine, lobster, nail polish, firecrackers, statues, sewing catalogs, pictures, Christmas cards."[12] The same regime's Ministry for the Promotion of Virtue and Suppression of Vice required men to wear long beards, short hair on the top of their head, and a head covering and women to wear *burqas*. Members of both sexes were beaten with sticks when they did not comply. Women were forbidden from being educated; ancient Buddhist art was destroyed.

The Taliban's influence on the civil war has been an enduring one. After the Bonn Conference in December 2001 and the fall of the Taliban government shortly thereafter, a lull in the war took place and hopes for a healthy political order in Afghanistan emerged. But by January 2007, the Taliban had regrouped and the war resurged. James Dobbins, a career diplomat and now researcher at the RAND corporation, testified before the U.S. House Armed Services Committee that the decades-long civil war had only worsened the country's religious cleavages and that, unlike the wars that savaged Yugoslavia in the 1990s and Iraq after the American invasion in 2003, Afghanistan's war has been the product of outside influences.[13] First, it was the Soviets and Americans in a global competition, then regional actors entered the fray as India, Iran, and Pakistan supported different factions to extend their own influence. As the war continued, divisions among Afghan ethnic, linguistic, and religious groups grew ever more hostile. These factors have mired Afghanistan in catastrophic violence that has not yet been quelled by the post-2001 reconstruction efforts and the government of Hamid Karzai. As of this writing, the country remains in chaos, and violence continues, with opposition groups that include a resurgent Taliban continuing to contest who will govern and what the role of religion will be in relation to the state.

INTEGRATION, RELIGIOUS ACTORS, AND THE STATE

When states deny religious actors autonomy and independence, and when those actors adopt political theologies that accept violence as a means to achieve their ends, the mix is volatile. While Afghanistan is not the only case of such actors and groups pursuing armed struggle, it offers a powerful cautionary tale. At the end of the chapter, we will see that present-day Iraq faces a strong risk of following Afghanistan's pattern.

The basic facts concerning religious civil wars reveal some clear and disturbing patterns. First, they are more destructive than nonreligious civil wars, causing more deaths among combatants and noncombatants alike.[14] Second, they last longer by an average of two years.[15] Third, civil wars where religion is a central component recur twice as often as civil wars lacking religious motivation. Fourth, they make up an increasing proportion of all civil wars; whereas religious civil wars constituted 19 percent of all civil wars started in the 1940s, they have made up nearly half of all such conflicts started since 1990.[16] And fifth, they increasingly involve Islam in particular; among religious civil wars occurring between 1940 and 2000, Islam was a factor 82 percent of the time. By comparison, Christianity was involved in 52 percent of these cases, while Hinduism was part of the dynamic in 16 percent of such wars.[17] As with terrorism, religious civil wars, due to the transnational nature of the beliefs that underpin some of the combatants and the transnational nature of the communities these combatants seek to mobilize, produce conflicts that have equally "glocalized" dimensions.

How has this come to be? More to the point, what circumstances within states have allowed religious civil wars to develop, wreak havoc domestically, and go on to pose a threat to international stability? This chapter, like the others in this volume, will concentrate on the intersection of political theology and the relationship between religious actors and states. It will ask where the possibility of religious civil war is likely to be increased or lessened by the domestic conditions created by these two factors.

WHAT IS CIVIL WAR, AND HOW DOES RELIGION RELATE TO IT?

Scholars disagree over how to identify a civil war. In recent years, for example, many have argued that the violence in Iraq following the invasion of the U.S. and its allies in 2003 has become a fully fledged civil war, while others have denied this claim.[18] What, then, qualifies as a civil war? Borrowing from Monica Duffy Toft's previous work, we use the following six criteria to differentiate civil wars from other forms of violence:

1. The war focused on determining which party would govern.
2. The number of organized combatant groups was at least two.
3. One of the combatant groups was the state.
4. On average, there was a minimum of 1,000 battle deaths per year.
5. The stronger combatant had to have sustained a minimum of 5 percent of the casualties.
6. At the beginning of hostilities, the war had to take place within the boundaries of a state or entity that was internationally recognized.[19]

There are two ways in which religion can matter in a civil war. First, it can influence the identities and loyalties of the players in the conflict—we call this influence "peripheral." Second, it can influence the political goals of combatant parties as well—we call this influence "central." In this sense, civil wars can be religious even when both parties adhere to the same religion. Tajikistan, for instance, experienced a civil war over whether it would become an Islamic republic.

Recalling a point from Chapter Two and a parallel with religious terrorism as described in Chapter Five, factors other than religion are frequently at play in a civil war that can be called "religious." Take Sudan's civil wars, for instance: "Religion is complicated by geography, demography, and colonization, and is a pivotal and contentious factor when imposed."[20] Although Saudi Arabia has not suffered a civil war, political scientist Steven R. David warns that the kingdom's "bad economy intensifies religious extremism, which in turn exacerbates divisions in the armed forces. The catalyst for civil war can therefore come from one of several different sources."[21] At the same time, underlying conditions alone—economics, demographics, history, and religion itself—rarely make a war; a government's response to potential volatility is often critical. But if religion is not all that matters, it still matters.

It would seem almost true by definition that civil wars are localized phenomena, occurring within state borders. However, they usually bear critical international consequences as well:

> The attention paid by the West to the wars in the former Yugoslavia should come as no surprise. Only recently have superpowers refrained from involvement in internal conflicts. Traditionally the case has been just the opposite. And with good reason: revolutions in France, Russia, and China sparked profound changes in the international system that remain with us today. During the Cold War, internal conflicts in Korea and Vietnam drew the United States into costly interventions, while domestic strife in El Salvador and Nicaragua dominated American foreign policy through the 1980s. For the Soviet Union, internal wars provided the source for both one of Moscow's greatest victories (Cuba) and one of its most costly defeats (Afghanistan).[22]

Why do civil wars affect the interests of foreign powers and the international community? Increasingly, this internationalization is fueled by religious dynamics. Due to the globalization of religious networks—a hallmark of the past generation's religious resurgence—one state's religious violence has the power to seep into the affairs of another. Rarely do the ideas of a religious opposition movement remain confined within its home territory; rather they spread across borders where others apply them to their own circumstances. This pattern can be seen plainly in the political theology and networks of Salafi-jihadism discussed in the previous chapter, which influence an increasing number of religious civil wars. Whereas religious opposition to the Saudi government helped to catalyze this movement, its goals have gained sympathy and following from Muslims elsewhere in the world, such as in Algeria, Indonesia, and Sudan.

Empirical Trends in Civil War Since 1940

Global data on religious wars help us to understand them better. Two main points stand out from an empirical study of civil wars from 1940 to 2010. As mentioned above, religious civil wars have increased relative to nonreligious civil wars. In addition, civil wars involving religion tend to cause more destruction than conflicts involving nonreligious issues. They are deadlier—for noncombatants as well as combatants—and they last longer on average.

Between 1940 and 2010, 44 religious civil wars occurred, accounting for 33 percent of all 135 civil wars. Of these 44 conflicts, 27 religious civil wars (or 62 percent) involved religion as a central element, while the remaining 17 wars (or 39 percent) involved religion as a peripheral one.[23] In the 1940s, the percentage of religious civil wars among all civil wars begun in that decade was 19 percent. The figure rose to 30 percent by the 1950s, though it fell to 22 percent during the 1960s. However, the proportion of civil wars with religion as a factor has steadily increased since the 1970s, when they constituted 36 percent of all civil wars. This figure reached 41 percent in the 1980s and 45 percent in the 1990s, and 50 percent from 2000 to 2010. As of 2010, 50 percent of the 16 ongoing civil wars have a religious basis.[24]

Where do religious civil wars occur? Data show that four regions are key. Of the 44 religious civil wars in question, Asia and the Pacific saw 20 (or 45 percent), the Middle East experienced 8 (or 18 percent), Africa underwent 8 (a further 18 percent), and Europe sustained 8 (or 18 percent). Within these regions, it appears that only 24 states have been host to all 44 religious civil wars. Table 6.1 below presents the distribution of religious civil wars across states, noting the year the conflict commenced as well as the identity of the combatants.

Islam is more likely than other traditions to be involved in religious civil wars.[26] The data from 1940 to 2010 reveal that one or more combatants identified with Hinduism in 7 religious civil wars (16 percent), with Christianity in 23 cases (52 percent), and with Islam in 36 (82 percent). Other religions, such as Taoism, Buddhism, and Judaism, appeared relatively rarely. Elsewhere, we see that Islam dominates religious civil wars that are intrafaith, or fought

Table 6.1

RELIGIOUS CIVIL WARS, 1940–2010[25]

STATE	START YEAR	COMBATANT
Afghanistan	1978	Mujahideen/Taliban
Afghanistan	2004	Taliban
Algeria	1992	Fundamentalists
Azerbaijan/Soviet Union	1988	Nagorno-Karabakh
Bangladesh	1972	Chittagong Hill
Burma	1948	Karens
Burma	1960	Kachins
Chad	1965	National Liberation Front of Chad
China	1950	Tibet
China	1954	Tibet
Cyprus	1963	Greek/Turk clashes
Cyprus	1974	Coup/Turk invasion
Ethiopia	1977	Ogaden
Georgia	1992	Abkhazia
India	1946	Partition
India	1948	Hyderabad
India	1956	Naga revolt
India	1965	Kashmir
India	1982	Sikh insurrection
India	1988	Kashmir
Indonesia	1950	Ambon/Moluccans
Indonesia	1953	Aceh revolt
Indonesia	1975	Timor-Leste
Iran	1978	Revolution
Iran	1981	National Council of Resistance of Iran/Mojahedin
Iraq	1991	Shiite insurrection
Iraq	2003	Insurgency
Israel/Palestine	1945	Independence
Lebanon	1958	First civil war
Lebanon	1975	Second civil war
Nigeria	1967	Biafra
Nigeria	1980	Maitatsine
Philippines	1972	Moro rebellion
Philippines	2000	Moro rebellion
Russia	1994	First Chechen war
Russia	1999	Second Chechen war
Sri Lanka	1983	Tamil insurgency
Sudan	1955	Anya-Nya
Sudan	1983	Sudan People's Liberation Movement
Syria	1979	Sunnis versus Alawites
Tajikistan	1992	Civil war
Yugoslavia	1991	Croatian secession
Yugoslavia	1992	Bosnian civil war
Yugoslavia	1998	Kosovo

between members of the same religion, while it shares the stage with Christianity among interfaith conflicts. In Table 6.2, the data demonstrate that 12 intrafaith wars took place, with Islam being represented in a striking 11 cases (or 92 percent of the time). Of the 32 interfaith wars, 26 (or 82 percent) involved Muslims as one of the combatants and 23 (or 72 percent) involved Christians. As Table 6.2 shows, conflicts between Christian and Muslim combatants comprised a majority of the interfaith cases (19, or 60 percent).

Under conditions of increasing modernization, democratization, and globalization, these trends in the religious characteristics of civil wars demand close scrutiny. A survey documenting the "global resurgence of religion" shows that religion is gaining ground primarily in seven regions of the world:

Table 6.2

INTRARELIGIOUS AND INTERRELIGIOUS CIVIL WARS, 1940–2010[27]

TYPE OF WAR	NUMBER OF CASES
Intrafaith	12
Islam	11
Christianity	1
Interfaith: State/Opposition	32
Christianity/Islam	13
Islam/Christianity	6
Hinduism/Islam	4
Hinduism/Christianity	1
Hinduism/Sikhism	1
Taoism/Buddhism	2
Islam/Buddhism	2
Buddhism/Christianity	1
Buddhism/Hinduism	1
Judaism/Islam	1
Total	44

"former Communist countries of Eastern Europe, Central Asia and the Caucasus, as well as Latin America, the Middle East, Africa, China, and Southeast Asia."[28] From what we saw above, these territories largely coincide with those regions where religious civil wars are more likely to occur.

Why is Islam so overrepresented? It is far too simple to look only at the text of the Quran, as many analysts do. Rather, a more compelling explanation lies in the relationship of Islamic states and Muslim actors to processes of democratization and globalization—and in just plain old geography and resources.

In terms of democratization, some of those countries that experienced civil wars also experienced at least some movement toward democracy as part of the global wave of democratization since the 1970s, as outlined in Chapter Four (though in a number of cases, such as Russia's, they also backslid and lost most, if not all, of their democratic gains). The political science literature strongly suggests that states undergoing transitions to democracy face a higher likelihood of suffering a civil war.[29] Tajikistan exemplifies this pattern, as does Algeria, Indonesia, Iraq, and Russia.

The second reason is globalization and the increasing facility with which ideas cross borders. More and more, ideas are transmitted through the Internet, which knows no state boundaries. For instance, the Internet has become a key feature of the global jihad movement, helping to spread a "culture of martyrdom" and the Salafi jihad.[30] In particular, the concept of jihad, which has been interpreted and practiced since ancient times by Islamic scholars, has undergone a renaissance and reinterpretation in the last couple of decades.[31] Jihad literally means "holy struggle" and can take two forms. The first is a person's internal struggle to overcome sin. This side of jihad has little to do with religious civil wars. The second is to struggle against external forces that are aggressing upon Islam—that is, to fight a "holy war." As an obligation to defend fellow Muslims and Islamic lands, jihad emerged in the 1980s among fighters against the Soviet-backed regime in Afghanistan as Afghans fought their civil war. Called to this battle, young Muslims traveled great distances to Afghanistan to defend Islam by killing Soviet troops and the Soviet Union's local allies. Motivated by a sense of religious obligation, supported by a never-ending stream of cash and weapons across Afghanistan's notoriously porous borders, these young men—the *mujahideen*—prevented the Soviets from achieving their political objectives at an acceptable cost.[32] Although military analysts in the West were apt to credit high technology (specifically, U.S.-made Stinger surface-to-air missiles) with the Soviet defeat in Afghanistan, to Islam's more conservative clerics and to many other Muslims as well, jihad—external jihad—was responsible for defeating a nuclear-armed, industrial state.[33] This helps to account for why, since the end of the Cold War, jihad has become the legitimizing principle of choice for Islam's most conservative clerics—many of whom either personally fought to defend the faith from "godless communists" or sanctioned others to do so. Globalization has helped, then, to facilitate the transmission of jihad and the transport of men (and women) to fight it.

A final reason for Islam's disproportionate role in civil war is geographic: the co-location of Islamic holy sites and concentrated petroleum reserves, which gives a range of outside actors a vested interest in the internal affairs of several Muslim-majority countries in the Arab Middle East. This fact has created both instability—the 1991 Persian Gulf War, for instance—and stability as outsiders propped up illegitimate regimes to insure a steady flow of oil. Such interference by non-Muslim outsiders, often seen by Muslims as infidels, has created resentment among local populations, some of whom felt emboldened or threatened enough to challenge the existing political order. The Iranian Revolution of 1979 and a host of challenges to the Saudi regime are partly the products of this dynamic.

In short, religion has dramatically altered the nature of civil wars as well as the intensity with which outsiders intervene to influence their outcome. Civil wars with religion as a component are peculiarly dangerous, in part because they are so susceptible to being transnationalized. Yet the precise factors that tend to generate religious civil wars still remain inadequately understood.

How to Understand Religion and Civil War

Political theology and the relationship between religious and political authority influence civil wars much in the way they influence terrorism. Religious civil war is more likely to occur in a state that either represses a religious actor or does not provide it with sufficient autonomy, and when a religious actor holds a political theology that advocates (or minimally does not condemn) the use of violence to achieve its political ends. When a state moves in the direction of conflictual integration, violence is more prone to break out. Conflictual integration is the most dangerous condition, since in repressing a religious actor, the state denies it independence and legitimate political participation. The religious actor turns to violence when it appears the only viable alternative. Tensions are also more likely to develop if a religious actor that is not privileged by the state espouses a political theology that inspires it to clash with the state, the privileged religious actor, or both. If the relationship between religious and political authority is one of independence, then change could be achieved by means of nonviolent action (e.g., via public debate or new elections). By contrast, in an integrated state a religious actor is more likely to turn to violence.

Religious civil war will be least likely to occur in states with conditions close to consensual independence. But this is not to say that religious violence will never occur in such an environment. As discussed in Chapter Five, the advent of Hindutva in India has generated high levels of informal violence against religious minorities, orchestrated by Hindu-nationalist groups to secure their goal of an integrationist Hindu state.[34] As Table 6.1 shows, Hindu-majority India has already been the site of no fewer than six religious civil wars (some of which remain unresolved) and has fought against insurgencies that have had Muslim, Sikh, and Christian elements, and the proliferation of anti-minority religious violence makes yet another religious civil war a non-trivial possibility. Growing hostility between minority Muslim populations and political authorities increasingly identified with Hinduism—especially at the state level in places such as Gujarat—is a perilous trend. Political scientist Anurag Pandey wrote as much in 2007: "[C]ollective identifiers of 'We and They,' of 'Hindutva' and 'Islamic Brotherhood,' will be more pronounced than before. We would then not be that far from a situation of near or actual civil war, which would further strengthen the BJP (Sangh Parivar) as well as promote Muslim separatism."[35]

The strife between China and Tibet during the 1950s provides us with an example of a relationship that has drifted toward conflictual independence. In this case, independence arises when the state represses all religious actors rather than simply privileging none. During the period from 1911 to 1949, Tibet enjoyed a sort of de facto political independence.[36] Beginning in 1951, however, Chinese forces occupied the region. An accord entitled the "Seventeen-Point Agreement," formulated by Beijing and Tibet, was adopted on May 23, 1951. Despite the fact that the document laid out Beijing's intention to "respect and coexist with Tibet's existing political, social, and monastic systems," the relationship established by the settlement was perceived as unequal and left many Tibetans uneasy about their future status within China.[37]

After several years of occupation, on March 10, 1959, a rebellion broke out in the Tibetan capital of Lhasa involving protestors opposed to both the

Chinese government and Communism. The document that Beijing issued following the March rebellion was called "Decisions on Several Policy Issues Concerning the Implementation of Democratic Reforms by Crushing the Rebellion in Tibet." In it, officials asserted that "the policy of respecting freedom of religious belief should be continuously upheld."[38] It was clear, however, that Tibet would be closely monitored and restricted.

The Chinese Communist Party (CCP) believed that suppressing the Tibetan rebellion would require it "to separate the political and religious spheres of Tibetan life."[39] Mao Zedong took for granted that Tibet belonged to China, and that the country would be unified only through the inclusion of a "liberated" Tibet.[40] In seeing this as the natural status quo, the CCP seemed to presume that Tibet's political and religious institutions could be peacefully and consensually integrated—in the long run, at least—with Chinese authority structures.

What have been the consequences of China's stance? The CCP failed to deal intelligently with religion as a potential factor in conflict, as historian Chen Jian has written:

> . . . Beijing's management of the Tibet issue was flawed all along by the Chinese leaders' inability to grasp that Tibet, with its distinctive historical tradition, religion, and culture, could not be subjugated through ordinary military and political means. Because Mao and his colleagues subscribed to the Marxist notion that "all struggles between nations and races are in essence struggles between classes," they made no real and consistent effort to understand Tibet's religion and culture. The Chinese Communists had long relied on a "united front" strategy to expand their own influence, and they stuck to this approach in Tibet, showing superficial respect for the Dalai Lama (and the Panchen Lama as well).[41]

Shortly after the March 1959 rebellion, the Dalai Lama fled to India. Yet even before that time, the issue of Tibet had caused strain between India and the People's Republic of China (PRC). China's long-term treatment of Tibet, which caused the conflict to spread beyond Chinese borders, thus had a hand in worsening relations between the two countries. The status of Tibet was a core factor in creating deep suspicion between China and India and leading to a series of crises.[42] The civil war between China and Tibet underscores just how such conflicts can have ramifications throughout the region.[43] Today, over 77,000 refugees from Tibet/China are present in India; more than 20,000 reside in Nepal.

In states closest to consensual integration, a religious civil war would seem most unlikely. Yet, two threats can force states into a situation that makes war more likely. First, the minority group (or a dominated majority) is repressed by the state, and second, the repressed group has or adopts a political theology that motivates it to oppose this repression through violence. As we discussed at length in Chapter Five, the origins of the ethno-religious Tamil Tiger terrorist organization (LTTE) in the context of growing Sinhalese-Buddhist hegemony in Sri Lanka exemplifies this pattern. The Sri Lankan case, like several other cases, such as that of Afghanistan, straddles the issues of terrorism and civil war. Though the Tamil Tigers were a terrorist organization, their conflict with the Sri Lankan government widened into a religious civil war that may have killed as many as 100,000 people between 1983 and 2009 (a war that was also internationalized, engulfing India in the late 1980s and leading to the assassination of Rajiv Gandhi by a female Tamil Tiger suicide bomber in 1991).

Religious civil wars are more likely to occur where integrated arrangements arise and marginalize at least one religious group. Once a state moves in this direction, it is unlikely to move away from it again, at least without a good deal of bloodshed. When religious dominance is part of the political objective of a group that manages to capture the state, other groups will become fearful that their faith will be undermined, suppressed, or even annihilated. What is now at stake is the very identity and survival of these other groups, whose members the state represses, imprisons, or kills off.

COMPELLING CASES

To illustrate the logic of our argument we examine five civil wars: Sudan, Chechnya, Algeria, Tajikistan, and Iraq. Sudan and Chechnya mirror each other insofar as both regions have endured two civil wars, with the first war in each case being a conflict of self-determination and nationalism in which religion played little role. The second civil war in both cases involved religion to a much greater extent, thanks in large part to global forces. The civil wars in Algeria and Tajikistan pitted secularist governments against Islamist groups that promoted integrationist ideas. Whereas Algeria continues to struggle for peace, Tajikistan is something of a successful case, having been able to integrate the opposing religious actor into state politics. Iraq, on the other hand, remains mired in political instability (at least at the time of writing), whose intricacies make it enormously complex. Some argue that Iraq actually contained four civil wars, involving various sects and militarized forces.[44]

Sudan (1955–1972 and 1983–2005)

At its core, Sudan's ongoing civil strife involves a disagreement over whether religion ought to be privileged in governance. Since winning independence from the United Kingdom in 1956, Sudan has experienced two brutal and destructive civil wars (1955–1972 and 1983–2005). Several northern regimes have fought against numerous southern alliances throughout the course of these two conflicts, with the principal rebel groups being the Anya-Nya during the first war and the Sudan People's Liberation Movement (SPLM) during the second. After two peace agreements, it remains unclear whether the more recent of these will hold or whether Sudan will succumb to a third bout of civil war.

On the subject of religion, Francis Deng, an expert on Africa and conflict management, has written that civil war in Sudan "culminates a long history in which the north has tried to spread its religion and language to the South, which has resisted these efforts."[45] This dynamic has pitted the mostly Arab and Muslim population of northern Sudan against the black African and non-Muslim population of the south. At the time of this writing, Sudan in ethnic terms is 52 percent black African and 39 percent Arab. Although factors other than religion have helped create a stark divide between the two halves of Sudan, religion is the most important cleavage. Islam and the Arabic language characterize the north while Christianity and English are central elements of identity in the south. As the British prepared to leave Sudan, the transfer of power favored northerners, leaving southerners feeling pushed aside in favor of an Arabic-Islamic Sudan. This ill-conceived transition yielded more civil service posts for the Arab population than for indigenous Africans from the south, causing the latter group to fear for its security.

The Khartoum government's assertion that Islamic law (*sharia*) should govern all of Sudan has been a major catalyst in Sudan's violence.[46] Beginning in 1958 under General Ibrahim Abboud, the government carried out an aggressive Islamization campaign against the south. In autumn 1983, following the southern rebellion that marked the beginning of Sudan's second civil war, the Nimeiri government imposed the "September Laws," which made *sharia* the basis of the national legal system.

The alignment of northern elites with fundamentalist Islam and the government's imposition of *sharia* throughout all of Sudan, even in those areas with non-Muslim populations, pushed religion into the center of Sudanese politics and helped to spark another civil war between the north and the south.

Conflictual integration has not, however, characterized Sudan throughout its life as a sovereign state. Sudan's first civil war was not religious. Religion was a factor in its second civil war because of a combination of local and global influences. The second war was driven by integrationist ideas. It was during that war that Osama bin Laden was first invited to Sudan by Hassan al-Turabi, the attorney general of the country. Bin Laden would stay in Sudan from 1991 to 1996, helping to elevate Islamist ideas to a more prominent position in Sudanese politics.[47]

Chechnya (1994–96 and 1999–)

Turning to the Chechen case, we see that the first civil war resembled that of Sudan as a conflict of self-determination. Chechnya's second civil war featured more religious elements, but religion had little traction there despite the government's attempts to sell the war as a battle based on faith and part of the global war on terror.

Before the onset of the first civil war, Chechnya was not immediately concerned with self-determination, let alone separatism based on religion. Initially, Chechen discontent was centered upon perceived Soviet indifference to local environmental concerns. The Chechen pattern followed that emerging throughout the rest of the USSR: as *perestroika* led to an "opening up" of the Soviet political scene in the late 1980s and people were allowed to voice their concerns over an increased range of issues, discontent with environmental conditions became one of the primary impetuses for public mobilization. This newfound motivation among local groups proceeded then to usher in a period of national evaluation and reflection among many of the USSR's ethnic minorities. The first mass public demonstration in Chechnya occurred in the summer of 1988, in the city of Gudermes, over a Soviet proposal to construct a biochemical plant. What was the primary issue? It was not Chechen independence from the state, but impending environmental degradation, the need to protect the local population, and the perception of Moscow and the Communist Party as indifferent to such concerns. These initial concerns and related demonstrations, however, gave rise to broader ones, and in a short time encouraged the emergence of questions about Chechen history, its role in the Soviet Union, and issues of national self-determination.

The first civil war between Russia and the self-declared autonomous state of the Chechen Republic of Ichkeria, or Chechnya, lasted from 1994 to 1996. In December 1994, negotiations that had begun in March 1992 ended when the two powers failed to reach an agreement over the scope of Chechen autonomy. The violence was then sparked when Moscow invaded the republic in the northern Caucasus.[48] In autumn 1999, another Russian invasion marked the beginning of the second such war. Boris Yeltsin made it clear that in his view, Russian territory was indivisible and that using force to suppress the Chechen independence movement was the only option left. In his published memoirs, he stated that during the session of the Russian Security Council when the decision to use force in Chechnya was made, "[t]he general position was *unanimous*: We cannot stand idly by while a piece of Russia breaks off, because this would be the beginning of the collapse of the country."[49] Moscow thus believed it had to intervene to prevent Chechnya and other regions from attempting independence, for an accumulation of secessions would threaten Russia's very survival.

From the Russian government's perspective, its relationship with religion had moved toward consensual integration with the Orthodox Church. In contrast, Chechen opposition perceived this relationship to be one of conflictual integration. It desired independence. During the course of both Russian-Chechen civil wars (1994–1996 and 1999–), the Kremlin has not acknowledged that the Chechen separatists have a legitimate cause. Influenced by a resurgence of Russian nationalism that was increasingly informed by a xenophobic Orthodox Church, Moscow sought to delegitimize the movement during the first conflict "by depicting the rebels as 'bandits' and 'Islamists.' "[50] Russian aggression against Grozny, the capital, beginning in 1999 was couched as a campaign against international Islamic terrorism.[51] Emil Souleimanov and Ondrej Ditrych recount the outlook of the Russian state:

> Russia's enemies in the North Caucasus were no longer national separatists, which they were predominantly perceived as being during the First Chechen War, but were now Islamist terrorists—criminals and fanatics who were interested not in securing freedom for their homeland, but were instead immersed in the totalitarian ideology of global *jihad*, striving to establish an Islamic caliphate. . . .[52]

Following the attacks of September 11, 2001, Moscow relied even more on the specter of global Islamic terrorism to support its campaign against

Chechnya. In this way, it seems that terrorism has a double link to civil war. In the first place, terrorism can exacerbate a conflict simply by virtue of being a tactic used in the war. The most famous and tragic terrorist act occurred during the Second Chechen War in September 2004 in Beslan, North Ossetia. Chechen fighters under the leadership of Shamil Basayev, a fighter driven by both religious zeal and Chechen nationalism, seized a primary school and took over 1,000 people hostage. The siege ended with the massacre of over 300 people, over half of whom were children.

Second, terrorism—whether real or imagined—can be a scapegoat that gives a state fighting a civil war a platform for legitimacy. Russia has relied on this second connection between terrorism and civil war:

> Not surprisingly, in the wake of September 11 the Russian govern-
> ment has given higher prominence to the terrorism "frame" in its
> interpretation of the Chechen War. Moscow has sought to persuade
> the West that the conflict in Chechnya is an acceptable and necessary
> part of a global war against terror. The Russian government seeks,
> at a minimum, noninterference from the West as it pursues its war.
> Beyond that, it would apparently welcome cooperation and an explicit
> endorsement of its fight against what it considers internationally spon-
> sored terrorists.[53]

Interestingly, the connections Vladimir Putin attempted to make between Chechen fighters and Osama bin Laden's Al Qaeda have not been fully substantiated.[54]

By refusing to recognize the Chechen movement as a reasonable one of national separatism, Russia has failed to deal effectively with these twin civil wars. As President Putin prepared to transfer power to Dmitry Medvedev in 2008, the Chechen civil war that began in 1999 was declared over. Still, some argue that the current lull in violence is more the effect of a temporary solution than a lasting peace.[55] Violence and suicide terrorism witnessed a marked increase in 2009, and continue into 2010.

In the end, the Russian government succeeded in fueling Islamism while attempting to stamp it out. There were warnings prior to the beginning of each civil war that Russia's emphasis on Chechnya's purported Islamic threat could in fact fuel a reactive religious fanaticism. The first president of the Chechen Republic, Dzhokhar Dudayev, stated in 1991 "that Islamic fundamental-ism in Chechnya presented no danger, but maintained that hostile actions by Russia could push Chechen nationalism onto a more extremist, Islamic path."[56] In fact, one account holds that Dudayev began to rely increasingly on Islamic connections for support—both within and outside of Chechnya—as it became clear that Moscow would not negotiate on Chechen sovereignty.[57]

There were, as scholar on religious peacebuilding Katrien Hertog notes, already traces of Islamism in Chechen politics. Islam, however, had long existed in Chechnya in a distinctly moderate form.[58] Over two centuries, Islam has retained strength despite outside efforts to force conversion; nine out of ten Chechens and Dagestanis identify as Muslim.[59] Furthermore, the strength of the Chechen Islamic faith has been attributed to the prevalence of Sufism among the group. Because Sufism is clan-based and less reliant on mosques than other Muslim institutions, it has been better able to withstand the attempts of the Russians and Soviets to force the Chechens to convert to Christianity or to Soviet secular ideology. Importantly, Chechens have not been as susceptible to outside influences in their understanding of what it means to be a Muslim, either. As political scientist Matthew Evangelista notes:

> The Sufi influence seems to account for why, according to survey data, religious belief and practice are far higher in Dagestan and Chechnya than in any other of Russia's Muslim republics, such as Tatarstan and Bashkortostan. The higher the level of religious practice, the more Islam can serve as a mobilizing force for resistance to Russian dominance, as it has done throughout the history of both Dagestan and Chechnya.[60]

Nonlocal, radical variants of Islam, however, have been able to take stronger hold in the Republic of Dagestan than in Chechnya.[61] In Dagestan, Islamism seems to be growing more extreme because of government policies that alienate moderate Muslims—for example, by referring to all Muslims as Wahhabis.[62] While this extremism seems to be localized for the moment, it has the potential to go global, especially if the local regional governments in coordination with the federal government continue to view all Muslims as threats to the existing political order.[63]

With the First Chechen War, Islam went from being a peripheral political concern to the Chechen population—a source of identity and a way of life— to being a central political focus—*the* source of national identity.[64] Russia's poor handling of the Chechen separatist movement thus provides an example of how religion can become a central consideration in a civil war where it did not have to be.

Tajikistan (1992–1997)

The civil war in Tajikistan is the only case we deal with that might be said to have a satisfactory outcome. This is because the Islamist opposition in Tajikistan is both moderate and fragmented. The Islamic Renaissance Party (IRP) led by Said Abdullo Nuri opposed the country's postindependence secularist government on a nationalist platform and did not aim to create an Islamic state or to pursue a new Islamic caliphate.[65] And second, because politics in Central Asia are often dominated "more by the tribal and ethnic allegiances than by ideology," Islamism is considered unlikely to underpin Tajik politics in any dominant fashion.[66]

At the time the war began, certain ethnic groups from the southern Kulyab region dominated the secularist government, causing opposition movements from other ethnic backgrounds to lash out against the ruling elite in order to gain a greater stake in power. The reasons why religious civil war emerged fit our pattern: An inability to participate in politics drove religious actors to seek their aims through violent means. Political scientist Mohammed Hafez notes this in his discussion of rebellion and its connection to state repression:

> In Tajikistan, rebellion and civil war broke out when neo-communist forces refused to cede any control of the government to the combined opposition of nationalists, Islamists, and democrats. Not only was the opposition ousted from power through mass repression, their organizations and parties were subsequently banned and suppressed. Indiscriminate repression against anyone suspected of supporting the opposition—often driven by regional and clan-based associations— produced hundreds of thousands of refugees, from whom the ranks of the rebels were recruited.[67]

From the government's perspective, it was a situation of consensual independence. In the minds of the mainly Islamist opposition, the status quo was moving in the direction of conflictual integration.

One reason why Islam appears to serve so often as the motivation behind uprisings, low-level conflicts, and full-on civil wars is its ability to unite. This is particularly true in the nations of the former Soviet Union, which at times have no ideological substance to fall back on in the absence of Communism.

As sociologist Mark Juergensmeyer has observed, this is one reason why Islam has traction in Central Asian civil wars:

> Indeed, Islam poses a serious threat to the secular governments of Central Asian nations, for without the ideological underpinnings of Marxist theory and the military and economic support of the Soviet Union, they have little on which to base their political authority. Some of the former Communists have turned to nationalism as a basis of support, but the boundaries of the five nations of Central Asia were loosely drawn and encompass a wide variety of ethnicities.[68]

In general, this combination of factors poses a relatively high risk of conflict. That is, if an integrated government feels threatened by a potential opposition group, it will likely seek to repress that group. In turn, this increased subjugation could inspire the use of violence.

The key to success in Tajikistan seems to have been the manner in which the government dealt with the IRP following the war. Specifically, the state's decision to accommodate the IRP and assign it a place in the political process created the potential for the party to become a less radical entity, pursuing its agenda through nonviolent mechanisms.[69] In contrast to other former Soviet states of Central Asia, Tajikistan has since 1999 allowed officially religious parties to take part in governance.[70] This policy is absent in regional neighbors such as Turkmenistan, Uzbekistan, and Kyrgyzstan. As part of a power-sharing agreement that still remains intact, President Imamoli Rakhmanov recognized the IRP as legal and brought the Islamic opposition party into the fold of public politics.[71]

Tajikistan's civil war cost the country tens of thousands of lives before a cease-fire was established. With the violence at a formal standstill as of December 1996, the combatants signed a June 1997 peace agreement in Moscow brokered by the United Nations. At the meeting, Russia backed the Tajik government, whereas the Islamists were represented by the United Tajik Opposition (UTO). In addition to setting up the parameters of power-sharing in the government, the agreement included amnesty and legalization of the Islamist parties and their press operations.[72] As not all members of the opposition have followed the arrangement, it is natural that Tajikistan experiences something short of complete peace.[73] But regarding the potential for Tajikistan to serve as a model for dealing with domestic unrest with a religious focus, historian Fabio Oliva has written that "the incorporation of a formerly armed Islamic opposition into the power structures along with the emergence of a moderate Islamic party represents an indisputable success."[74]

Algeria (1991–2002)

In Algeria, supporters of the Islamic Salvation Front (FIS) took up arms after the cancellation of an election in 1992 that promised a parliamentary victory for Islamists. Since that time, approximately 150,000 people have been killed in an ongoing struggle between Islamists and the regime.[75]

In contrast to Tajikistan, Algeria's civil war (1991–2002) is instructive in a negative sense. The Algerian political elite managed domestic strife poorly, without consideration of the consequences, which came to include a civil war and lingering violence. Algeria's precarious situation can be attributed largely to the way it handled Islamist opposition forces in the early 1990s.[76] Here a secular, socialist government privileged certain religious forces in a relationship of consensual integration while excluding others in a relationship of conflictual integration. This dynamic exacerbated tensions and fueled the opposition movements that would contribute to the country's civil war.[77] Due to this combination of factors, violence erupted in the first days of 1992. The civil war began in earnest at that point, once the government had annulled a December 1991 general election in which the Islamic Salvation Front was poised to defeat the National Liberation Front.[78] According to a plan made public shortly after voting, the FIS desired "to expand sharia law to all areas of public and private life in Algeria, including in particular women's dress and work. The group also declared its intent to reform government at all levels."[79] And unlike Tajikistan's IRP, the FIS stated that its goal was turning Algeria "into an orthodox Islamic state."[80] This ill-fated election was the result of decades of discontent under a military-backed socialist regime. True, unhappiness with the incumbent elites stemmed from more than just a conflicting political theology, with many analysts making the case that it was not necessarily support for the Islamists, but rather a protest vote against the incumbent governments' corruption. The religious party was a credible alternative.[81]

The democratic election of a group with an agenda thought to be conservative and religious caused growing alarm among the secularists already in power. Up to 1992, however, the FIS was in fact less radical than the group was made out to be. At a minimum, it was willing to engage in political compromise, but the government's repressive actions served to radicalize and intensify the Islamist cause.[82] Prior to the 1992 elections, the party's strategy was one of "tactical militancy" and accommodation: "It was not a revolutionary party that aimed to build an Islamic state at any cost and irrespective of the means. In other words, unlike the radical groups that wanted to overthrow the system through armed struggle and shunned democracy as un-Islamic, the FIS was clearly against revolutionary violence in this period."[83]

As a result of the backlash against Islamist forces in the first days of 1992, FIS leaders and activists were pushed underground. With a more fragmented and less visible Islamist movement, it was impossible to gauge or attempt to deal with a possible threat from that quarter.[84] Rather than taking a productive step toward solving a complex dispute, the government in Algiers only made the situation worse.

An extreme form of Islamism thus grew in Algeria, causing some to characterize the country as posing "the increasingly widespread quandary of how to sift moderate political Islam from Islamic militancy and terrorism."[85] With the Islamists and the secular political elite both being portrayed as uncompromising, one must ask how Algeria hopes to move away from conflictual integration and into a more consensual arrangement. In the wake of 1992, the desire on the part of the Islamists to compromise was lessened due to its total exclusion from the political sphere.[86] By the year 2002, however, "much of the Islamic resistance had been defeated or diffused by an amnesty program aimed at reconciling dissident elements."[87] Additionally, the 2004 reelection of President Abdelaziz Bouteflika to a second term in office—an outcome deemed legitimate by international observers—could be a step in the right direction. The various amnesty programs established by the Bouteflika administration have largely avoided delving into past events, instead emphasizing the future of Algeria by offering reconciliation to parties "with blood on their hands," including terrorists.[88] Bouteflika is viewed as someone who is amenable to both sides and might be able to bridge the divide between them—perhaps bringing peace to Algeria.

In view of the relative success found by Tajikistan in accommodating Islamist parties and integrating them into the government, Algeria might also benefit from this strategy. Increasing political openness in Algeria would likely do much to bolster moderate Islam and quell radical voices.[89] This assessment of Algerian politics falls in line with one of our key predictions: that where religious actors possess the freedoms necessary to pursue their goals through political means, the risk of violence—in the form of terrorism, civil war, or both—will generally be lower.

The FIS has been outlawed in Algeria since March 5, 1992. While some

former leaders of the FIS have been pardoned and are monitored by authorities, others are in exile abroad. All are banned from participating in Algerian
politics.[90] Despite a cease-fire being declared in September 2007, sporadic violence continues to plague Algeria. The group called Al Qaeda in the Islamic
Maghreb now holds considerable influence there, and is currently "North
Africa's most active militant group."[91]

Iraq (2004–)

Since the March 2003 American-led invasion of Iraq, religious groups in that
shattered country have understood themselves to be engaged in a civil war,
whatever the hesitations of others in using the term. For these groups, the
centrality of religion to the conflict is demonstrated in three key ways. First,
Sunni and Shiite Muslims identify themselves and their situation more in
religious terms than with respect to other sources of identity. Second, they
use religious language when articulating threats and when singling out the
enemy. Third, they draw on religious connections when seeking aid from
foreign sources. In addition to conflicts between Sunnis and Shiites, there
is now evidence that fighting is taking place among various Shiite groups.[92]
With religion at the heart of Iraq's civil war, it is unlikely that a negotiated end
to the fight will be easily attained, despite the strides the country has made
towards democracy we noted in Chapter Four. Compounding this problem,
the number of religious actors has grown, making it more difficult to reach a
compromise or to identify the right partner for negotiation.[93]

Some have made the case that Iraq has essentially experienced four civil
wars. In all four cases, the cause of the violence is not simply religion but
also that actors have intertwined religion and the use of violence with other
interests such as politics, the economy, and control over territory and natural
resources. To combat or even analyze this explosive mixture is a cumbersome
task, and it has been a major obstacle to coalition progress in Iraq since 2003.
So far, U.S. Secretary of Defense Robert Gates has most succinctly stated the
problem of the four wars: "One is Shi'a on Shi'a, principally in the south; the
second is sectarian conflict, principally in Baghdad, but not solely; third is
the insurgency; and fourth is Al Qaeda, and Al Qaeda is attacking, at times,
all of those targets."[94]

Despite a democratic political system that maintains a constitutionally
grounded, consensual independence between political and religious authority, and despite powerful segments of the Shiite leadership that support a
democratic form of consensual independence, religiously motivated spoilers

exist on both the Sunni and Shiite sides. Their willingness to inflict large-scale violence produces continuing instability and insecurity. At the same time, Shiite resentment of past Sunni rule combines with Sunni resentment of current Shiite dominance in politics to produce general dissatisfaction. Iraq's Shiite population, now estimated at 60 to 65 percent of the country's population, was long dominated by the minority Sunnis, who make up 32 to 37 percent of the whole. Decades-long Sunni rule under the Ba'ath Party was possible under the authoritarian leadership of Saddam Hussein. In the absence of a ruthless despotism keeping the various religious actors and factions in line, mutual accommodation will be elusive.

The Iraqi case goes far in demonstrating the comparative success of the accord reached by Tajikistan. In a draft plan for the postwar administration of Iraq issued in April 2003, one can see how dim the hopes were even at the start of the conflict for a stable Iraq. In its Section 1.6, covering security concerns in the country, the *Unified Mission Plan for Post Hostilities Iraq* demonstrates this outlook:

> The potential for instability, likely to exist for some time after the war is over. The most probable threat will come from residual pockets of fanatics, secessionist groups, terrorists and those would seek to exploit ethnic, religious, and tribal fault lines for personal gain. The threat from these groups would manifest itself in high impact tactics such as car or suicide bombings, sniping, and "hit and run" raids. A high level of such attacks will have an adverse impact on the creation of stability, a prerequisite for self-sustaining peace. [*sic*][95]

Another faction that stands in the way of a unified and stable Iraq is the Kurdish population. Concentrated in northern Iraq, ethnic Kurds make up 15 to 20 percent of Iraq's population. They are largely focused on maintaining autonomy in the north rather than on the civil war and, as a result, have contributed little to the fighting. Nonetheless, the Kurdish bid for independence could play a role in the eventual breakup of Iraq, should it formally separate into three areas—Sunni, Shiite, and Kurdish.

CONCLUSION

Today, there exists a conspicuous relationship between religion and civil war. Paralleling the argument of this book about a religious resurgence, the rise in the proportion of civil wars with religion as a basis either peripherally or centrally emerged in the 1970s. This trend is traceable to the three broad trends that explain the global resurgence of religion more generally: modernization, democratization, and globalization.

Colonialism collapsed in the late 1940s, 1950s, and 1960s. Although the Western powers departed, they left behind their secular ideologies of Communism, liberalism, and socialism. The systems based on these ideologies promised much but delivered little. By the 1960s, alternatives were sought. Religion had never disappeared. Those religious elites and organizations that survived were in a good position to try to deliver what these other systems failed to produce. Modernization and the failure of secularization thus privileged religious actors who were able to tap into existing networks and institutions and challenge the state's legitimacy and authority. However, where secularist and nationalist authoritarian regimes sought to block what they considered their divinely ordained ascendancy, the result in numerous cases was civil war.

Furthermore, as more states democratized, ideas about the proper place of religion in relation to states entered the political fray. The pressure for political systems to become more transparent and accountable to their citizens has meant that different sectors of society have been able to advance their agendas in the political sphere. What this means in practice is that, as religious populations have grown, so too have their influence in politics. All too often, however, democratic transitions throughout the world have been slow and incomplete, or have only served to establish "illiberal democracies" that effectively favor one set of religious or ethnic actors over another. The simultaneously volatile and often abortive nature of numerous democratic transitions—which have held out the promise of all-inclusive democratic participation only to produce a non-democratic reality—has also generated its fair share of religious civil wars.

Finally, religious actors are transnational actors, and as globalization increased propitiously in the 1970s and into the 1980s, it is not surprising that they were able to harness ideas and technologies to challenge their states. Although civil wars are largely local fights contained within the borders of a state, they are not immune to global dynamics.

Amid this resurgence of religion in civil wars, we can also see a more particular increase in two areas: religious civil wars underpinned by Islam; and wars that are driven by other integrationist ideas. Given these uncomfortable realities, it is essential to try to address head-on how policy-makers might attempt to counter the sort of Islamism that appears to be a prevalent factor in contemporary religiously based civil wars.

If the answer to religious violence were truly to be found within religion itself,[96] we would do well to pay more attention to a strand of Islam that more often than not serves as a voice of moderation: Sufism. The roots of Sufi brotherhoods, or *tariqahs*, run deep, having emerged in the early ninth century C.E. Today, around one-fifth of Muslims around the world identify as Sufi, though many more are familiar with Sufism as a cultural influence.[97] As historian and religious studies scholar Philip Jenkins has written, Sufi brotherhoods have done much to expand the global reach of Islam while also invigorating the religion as a whole. On the subject of religious violence, he notes that Sufis constitute "a global web of devout religious brotherhoods that by all logic should be a critical ally against extremism."[98] The presence and strength of Sufi Islam seems indeed to tamp down the force of radical Islam: "Where Islamists rise to power, Sufis are persecuted or driven underground; but where Sufis remain in the ascendant, it is the radical Islamist groups who must fight to survive."[99] This effect—along with the apparent strength of Sufi movements at present—holds out hope for an antidote to extremism.

The idea that Sufis "are potentially the greatest hope for pluralism and democracy within Muslim nations" should grab our attention in light of our stress on the danger of integration.[100] That is, Sufi groups could be extremely helpful religious actors to have on the ground in places where integration dominates. Promisingly, Sufi groups have proven themselves generally averse to imposing their own religious views on those whose conscience dictates otherwise. For example, consider Fethullah Gülen, a Sufi religious leader in Turkey. He opposes state enforcement of Islamic law because most "Islamic regulations concern people's private lives and only a few bear on matters of governance. . . . Because religion is a private matter, the requirements of any particular faith should not be imposed on an entire population."[101]

In terms of policy measures, it seems clear that healthy Sufi movements ought to be protected. As a potential threat to Islamists, they are often the targets of rival extremist movements. Yet, because they are natural allies of moderate regimes and of Western governments, a common basis of understanding could be established with them.[102] While we ought not to rely only upon moderate Sufi brotherhoods in the fight against extremism, they provide a good model for the kinds of religious allies policy-makers should look for not only among Muslims but also among all religious actors that might resort to violence.

Chapter Seven

MILITANTS FOR
PEACE AND JUSTICE

THE SETTING IS THE MAIN CONFERENCE ROOM OF THE
Farnesina Palace, home of the Foreign Ministry of Italy in Rome, in
fall 1992. Seated on a dais are Joaquim Chissano, president of Mozambique;
Afonso Dhlakama, president of RENAMO (Resistência Nacional Moçambi-
cana), Mozambique's insurgency movement; Emilio Colombo, Italy's foreign
minister; and other African heads of state and foreign officials. The dignitaries have just concluded an agreement to end the civil war in Mozambique, a
war that lasted for sixteen years and resulted in over a million deaths.

Though significant for Mozambicans, the agreement was only one of several that ended civil wars at the close of the Cold War. Far more remarkable
was who negotiated the agreement and how it was concluded. Seated prominently with the dignitaries were also four other people: Mario Raffaeli, an
Italian member of Parliament; Don Jaime Gonçalves, the Catholic archbishop
of Beira, Mozambique; Professor Andrea Riccardi, president of the Community of Sant'Egidio; and Don Matteo Zuppi, a priest and member of the Community of Sant'Egidio.[1]

The Community of Sant'Egidio? This group was the key mediator of the
peace in Mozambique. But who are they? In 1968, a year of political ferment
all across Europe, a handful of students at Rome's Virgil High School decided
to put their Catholic faith into practice by gathering regularly to pray together
and to befriend the city's poorest inhabitants. During the 1970s, their ranks
grew as they expanded their work to include addicts, orphans, the handi-
capped, and the elderly poor and extended their network into countries like

Albania, Ethiopia, Somalia, and Vietnam. The Catholic Church declared them a "public lay association" and gave them an abandoned convent in the Trastevere district of Rome, linked to the Church of Sant'Egidio (St. Giles), from which they took their name. Today the community includes over 50,000 members spread over seventy countries.[2]

That Sant'Egidio mediated Mozambique's peace agreement defies conventional wisdom. Peace agreements are supposed to be negotiated by states and international organizations that can provide material rewards and enforce the peace through security measures. To be sure, such "realist" factors mattered here: The diplomatic roles of the United States, the United Nations, and Italy were essential, as was the end of the Cold War, which dried up Soviet support for Mozambique's Marxist government. But seasoned diplomats have observed that Sant'Egidio was indispensable. How so?

Consistent with its modus operandi, members of the Community formed a network of friendships in Mozambique during the 1970s, one that included leaders from both sides in the civil war and Catholic Church officials, most importantly Bishop Jaime Gonçalves. From this human infrastructure, Sant'Egidio helped to open up religious freedom for the Catholic Church in Mozambique as well as bring desperately needed economic aid to the country in the 1980s. At the end of the decade, when both sides showed an interest in a settlement, Sant'Egidio, along with leaders of the Catholic Church in Mozambique and the Mozambique Christian Council (a coalition of Protestant churches), brought the parties into nine rounds of peace negotiations, which Sant'Egidio conducted at its Trastevere headquarters between 1990 and 1992. Trastevere was itself symbolic, having been a crossroads and meeting place for members of diverse cultures from the time of the Roman Empire. It was here that the Community brought together what one diplomat has called an "idiosyncratic bouillabaisse" of actors, including the main disputant parties, U.N officials, representatives of ten different governments, including Italy and the United States, as well as "Tiny" Rowland, a morale-boosting British businessman.[3]

The General Peace Accord was signed on October 4, 1992—the Feast Day of St. Francis of Assisi, a medieval saint and a great peacemaker. Unlike many other peace agreements, 43 percent of which relapse into violence within five years, this peace would last.[4] Sant'Egidio remained committed to Mozambique, carrying out major projects to fight AIDS and to bring relief to victims of massive flooding there in subsequent years. On the reputation of its diplomatic work, Sant'Egidio also undertook mediation efforts in other countries around the world, including Algeria, Burundi, Congo, Guatemala, Ivory Coast, Kosovo, Liberia, and Uganda.

Just as religious actors foment civil war and terrorism, as we saw in the last two chapters, so, too, they promote peace and reconciliation in the wake of civil war, genocide, and dictatorship, the subject of this chapter. When they do, they draw from the motivations, doctrines, and communities that their religion entails. Sometimes they pursue peace with fervor equal to the religiously violent, acting as what historian R. Scott Appleby calls "militants for peace."[5]

Our claims about religious activities for peace support the larger claims of the book. Reflecting our first argument—that a religious resurgence has characterized the past generation—Sant'Egidio's peacemaking efforts are one of the most vivid examples of a global outbreak of religious initiatives for peace during the last four decades, the same period in which religious actors also intensively promoted democracy, terrorism, and an increasing proportion of civil wars.

Within the Catholic Church, Sant'Egidio's work reflected the same surge of activist energy that included the mediation and reconciliation efforts of several national Catholic churches as well as the Catholic Wave of democratization described in Chapter Four—all fruits of the Second Vatican Council. Within all religions, peace efforts during this period conspired with—and were not quelled by—the forces of modernity: transnationalism, technological modernization, globalization, and democratization. The transnational reach that Sant'Egidio established in the 1970s proved essential for bringing together the relevant parties for peace in Mozambique. Crucial, too, was the ability of community members to fly back and forth and to communicate efficiently between Italy and Africa. As a group of laypeople and citizens who could speak, act, and assemble freely and flexibly within the political context of the modern Italian Republic, Sant'Egidio practiced a politics distinctive to an age of globalization and democracy.

Reflecting the book's second argument—about the importance of independence and political theology—Sant'Egidio's success also lay in the fact that it was a quintessential institutionally independent actor. In the spirit of the Second Vatican Council's teachings, it had no formal ties to a state and no stake in political or economic power. In the Mozambique negotiations, one of the most difficult issues in getting the parties to the table was the government of Mozambique's unwillingness to recognize the legitimacy of the rebel movement, RENAMO, which it had previously dismissed as rogue bandits. It was only because Sant'Egidio did not carry the official authority of a sovereign state or of the U.N. that the government negotiators were willing to sit at the same table with their opponents. Likewise, those religious actors that are most effective in promoting peace are ones who are most independent from their state.

Sant'Egidio's political theology mattered, too. Its themes of promoting social justice and peace through direct outreach to the poor, reconciliation, and the building of friendships with political actors on all sides of a dispute arise from its interpretation of the New Testament as well as from the teachings of the Second Vatican Council of the 1960s. We shall see how other religious peacemakers, too, are steered by their distinctive ideas.

The rest of this chapter is divided into three sections. The next section offers a landscape of the religious peace-building efforts that have arisen around the world in the past generation and shows how they have benefited from the forces of modernity. Two subsequent sections demonstrate how religion-state relationships and political theology together influence which religious actors are likely to be effective peace-builders through a closer look at two separate types of activities: (1) the mediation of civil wars; and (2) the shaping of transitional justice, or the way in which societies deal with the injustices of the past.

RELIGION AND THE PROMOTION OF PEACE

What does it mean for a religious actor to promote peace? That depends on what exactly peace is. The major religious traditions contain centuries of thinking about this issue. Most teach that peace is more than a "negative" condition in which swords have ceased to clash but also a "positive" state of affairs where they have been turned to ploughshares—that is to say, oppression and injustice have been alleviated. This is the meaning of the Jewish *shalom*, of its close Islamic equivalent, *salaam*, and of the New Testament's *eirene*, the Greek word from which *shalom* is translated.

The promotion of peace, then, can be understood as any activity carried out by a religious actor that is aimed at transforming a condition of violence or deep injustice into one of greater *shalom*, or "just peace." This includes: the mediation of civil wars, the conduct of truth commissions, interreligious dialogue, trauma-healing in developing world villages, or war. The last example may seem paradoxical, but in fact the dominant thinking about war in virtually all of the major religious traditions is a version of the "just-war doctrine," which holds that war may be justified only under certain conditions, one of which is that its conduct be intended to bring about a just peace. True, most religious traditions also include pacifist strands, but these remain minority voices (albeit ones that often carry innovative ideas for peacemaking). In the present chapter, though, we leave aside the question of the justice of war and focus on what is usually meant by the promotion of peace: those activities that are designed to reduce war, end war, and alleviate forms of injustice that lead to war.

The Global Rise of Religious Efforts for Peace

Religious peacemaking is at least as old as St. Francis of Assisi, who journeyed to Egypt to speak to Muslim Sultan Melek al-Kamil about peace and conversion during a battle of the Crusades; as Moses Maimonides, who devised rituals of *teshuva*, or repentance, for medieval Jewish communities; and as Islamic reconciliation rituals of *sulh* and *musalaha* that date back centuries.

More recently, in the nineteenth century, Protestant Evangelicals lobbied to end slavery and the slave trade in Britain and the United States, spearheaded the feminist movement in the United States, and launched humanitarian organizations like the International Committee of the Red Cross, the brainchild of Swiss Calvinist Henry Dunant. In the twentieth century, U.S. President Woodrow Wilson was inspired in good part by his Presbyterian faith to found the League of Nations, while Protestant churches were also important lobbyists for the United Nations.[6] A much more religiously diverse group of individuals—including a Catholic, a Confucian, a Hindu, and a Muslim—worked with Eleanor Roosevelt in negotiating the landmark Universal Declaration of Human Rights in 1948.[7] Religious leaders also propelled two major nonviolent movements for social justice in the midtwentieth century. Mahatma Gandhi, who reinterpreted Hinduism and combined elements of the New Testament with it to form his approach to resistance known as *satyagraha*, or soul force, led India's independence movement. With Gandhi's success as an important inspiration, Martin Luther King drew upon both Old Testament prophetic writings and Jesus' Sermon on the Mount to craft his leadership of the civil rights movement in the United States.

Although it is not often thought of as a religious movement for peace, European federalism, which began as the European Coal and Steel Community in 1950 and eventually became today's European Union, has important origins in Catholicism and its views of peace. Seeing the initiative as a way to check the idolatrous and unaccountable authority of the Westphalian sovereign state, which had sundered European Christendom and eventually wrought the horrors of World War I, World War II, and the Holocaust, the Vatican gave federalism its enthusiastic endorsement. Most of the initiative's founding fathers were Catholics who thought along similar lines: German Chancellor Konrad Adenauer, Italian Prime Minister Alcide De Gasperi, French Foreign Minister Robert Schuman, and French businessman Jean Monnet, who was federalism's chief architect. Indeed, over the course of its history, Catholic Christian Democratic parties and voters have consistently been European federalism's strongest supporters.[8]

Already these activities for peace, all of which predated the late 1960s, the period of our resurgence, create a problem for the secularization thesis, which thought that religion was not only fading in its influence but was irrational, tribal, and violent. To the contrary, religious actors have been key advocates of norms and values that came to be ensconced in international law and international organizations. But it was during the second half of the twentieth century that efforts to promote peace multiplied, diversified, and spread among many world religions. These efforts contributed to the evolution of religion from being private and passive to assertive and politically involved.

Within Christianity, Protestants were forerunners of this expansion, as the foregoing examples suggest. In the past generation, operating through the structures of the large Protestant churches (Methodist, Baptist, Anglican), through associations like the World Council of Churches and the U.S.-based National Association of Evangelicals, through more local churches and organizations or simply as individuals, Protestants have promoted human rights, religious freedom, protests against war, conflict resolution, economic relief and development, ecological protection, and initiatives to fight AIDS and other diseases.

An active commitment to peace can also be found in the Catholic Church prior to the last generation. Pope Benedict XV has been called "the Pope of Peace" for his pleas for an end to World War I. But this commitment ballooned following the early 1960s, when Pope John XXIII penned his encyclicals *Mater et Magistra* (1961) and *Pacem in Terris* (1963) and convened the Second Vatican Council. Peace emerged through several themes. One, stressed in *Pacem in Terris* and Council documents, was a view of war not merely as a practice to be judged according to criteria of justice but as itself a problem for humanity, a view provoked by the death toll of World War II and by the potential for holocaust in nuclear weapons. Disarmament, negotiations, and international law and organization were the Church's resulting prescriptions. Second, the Church fully and centrally embraced human rights and gave them a robust theological foundation in theology and natural law. Third, in *Mater et Magistra* the Church first made economic development for the world's poor a central plank of its social teachings. Finally, the Church proclaimed the furthering of social justice as a "constituent element of preaching the gospel," as a 1971 synodal document put it, and called on lay people to undertake it. All of this yielded an outbreak of pursuits of peace over subsequent decades, enabled by a transnational structure that links national churches with the Vatican and with one another.

Pursuits of peace can also be found in the Orthodox Church, though these have come later due to its immobility under Communist regimes and other suppressive states like Turkey. The Ecumenical Patriarch Bartholomew I of Constantinople, who is "first among equals" in the Orthodox Church, has vigorously promoted stronger ties among national Orthodox churches; dialogue with the Catholic Church, Protestant churches, Jews, and Muslims; and environmentalism, the latter earning him the sobriquet, "the Green Pope." Archbishop Anastasios Yannoulatos of Albania is active in the World Council of Churches, has long spoken for reconciliation, religious and communal dialogue, and sustainable peacebuilding, and is famous for sheltering Kosovar Albanian Muslim refugees in Orthodox facilities during the violence in Yugoslavia of the 1990s. Proponents of peace, both hierarchical and lay, can be found in multiple national Orthodox churches as well.[9]

The rise of Engaged Buddhism, involving advocacy for peace, environmentalism, nonviolence, human rights, and social transformation, strongly reflects, though its beginning somewhat predates, the global rise of religion as a transnational global force. Arising first in the 1950s, it corresponds to a period in which a militant nationalist form of Buddhism arose in Sri Lanka while Buddhists sharply increased their global activism through worldwide missionary efforts. Through modern communication as well as transnational links within the Buddhist community, Engaged Buddhism has spread from country to country and is now found most strongly in Cambodia, Vietnam, Thailand, Korea, Japan, and Taiwan, where it has sought to influence the policies of governments, sometimes against intense opposition. A leading early figure was B. R. Ambedkar, the Indian "untouchable" who rose to become India's first law minister, chief draftsman of its 1947 constitution, and leading opponent of its caste system—and who converted to Buddhism in 1956. From his exile in India, the current Dalai Lama has developed teachings on nonviolence and peace over several decades and won the Nobel Peace Prize in 1989. Vietnamese Zen Master Thich Nhat Hanh, a theorist of peace and nonviolence and opponent of the Vietnam War, and Burmese dissident for democracy Aung San Suu Kyi also embody Engaged Buddhism.[10]

One of the most remarkable expressions of Engaged Buddhism took place in the "killing fields" of Cambodia, where, in the latter 1970s, Pol Pot's Khmer Rouge carried out a genocide that killed 2 million people and attempted to exterminate the Buddhist religion as well as other alleged "forces of reaction." In an effort to bring healing to Cambodia over a decade after the killing, monk Samdech Preah Maha Ghosananda led the *Dhammayietra*, or peace walks, beginning in 1992. Even as a child, Ghosananda had gained a reputation for kindness. One story has it that when his parents left him alone to tend their shop, he gave away their goods to passersby. He repeated the same practice throughout his life, even to the chagrin of his temple authorities. During the genocide, the death of his entire family and most of his friends left him stricken with grief. He decided to remain in the forest, where he practiced mental control and prepared himself for service. When Vietnam defeated the Khmer Rouge in 1979, Ghosananda began to teach peace. He drew from a political theology rooted in Theravada Buddhism holding that social peace and the inner peace of individuals are inseparable and interdependent. He also practiced a fierce independence from both the Vietnamese Communist occupiers and the Khmer Rouge, who became the armed opponents in a civil war. He even extended his ministry of peace to members of the Khmer Rouge.

The first *Dhammayietra* began in a refugee camp on the Thai border, traveled through Khmer Rouge territory, and ended in Phnom Penh, the capital. Scores more marchers and supporters joined their ranks along the way, often braving extreme heat, hunger, landmines, and violent attacks. Instances of reconciliation began to emerge, including soldiers laying down their arms and renouncing killing and walkers meeting relatives whom they had not seen for decades. Repeated annually, the walks became a national symbol of peace and helped to advance causes like refugee repatriation and landmine removal. Ghosananda came to be known as the "Gandhi of Cambodia" and was nominated for the Nobel Peace Prize five times.

Within Islam the same political resurgence that brought increased demands for more assertive forms of *sharia* law, civil war, terrorism, and democratization movements also brought peace initiatives. The Wajir Peace and Development Committee of Kenya, the Centre for Research and Dialogue in Somalia, the Islamic Community of Bosnia-Herzegovina, the Sudanese Women's Initiative for Peace, the Salam Institute for Peace and Justice in the United States, and similar Muslim organizations throughout the world promote cooperation between Muslims and people of other faiths, mediation and conflict resolution, peace initiatives, and the dissemination of religious teachings on peace and reconciliation.[11]

Embodying Islamic peacebuilding in the age of religious resurgence is Sakena Yacoobi, a devout Afghani Muslim woman who founded the Afghan Institute of Learning (AIL) to train and educate women and girls in equality, peace, nonviolence, and practical skills in 1995—that is, under the reign of the Taliban, the revivalist Islamic regime that harshly restricted opportunities for women among its many repressive activities. In her literacy classes, Sakena has helped her students to read the Quran, which she believes teaches human rights and gender equality. Over 8,500 female Afghan teachers have been trained under her direction. Today, AIL services—which also include skills education, health care, counseling, and language training—reach 350,000 women and children every year in four Afghan cities as well as Peshawar, Pakistan. Under the Taliban, Sakena's work was highly risky. "If someone had caught the class," she explains, "every one of them in it would have been killed or jailed."[12]

Mahatma Gandhi, of course, was the great interpreter of Hinduism as a religion of peace, having drawn from the Vedas concepts like *ahimsa* (nonviolence), *kshama* (forgiveness), and *shanti* (peace). Just as Gandhi was assassinated by a Hindu nationalist, it might seem that the rise of Hindu nationalism in subsequent decades has eclipsed his interpretation of the tradition with its own marriage of religion and nation, its notions of memory and revenge, its call for the revival of the caste system, and its view of Islam as foreign. Groups that practice and spread Gandhi's approach, however, remain, including the Brahma Kumaris, the Chinmaya Mission, the International Society for Krishna Consciousness, the Ramakrishna Mission, and the Swaminarayan community.[13]

Strategies of Peace

If peace is a major theme in the global resurgence of religion, what sort of activities does it involve? Many examples have already been offered. But they can be divided into three broad categories, depending on the nature of the religious actors engaged in the peace process.

The first is interreligious dialogue, efforts by representatives of different religions to understand one another better but often also to reduce tensions and to build common initiatives for peace and justice. The World's Parliament of Religions, which met in Chicago in 1893, is one of the earliest examples. Here again, Protestants were early players, founding the World Council of Churches in 1948 to bridge denominational differences. But here, too, the practice vastly expanded from the 1960s onward, so much so that dialogue has become a major feature of religious politics in the past generation. The Second Vatican Council's embrace of interreligious dialogue brought the Catholic Church into ongoing conversation with other Christian churches and virtually every other major religion, as well as with Marxists and atheists. Some of the fruits have been dramatic, as when in 1999 the Catholic Church and the Lutheran World Federation achieved a common understanding of justification by faith, the central issue that sparked the Protestant Reformation in 1517. In 1970 the World Conference of Religions for Peace was first convened in Kyoto to bring together leaders of world religions to cooperate for peace. In 1993, a centennial Parliament of the World's Religions was held and led to a series of subsequent parliaments.

Sometimes, dialogue can emerge in unexpected ways. In his Regensburg Address of 2006, Pope Benedict XVI provoked a global storm of controversy, including rioting and violence in several Muslim locales, through his quotation of a medieval Byzantine emperor: "Show me just what Mohammed brought that was new, and there you will find things only evil and inhuman, such as his command to spread by the sword the faith he preached." What ensued, though, was a response by thirty-eight global Muslim religious leaders, Benedict's own conciliatory visit to a mosque in Turkey, a later statement by 138 Muslim leaders, and eventually a Catholic-Muslim dialogue that has focused on substantive areas of justice like religious freedom. This dialogue was a global one, facilitated by the rapid communication and short news cycles that the Internet and cable news networks make possible.

Another broad category of peace efforts, carried out by thousands of religious actors around the globe, is what might be called "civil society initiatives." These are efforts to overcome violence, social division, and injustices by working directly with the middle or grassroots layers of society. Representative of the trajectory of these efforts is the history of Catholic Relief Services, one of the largest relief and development agencies throughout the world. Founded in 1943, for most of its history it focused on economic development and disaster relief. Particularly after the Rwandan genocide of 1994, however, the organization came to believe that economic development was inseparable from the building of peace and so began to launch projects that stressed interethnic dialogue, the reintegration of ex-combatants into society, and training in peacebuilding.[14]

In the midst of ethnic conflicts and civil wars around the world can be found initiatives of a similar spirit. A Pentecostal Christian pastor and Muslim imam in Nigeria who were once bitter enemies became friends through finding teachings about forgiveness and peace in their mutual scriptures and are now partners in promoting interfaith mediation.[15] In the Philippines and Central America, religious people have established village-level "zones of peace." Others conduct mediation between warring communities, trauma healing, education in conflict resolution and reconciliation, advocacy with governments and international organizations, and public rituals of healing and remembrance. Some of the organizations that conduct work for peace, like Catholic Relief Services, are tied to global religious communities and illustrate the transnational nature of peacemaking efforts. Others work alone. Some work for peace remains largely confined to civil society; other efforts bring governments into their network of influence.[16]

Those efforts that directly and primarily engage governments, in collaboration, criticism, or opposition, belong in a different category. The role of the religious in democratization movements as documented in Chapter Four can be placed in this category insofar as they involve the nonviolent promotion of justice. So can the direct mediation of peace agreements and the shaping of transitional justice institutions, both described below.

In all of these efforts, at all levels, there are certain assets that "faith-based" actors bring to peacemaking. Religious leaders profit from the authority that they enjoy in their religious communities. Leaders and laity alike are motivated and informed by divine purposes as expressed through their scriptures and traditions. They also deploy religiously derived concepts of peace, justice, and mercy, along with rituals, authority structures, and spiritual charisma, in the actual work of peace. Finally, as John Paul Lederach, an experienced Mennonite peace-builder, has observed, a focus on personal relationships is a distinct quality of religious peace efforts.[17]

But some religious actors are more likely to be successful promoters of peace than others. Why? Here we advance our argument about the importance of political theology and the relationship between religious and political authority and apply it to two of the most dramatic areas where religion makes a difference: peace settlements and institutions for transitional justice.

Before proceeding, though, it is worth observing at the outset a notable feature of our findings regarding these two activities: the heavily Christian, especially Catholic, character of religious involvement in them. To be sure, as the chapter has shown thus far, peacemaking activities, just like terrorism and civil war, occur in every major religion and deserve recognition wherever they are found. Mediation and transitional justice themselves include several cases of Muslim involvement. Still, Christianity shows up disproportionately. Why?

Much of the explanation lies in the simple fact that the events that have elicited mediation and transitional justice—namely civil wars and transitions from dictatorship to democracy—have themselves occurred widely in countries with Christian populations. Indeed, the frequency of dictatorship and civil wars among Christians forbids any interpretation of Christian triumphalism. Many of the cases of transitional justice have involved the movement of authoritarian regimes toward democracy. As political scientist Samuel P. Huntington has pointed out, a preponderance of the transitions in the Third Wave of democratization occurred in Christian countries.[18] As we have seen, the Third Wave was largely a Catholic Wave. This was true because, as late as the early 1970s, dictatorships were still exceedingly common in Catholic countries. Although Christian populations have not been involved in civil wars in the same proportion that they were involved in transitions to democracy, they have fought civil wars widely, both against each other, as in Burundi, El Salvador, Guatemala, Mozambique, Nicaragua, Northern Ireland, Rwanda, and Yugoslavia, and against members of other faiths, as in Sudan and Timor-Leste (East Timor).

Another factor behind Christianity's share of mediation and transitional justice is the fact that these activities require access to top elites in governments and opposition forces—the kind of access Christian churches are able to secure because they are often centrally, hierarchically, and transnationally organized. Yet this kind of organization is much more likely to be found in large, historic Protestant churches than in small, independent, Pentecostal and evangelical churches and it is even more likely to be found in the Catholic Church. The political clout of the Catholic Church is further enhanced by the Vatican's status as a sovereign state and member of the United Nations. Islam, by contrast, contains few organizations of similar structure. Even the populous and transnational Muslim Brotherhood is far more fragmented in its leadership than the Catholic Church or the multinational Protestant churches. But as the next section of our chapter shows, both Muslim and Buddhist peace efforts are more common on the more localized, grassroots level.

The final reasons for the disproportionately Christian and Catholic involvement are ones that arise from our arguments about political theology and the relationship between religious and political authority. As detailed in Chapter Four, the Second Vatican Council placed the Church squarely behind human rights and democracy. In many cases of transitional justice, church leaders also embraced what we will call a political theology of reconciliation. As for the independence of church and state, the Vatican transmitted ideas of human rights and democracy throughout the global church through its unusually robust transnational structure, itself a fortifier of independence. Similar patterns regarding political theology and independence can be found in Protestant churches. In comparison, in neither the Orthodox Church nor other religions has political theology or institutional independence of this sort become as widely shared. But even in the Christian cases, variation must always be noted. Along with great peacemakers like Anglican Archbishop Desmond Tutu can be found the major Rwandan churches, acquiescent in genocide, the Argentinean Catholic Church, which was cozy with a dictator-ship during the "Dirty Wars" of 1976–1983, and the violent former dictator of Guatemala, Rios Montt, a Pentecostal.

RELIGION AND THE MEDIATION OF CIVIL WARS

As the preceding tapestry of religious peace efforts makes clear, mediation is only one way in which the religious promote peace. But it is an important way. By mediation, we mean the direct involvement of a third party in negotiating an end to a civil war. Here, the third party is a religious actor who speaks and negotiates directly with official representatives of the government as well as the leaders of the rebel opposition movement. Mediation is not arbitration, where a third party is authorized to make a judgment by which the dispu-tants have agreed in advance to abide. Rather, it involves the facilitation of a negotiation, one that can often be difficult to forge, in good part because even to acknowledge the legitimacy of the other side is a concession that one side does not want to make, as the Mozambique case illustrates. Mediation is a direct, discernible, and often dramatic form of religious influence—and one in which much is at stake. Civil wars have taken over 16 million lives in the last half century, far more than have been lost through international disputes during the same period. And civil war settlements have a high rate of collapse. The breakdown of the Arusha Accords in Rwanda in 1992 resulted in a genocide of more than 800,000 deaths; the collapse of peace negotiations in Angola in 1991 led to a war that left 350,000 dead. In helping to achieve a lasting peace settlement through mediation, religious actors make a marked difference for peace.

The mediation of negotiated agreements to civil war endings has increased dramatically since the end of the Cold War. Civil wars can end in two ways. One is the victory of one side. The American Civil War, for instance, ended in 1865 at the Appomattox Court House with the surrender of Confederate General Robert E. Lee to Union General Ulysses S. Grant. The other is a negotiated settlement, like the end to the war in Mozambique. In any one decade between 1940 and 1989, from 75 to 100 percent of civil wars concluded with a military victory, while a mere handful were resolved through negotiation. But then, after 1989, a markedly increased 42 percent of civil wars came to a close through negotiations, outpacing the 40 percent that ended in military victory.[19] A greater number of civil wars indeed ended through negotiations between 1989 and 2004 than in the previous two hundred years.[20] These numerous instances of a single type of event provide grist for comparison in answering the question: Among those negotiated victories in which religious actors served as effective mediators, what characterizes these religious actors?

In part, they are often independent of the state in their authority. Only if they are not perceived as a partisan, collaborator, or instrument of the state can they be an effective bridge between the state and another party. But here, independence takes on a more complex form than it has previously in this book. Not only must the religious actor be independent of the state but it must also operate at a distance from the armed opposition movement with which it negotiates. At times, religious actors, usually those committed to radical visions of social justice, become collaborators with rebel movements in their opposition to the state. As a result, they will not be perceived as having the impartiality needed to be effective intermediaries. Independence is indeed a vital ingredient of the moral authority that earns the religious actor both prestige and trust among the negotiating parties.

The religious mediator also holds a certain kind of political theology. Broadly, this may be called a theology of peace. Far more than the mere idea that an end to war is desired, a theology of peace calls for dialogue, reconciliation, the reduction of arms, and for the transformation of unjust social structures, abject poverty, regimes that practice human rights violations, and unaccountable military forces. It roots these themes in the very claims of its faith.

Religious actors who both enjoy institutional independence and embrace a political theology of peace are likely to be the most effective mediators. When one or both of these is lacking, it is unlikely to be effective. This is what the evidence from twenty-six cases teaches. All but one occurred between 1989 and 2005, the limit years of the Peace Agreement Dataset of the Uppsala Conflict Data Program, arguably the most authoritative source of data on negotiated agreements.[21] The one exception is the Vatican's negotiation of the Beagle Channel dispute between Argentina and Chile, which we include because it is one of the most dramatic cases of religious mediation on record.[22] We also include a couple of cases where an important instance of religious mediation occurred but where no peace agreement resulted.

We divide the religious mediation of peace agreements into three categories: strong mediation; weak mediation; and little-to-no mediation. Strong mediation indicates that a religious actor was directly and vitally involved in negotiating an agreement or series of agreements between a government and one or more armed opposition movements. Were it not for its role, a particular peace agreement probably would not have come about. Weak mediation means that a religious actor played a genuine mediating role, communicating between representatives of the warring factions, but that its role was dispensable. It was one of several negotiators and perhaps not the most important. The agreement in question could easily have still occurred without it. Finally, the negative cases are ones where religious actors were not involved in mediation at all. They may well have played other roles in forging peace in a civil war, perhaps within civil society. But their role was not that of a mediator. Table 7.1 summarizes the findings.

Strong Mediation

Some of the strongest instances of religious mediation for peace, where religious actors played a direct and crucial role, have been those carried out by the Community of Sant'Egidio. On the strength of its reputation from Mozambique, Sant'Egidio was invited to mediate other civil wars. In these sites, too, it continued to profit from its position as an actor with few formal ties with any of the parties and no political stake in the issues at hand. Even more importantly, its theology of dialogue and reconciliation and its "methodology" of personal relationship allowed it to achieve important agreements.

One such agreement was achieved in a largely Islamic country, Algeria. As we discussed in Chapter Six, Algeria's civil war between the government of the National Liberation Front (FLN) and Islamist opposition factions began in 1991 when the secularist government, supported by the military, canceled the second round of national elections, which it feared the Islamic Salvation Front (FIS) would win. In late 1994 and early 1995, Sant'Egidio brought the parties to Rome and negotiated a "platform" consisting of a declaration of principles by which a wide spectrum of factions committed themselves to democracy and a peaceful solution to the crisis. Although the Algerian government refused to sign, the platform remained the basis for ongoing negotiations as the country's bloody civil war continued.[23]

In 1996, Sant'Egidio became the key mediator in talks between the government of Uganda and its opponent, the Lord's Resistance Army. The Community continued to play this role into the early 2000s, though it would come to share it with Pax Christi, a like-spirited lay Catholic organization, as well as the Acholi Religious Leaders Peace Initiative, a coalition of Catholic, Protestant, and Muslim leaders in Northern Uganda. That same year, Sant'Egidio succeeded in forging an agreement between Serbia and Kosovar Albanians on educational issues, one of their central sources of contention, an agreement that unfortunately broke down in 1999 when NATO undertook its bombing campaign of Serbian forces. In 1996, Sant'Egidio also succeeded in bringing the main factions in Guatemala's civil war to Rome, Paris, and San Salvador and finally facilitated the signing of an agreement in Mexico City. Sant'Egidio also mediated an early round of peace talks in Burundi in 1996, helped to mediate a civil war in Liberia in 2003, and was an observer in Ivory Coast's peace negotiations in 2003.

Ranking also among the strongest instances of religious mediation is another case involving the Catholic Church, though not a lay group but rather the church hierarchy in the Vatican itself: the Beagle Channel dispute between Argentina and Chile in the late 1970s and early 1980s. This maritime boundary quarrel dated at least as far back as 1915, resurfaced in the 1970s, and brought the two countries to the brink of war in late 1978. It was at that point that both parties accepted the mediation of the Vatican, which would proceed for five years under the leadership of Pope John Paul II and his special diplomatic representative, Cardinal Antonia Samoré, who became

Table 7.1

CASES OF MEDIATION BY RELIGIOUS ACTORS

RELIGIOUS ACTOR	CONFLICT	STRENGTH OF MEDIATION	RELATIONSHIP WITH STATE	POLITICAL THEOLOGY
Community of Sant'Egidio	Algeria	Strong	Consensually independent	Peace and reconciliation through personal friendships
Community of Sant'Egidio	Uganda	Strong	Consensually independent	Peace and reconciliation through personal friendships
Community of Sant'Egidio	Kosovo	Strong	Consensually independent	Peace and reconciliation through personal friendships
Community of Sant'Egidio	Guatemala	Strong	Consensually independent	Peace and reconciliation through personal friendships
Community of Sant'Egidio	Liberia	Strong	Consensually independent	Peace and reconciliation through personal friendships
The Vatican	Argentina-Chile	Strong	Consensually independent	Peace, human rights, reconciliation
Archbishop Arturo Rivera Y Damas	El Salvador	Strong	Consensually independent	Peace, human rights, reconciliation
Lutheran World Federation	Guatemala	Strong	Consensually independent	Peace, human rights, reconciliation
Archbishop Rodolfo Quezada Toruno	Guatemala	Strong	Consensually independent	Peace, human rights, reconciliation
Colombian Catholic Church	Colombia	Strong	Consensually independent	Peace, human rights, reconciliation
U.S. Senator John Danforth	Sudan	Strong	Consensually independent	Peace, human rights, reconciliation
Catholic and Muslim Communities	Ivory Coast	Weak	Consensually independent	Peace, human rights, reconciliation
Coalition of Catholic and Protestant Churches	Congo	Weak	Consensually independent	Peace, human rights, reconciliation
Community of Sant'Egidio	Burundi	Weak	Consensually independent	Peace and reconciliation through personal friendships
Community of Sant'Egidio	Ivory Coast	Weak	Consensually independent	Peace and reconciliation through personal friendships
Catholic Bishops of Angola	Angola	Weak	Consensually independent	Peace, human rights, reconciliation
Catholic Bishops-Ulama Forum	Philippines	Weak	Consensually independent	Peace, human rights, reconciliation
Muslim Leaders of Somalia	Somalia	Weak	Consensually integrated	*Sharia* law, favors strong government promotion of religious norms
Catholic Cardinal Obando y Bravo	Nicaragua	Weak	Conflictually independent	Peace, human rights, religious freedom

Bishop Carlos Belo	Timor-Leste	Weak	Consensually independent	Peace, human rights, democracy
Muslim Leaders in Chad	Chad	Weak	Official version of Islam consensually integrated; other versions conflictually integrated	*Sharia* law, favors strong government promotion of religious norms
Monk Samdech Preah Maha Ghosananda	Cambodia	Weak	Made official religion of Cambodia (consensual, borderline independent/integrated) shortly before negotiations	Peace, reconciliation, interdependence of personal and societal peace
Protestant Churches and Religions for Peace—Liberia	Liberia	None	Consensually independent	Peace, human rights, reconciliation
Muslim leaders	Mali	None	Consensually independent	Peace, human rights, democracy
Catholic, Anglican, and Presbyterian Churches	Rwanda	None	Consensually integrated	Stress on personal piety and salvation over justice
Buddhist Sangha	Sri Lanka	None	Consensually integrated	Strong government promotion of Buddhist homeland

known as "the Vatican Kissinger." The Church's ability to bring the dispute to a successful settlement in 1984 arose from its independence from the authority of either government, its prestige as an international religious body with diplomatic status as a sovereign state, its prestige within Argentina and Chile, both heavily Catholic countries, and a reputation for peace and reconciliation reinforced by the teachings of the Second Vatican Council.[24]

Another outstanding instance of religious mediation again involved the Catholic Church, but this time a national church—that of El Salvador under the leadership of Arturo Rivera y Damas. Rivera served as the lead mediator in the negotiation of El Salvador's civil war between 1980 and 1990, after which the United Nations took over and mediated until the war's settlement in 1992. How Rivera came to this position is indeed a story of political theology and a relationship between church and state. In the early 1970s, Rivera was the only "progressive" among El Salvador's five bishops, speaking for the cause of the poor, calling for change in Salvadoran social structures, and denouncing the human rights abuses of Salvador's military government, much in the spirit of the liberation theology movement that swept through Latin America in the

1960s and 1970s. In 1977, when Oscar Romero became archbishop of El Salvador, he joined Rivera in his stance after government forces brutally murdered his close friend, a Jesuit priest. In 1980, Romero himself was assassinated, and the country's civil war began in earnest. It was then that Rivera, in part because of pressure from the Vatican, shifted his stance to a more impartial one, skillfully denouncing the human rights abuses of both the government and the rebel forces and adopting the language of reconciliation. It was from this standpoint that Rivera became one of the great religious mediators.

Other religious actors who served as strong mediators are worthy of mention. In Guatemala, the Lutheran World Federation played a mediating role much like Sant'Egidio's but earlier in the peace process, making possible the Oslo peace talks of 1990. Churches within Guatemala, both Protestant and Catholic, also participated heavily in a peace process notable for the unusually strong involvement of civil society actors. Catholic Archbishop Rodolfo Quezada Toruño was the lead mediator between government and rebels in several episodes from 1987 to 1993, after which he yielded mediation to the United Nations and later Sant'Egidio. His role was made possible by the shift in 1984 of the Guatemalan Catholic hierarchy away from an integrated relationship with the country's dictatorship toward a position of distance from the government and embrace of advocacy for the poor and landless and denunciation of human rights abuses.[25] In Colombia, too, a strong Catholic Church that is independent of Marxist rebels, right-wing paramilitary units, and the government has served from the 1990s to the present as a prime mediator in its civil war of four decades.[26]

Finally, an end to Sudan's long civil war of 1983–2005 was mediated by U.S. Senator John Danforth, whom President George W. Bush had appointed as his Special Envoy for Peace in Sudan in 2001. Because Danforth had been ordained an Episcopal priest prior to launching his career in politics, he garnered great respect as a "man of God" among both Muslim and Christian leaders in this highly religious civil war (recall Chapter Six). It was not only Danforth's religious status but also his own religious awareness that proved essential to his success in bringing the parties together where others had previously failed. One of Danforth's crucial stratagems, for instance, was his utilization of the Sudanese Inter-Religious Council, a forum that brought Muslim and Christian leaders together to work out disputes between their communities. The forum itself had been established by the International Center for Religion and Diplomacy, an NGO dedicated to achieving peace through mobilizing religious traditions.[27]

Weak Mediation

Cases of weak mediation by religious actors fall into two broad patterns. In some cases, religious actors who are independent and espouse a theology of peace carry out strong peace-building efforts within civil society—true to our expectations—yet their activities spill over into mediation only to a limited extent and far less than in the cases above.

In Ivory Coast, a high degree of cooperation between the country's Catholic and Muslim populations—involving dialogue, cooperation on peace and human rights, forums of reconciliation and the like, between clerics and laypeople—prevented its civil war of 2002 from turning into a religious dispute and sometimes spilled over into mediation efforts. A coalition of Catholic and Protestant churches in Congo also shared an independent status and a political theology of peace, held a national consultation on peace in February 2000 that resulted in formal discussions with the government, and later met with heads of state in Congo and Rwanda, meetings that approached mediation. In Burundi's civil war, which took around 200,000 to 250,000 lives between 1993 and 2000, the Community of Sant'Egidio helped to initiate comprehensive talks in 1997. But soon thereafter, Tanzanian elder statesman Julius Nyerere took center stage and upon his death was succeeded by former South African President Nelson Mandela, who led the negotiations resulting in the Arusha Accords of 2000. In all three cases, the involvement of several foreign governments in the peace negotiations crowded out religious actors, thus resulting in weak mediation by religious actors.

In Angola's civil war, religious actors did not make efforts to build peace until the early 1990s. Historically, its Catholic Church had enjoyed a classic consensually integrated relationship with the Portuguese colonial state. In 1974, Angola achieved independence and came under the rule of a Marxist government that suppressed the Church in a classic conflictually integrated fashion but then, over the next two and a half decades, gradually restored more and more of the Church's freedoms. The large Protestant churches, Baptist, Methodist, and Congregrationalist, by contrast, had been opponents of colonialism and were thus allowed their independence by the Marxist regime. The other main religious actors were smaller evangelical Protestant churches, which embraced an apolitical theology of personal salvation. By the 1990s, though, associations of all three types of churches came to advocate, teach, and organize around a theology of peace. It was the association of Catholic bishops that engaged in some actual mediation, bringing together government representatives, political parties, twenty-two churches, and civil society organizations into a peace congress in the year 2000. It was the association's suppression and wariness of challenging the government up to this point that prevented earlier and stronger peace efforts on its part.[28]

Two other examples of the same pattern are the Philippines and Somalia. The Philippines, particularly the southern region of Mindanao, is another site of extensive peace-building efforts within civil society. These include a Catholic Bishops–Muslim Ulama forum, whose members sometimes served as advisors and informal bridge-builders in the negotiations between the government of the Philippines and the Moro Islamic Liberation Front that occurred in the mid-1990s. In Somalia, the vast majority of whose population is Muslim, U.N. Secretary-General Boutros Boutros–Ghali hosted a meeting in January 1993 of warlords, clan elders, and religious leaders that led to a peace agreement later that year.[29] In both cases, other high-level actors occupied the space of mediation, leaving room for religious actors to play only a weak role.

In a second pattern of weak mediation, a religious actor possesses a theology of peace but lacks political independence of the complex sort that is needed for strong mediation. In two cases, this was because the religious actor was a partisan of one side of the struggle—but not so partisan as to preclude its political efforts from spilling over into limited mediation. The actor in question was the Catholic Church in both Nicaragua and Timor-Leste. In Nicaragua's civil war of the 1980s, Cardinal Miguel Obando y Bravo was a strong opponent of the Marxist Sandinista government, which he saw as a threat to the freedom of the Church, and sometimes closely allied himself with the opposition forces, known as the Contras. In the late 1980s, however, he took a more conciliatory position toward the state, especially as a peace agreement and national elections came near, and played a small mediating role in reintegrating the Contras into Nicaraguan society. By contrast, Nicaraguan Protestants, far less partisan, successfully mediated land disputes between the government and indigenous peoples of the East Coast of the country.[30] Likewise, in Timor-Leste, Bishop Carlos Belo deployed the language of human rights and democracy in becoming a leading spokesman for Timor-Leste's struggle for independence against Indonesia (1975–1999), a highly partisan position, but also spoke of dialogue and reconciliation and offered his services for mediation.

A couple of other cases of weak mediation involved religious actors who lacked independence from their state. The Muslim community in Chad conducted mediation only at the tail end of a series of peace negotiations spanning the 1990s and into the 2000s, yet was not strongly independent of political authority. In Cambodia, Ghosananda, who had become the supreme patriarch of that country's Buddhist community in 1988, led a delegation of monks to the peace talks that eventually ended the country's civil war in 1991. But the monks did not play an instrumental role. By and large, the Buddhist community was still recovering from the Khmer Rouge's attempt to eradicate it in the late 1970s and the severe restrictions that the Vietnamese-controlled government placed on Cambodian Buddhism in the 1980s. It was only in 1988 that this conflictual integration was lifted and Buddhism once again became the country's national religion.

Lack of Mediation

What about cases in which peace agreements came about with no (or negligible) mediation on the part of religious leaders? Like weak mediation, a lack of mediation sometimes obtains in cases in which religious groups contribute to the peace process in civil society but—for reasons particular to the case at hand—not through mediation of an official agreement. In Liberia, for instance, Protestant churches as well as the international coalition, Religions for Peace–Liberia, a part of the World Conference of Religions for Peace, promoted dialogue and reconstruction efforts in the peace settlements of 1994 and 2003. In Mali, leaders of the country's strong Muslim community brought together hostile groups amid the agreements that ended the country's ethnic conflict in 1991–1992. But in both cases the involvement of other powerful mediators left little room for religious groups to operate at an elite level.

In other cases, the reason for the lack of religious mediation was one very much in line with the argument here: The country's main religious communities were strongly integrated with the state and thus lacked the political distance necessary for serving as an effective bridge to the opposition. Rwanda's main churches—Catholic, Anglican, Presbyterian—played no mediating role in the Arusha Accords of 1993, whose breakdown led to the genocide of the following year. True to our argument, these churches already had been integrated with the Rwandan state as far back as colonial times. Stressing personal piety and salvation over social justice, they carried little in the way of a robust political theology. When the genocide arrived, killing an estimated 800,000, church leaders were largely acquiescent, some lower-level clergy partcipated, and many laypeople took part as well (though a few resisters ought to be noted, too).[31] In Sri Lanka's civil war, the closely woven relationship between the Buddhist *sangha* and the government and the high level of support among monks and Sinhalese-Buddhist groups for all-out war against the Tamil Tigers left little room for a mediating role. Only a few small Buddhist groups and a couple of interfaith coalitions worked actively for peace.

To summarize the above survey, in eleven cases of strong mediation, all involved a religious actor who both practiced a consensually independent relationship with the state and embraced a theology of peace. In eleven cases of religious actors who practiced weak mediation, seven were consensually independent from the state, while nine embraced a theology of peace. In four cases of religious actors who played no mediating role, only two enjoyed consensual independence from the state, two were consensually integrated, and only two embraced a theology of peace. Altogether, these cases show that religious actors mediate best when they keep a distance from both state authority and armed opposition groups, and when they carry a political theology that stresses peace and social justice. But these factors alone are not always adequate. Other mediators, including the United Nations, outside governments, and secular nongovernment organizations also involve themselves in peace negotiations and sometimes leave little room for the religious.

RELIGION AND TRANSITIONAL JUSTICE

Another global trend of the past generation has been a proliferation of efforts to address human rights violations and atrocities committed during past periods of injustice, both in the wake of civil war settlements and following transitions away from dictatorship in the Third Wave of democracy. Demands for justice vary greatly. "If they can just show us the bones of my child, where did they leave the bones of my child?" asks the mother of one missing South African political activist.[32] Mhleli Mxenge, the brother of a South African human rights activist who was murdered by the South African government, held a very different view: "[Some people] say that offering amnesty helps the truth come out. But I don't believe that knowing alone makes you happy. Once you know who did it, you want the next thing—you want justice!"[33] Still a different perspective came from Guatemalan Bishop Juan Gerardi, who presented the report of the Recovery of Historical Memory Project in the cathedral in Guatemala City on April 24, 1998, with the words "[y]ears of terror and death have displaced and reduced the majority of Guatemalans to fear and silence. *Truth* is the primary word, the serious and mature action that makes it pos-

Truth is the primary word, the serious and mature action that makes it possible for us to break this cycle of death and violence and to open ourselves to a future of hope and light for all."[34] Two days later, he was assassinated. South African Archbishop Desmond Tutu offered still another view when he wrote, "There is no future without forgiveness."[35] The political institutions and practices that countries adopt to meet demands like these are what is known as transitional justice.[36]

How Do Countries Pursue Transitional Justice?

Two broad approaches have emerged. The first is "punitive justice," whose goal is accountability for human rights violators, either through courtroom trials and punishment or through "vetting" processes that debar certain perpetrators from government positions. Punitive justice was at the center of debates over how to treat former dictators in Latin America during the 1980s: punish or pardon? It is also the motivating ideal behind two international criminal tribunals in the 1990s for Yugoslavia and Rwanda that resurrected the precedent of the Nuremberg Trials after World War II and eventually took permanent form in the International Criminal Court in 1998.

Other countries, like South Africa and Guatemala, have stressed a different goal: discovering and publicly revealing the truth about past atrocities. This second approach can be called "truth recovery." Here, the quintessential institution is a truth commission, an official body whose purpose is to report publicly the human rights violations of a given period. Truth commissions are also a recent innovation in global politics. South Africa's Truth and Reconciliation Commission is the most famous to date. It was preceded and influenced by Chile's Commission on Truth and Reconciliation, and was imitated and developed by subsequent commissions in Sierra Leone, Timor-Leste, Guatemala, Peru, and elsewhere.

Realities on the ground are often more complex than either model alone can capture. Some countries, like Germany, Sierra Leone, and Timor-Leste, have adopted a combination of the two approaches. Other institutions and practices combine with or elude one or both of the two approaches: reparations, public apologies, memorials, museums, acts of forgiveness, and civil society efforts. Still, these two approaches remain dominant. Figure 7.1 arrays nineteen countries that have undertaken transitional justice over the past generation according to the respective strength and weakness of their punitive justice and truth recovery efforts.

Figure 7.1

COUNTRIES WITH TRANSITIONAL JUSTICE EFFORTS

TRUTH COMMISSIONS

PUNITIVE JUSTICE	Nonexistent	Weak	Moderately Weak	Moderately Strong	Strong
Nonexistent	Bulgaria, Northern Ireland, Romania, Russia				**Peru**
Weak		Poland		**Brazil,** El Salvador	**Guatemala, South Africa**
Moderately Weak	Czech Republic			Argentina	**Sierra Leone, Timor-Leste**
Moderately Strong	Greece	Rwanda, Former Yugoslavia		**Chile, Germany**	
Strong					

Religion's Influence on Transitional Justice

Why do countries adopt certain combinations of approaches? Impossible to ignore is the balance of power in a transition. If a shift to democracy involves the overthrow of a dictator, or if a civil war ends through the decisive defeat of one side, then the new regime will be able to conduct trials. If the end of a dictatorship or civil war is a negotiated one, then trials will be less likely, while truth commissions—which do not themselves land human rights violators in jail—will be more likely. But in many cases, power proves too simple an explanation. In Chile, for instance, the Supreme Court upheld amnesty for General Augusto Pinochet and his generals at the time of his negotiated departure from power in 1990, but human rights lawyers subsequently secured many important prosecutions and convictions. Other influences matter, too: parties, politicians, courts, and civil society organizations in the countries in which transitions take place as well as international organizations like the United Nations. Ignored in most analyses is still another actor: religious leaders and communities.

It is difficult to establish precisely how much influence religious actors have on countries' choices for transitional justice. Few observers of South Africa's Truth and Reconciliation Commission, though, can avoid the indelible association of its tenor and conduct with the purple robes, pectoral cross, and pastoral charisma of Anglican Archbishop Desmond Tutu. In Guatemala, the Catholic Church under Bishop Juan Gerardi actually constructed and conducted an entire truth commission. Here again, two global trends intersect: the rise of religion and the rise of transitional justice. In Figure 7.1, those countries in which religious actors played an influential role are highlighted in boldface. There are eight of them. The chart suggests a strong link between religious involvement and truth recovery and a weaker link between religious involvement and punitive justice. A closer look at the cases shows that where religious actors exerted a direct influence they usually did so to promote truth commissions and other measures for truth recovery. Only in the cases of Timor-Leste and Germany did a religious leader strongly advocate punitive justice.

When religious leaders and communities do exert influence on transitional justice—mostly for truth commissions, sometimes for trials and vetting—they do so at two stages: first, upon the formation of institutions and practices; second, upon their implementation. Concerning formation, religious actors lobby their governments, both publicly and privately, sometimes take part in the negotiation of truth commissions, and, through their public voice, inject concepts like reconciliation, forgiveness, and apology into the public debate. In some cases, such as Brazil, Chile, and Guatemala, churches have themselves gathered information on human rights violations. After institutions for transitional justice have been established, religious actors may help to build and conduct them. Religious organizations sometimes share in the selection of truth commissioners; their leaders sometimes serve as truth commissioners. As chair of South Africa's truth commission, Tutu gave truth recovery a distinctively religious cast, beginning hearings with prayer and presiding while participants broke out into hymns in the wake of particularly wrenching testimonies. In some truth-recovery efforts, religious communities testify as corporate entities about their own role in past injustices. Often, they will support truth commissions through logistical support, finding and encouraging victims and witnesses, and providing counseling and debriefing sessions following hearings. In the implementation phase, too, religious communities can commend ideas like forgiveness and reconciliation to political leaders and to the public at large.

What distinguishes those religious actors who are influential from those who are not? In most of the influential religious communities, a political theology of reconciliation is held in common among leaders and wide swaths of the rank and file. The reigning conception of transitional justice among Western governments and powerful international organizations like the United Nations and the World Bank has been the "liberal peace," which stresses human rights, democracy, and the prosecution of human rights violators.[37] Reconciliation, by contrast, while encompassing human rights and democracy and not necessarily rejecting punishment, is a more holistic conception that denotes restoration of right relationship and embraces apology, forgiveness, acknowledgment, and the healing of memories. It is held disproportionately, though not exclusively, by the religious and constitutes an alternative approach. Testifying to the power of global communication and transnational networks, the idea has migrated from site to site during the age of transitional justice. Reconciliation in politics surfaced in early-twentieth-century Christian theology, then found its way into the language of religious activists in the struggle against apartheid in South Africa. Chile was the first country to use the term in the title of its truth commission and directly influenced South Africa's commission. South Africa then inspired other countries to take up reconciliation, either in their truth commissions or in civil society efforts: Northern Ireland, Peru, Sierra Leone, Timor-Leste, and elsewhere.

Like religious actors who mediated peace settlements, those who shaped transitional justice had long practiced independence from the state. Here, too, many derived their moral authority precisely from the conflictual independence that they were able to maintain through heroic opposition. Here, too, religious actors who did not shape transitional justice were often ones whose authority and independence had been at least partially surrendered to the state.

Cases of Strong Religious Influence on Transitional Justice

A closer look at cases where religious actors did and did not shape their governments' approach to transitional justice shows that the influential ones both espoused a political theology of reconciliation and enjoyed institutional autonomy from political authority.

The most direct and powerful case of religious influence is that of the Catholic Church in Guatemala, which, judging the government's proposed truth commission to be too weak, conceived and launched its own truth commission, the Recovery of Historical Memory Project (REMHI), in 1995. Unearthing 14,291 cases of human rights violations involving 52,427 victims, covering crimes of both the guerilla opposition movement and the far more numerous crimes of the government, REMHI remains one of the largest truth recovery efforts in the world today. *Nunca Más* (Never Again), REMHI's final report, calls Guatemalans to repentance, forgiveness, and reconciliation, reflecting the prevalent political theology of the Guatemalan Catholic Church. This was a church, too, in which significant parts of the hierarchy and grassroots alike had asserted their independence from the country's military dictatorship in the 1980s and had become a vocal critic of the human rights violations that this dictatorship had committed during Guatemala's civil war.[38]

Elsewhere in Latin America, churches in Chile and Brazil were important shapers of transitional justice. Under the dictatorship of Pinochet, the Catholic Church's Vicariate of Solidarity secretly gathered and spirited out of the country evidence of torture and other human rights violations that would later prove crucial both for Chile's truth commission and for prosecution of regime members. Protestant churches gathered evidence as well. In Brazil, members of the Catholic and Protestant churches had been conducting similar work since the 1960s. The Catholic Church in Chile, along with President Patricio Aylwin and other Christian Democratic politicians whose faith inspired their politics, then became strong advocates of Chile's truth commission of 1990–1991, speaking the language of reconciliation, apology, and forgiveness.

In both countries, large sectors of the Catholic Church and certain Protestant churches had carried out opposition to the national regimes—conflictual independence—for several years: the Chilean Catholic Church since the mid-1970s, the Brazilian Catholic Church since the late 1960s. In Chile the Justice and Peace Commission was an important source of opposition, as were human rights groups with a religious component like the Sebastian Acevedo Movement Against Torture. The visit of Pope John Paul II to Chile in 1987 was also pivotal in raising awareness of human rights violations.[39]

South Africa's Truth and Reconciliation Commission remains the world's most famous—as well as its most religious. We have mentioned commission chair Tutu's religious regalia and the role that he gave to prayer and song during the hearings. In public forums—speeches, interviews, and his book, *No Future Without Forgiveness*—Tutu explained the commission's work in terms of Christian theology. Some Muslim leaders supported the commission out of their religious beliefs. In addition, religious communities provided the commission with staff, publicity, spiritual and psychological counseling for victims, encouragement of their own members to take part, and appearances at hearings for faith communities. The communities that played this role most strongly were precisely those that most strongly and actively opposed the apartheid state, drawing from a political theology of reconciliation in doing so.

Religious actors contributed vigorously to truth commissions in the wake of three civil wars that ended in the late 1990s and early 2000s in Peru, Sierra-Leone, and Timor-Leste. All of these actors had remained independent from the state during the war and espoused a political theology of reconciliation. Both Catholic and Protestant churches lobbied for and contributed to Peru's Truth and Reconciliation Commission, including supplying three of its seven commissioners. In Sierra Leone, Christian and Muslim leaders formed an interreligious council during the civil war that gave shelter to refugees, helped to mediate peace (as we have seen), assisted in shaping the truth commission, and then contributed to healing and reconciliation ceremonies in the wake of hearings—and in all of this voiced a political theology of reconciliation. Similar to South Africa, Sierra Leone's truth commission was chaired by a religious leader, Methodist Bishop Joseph Humper, and involved Islamic leaders playing prominent roles as well. The Catholic Church of Timor-Leste, led by Nobel Peace Laureate Bishop Carlos Belo and other leading prelates, both strongly urged the trials of top human rights violators and lent their support to the country's Commission for Reception, Truth, and Reconciliation, furnishing it with two of its seven commissioners and promoting its community reconciliation panels.[40]

In Germany following the fall of the Berlin Wall in 1989 and national reunification in 1990, churches played two sorts of roles, but ones that corresponded to their political theology and to their relationship to the Communist East German state. Contributing to both the Gauck Commission, which vetted state employees, and to the Enquete Commission, the rough equivalent of a truth commission, were Protestant pastors who had been dissidents—that is, conflictually independent—from the Communist government and who often framed their proposals in terms of reconciliation. Playing little role at all in these proceedings was the hierarchy of the national Protestant churches, which had practiced a partnership—that is, an integrated relationship—with the Communist government.[41]

Cases of Weak Religious Influence on Transitional Justice

In a number of other cases, religious actors exercised a minimal influence on institutions of transitional justice. Confirming the flip side of our argument, these same actors practiced an integrated relationship with political authority during the period of dictatorship or civil war, lacked a political theology of reconciliation, or both.

Take Rwanda, for instance, whose large established churches—Catholic, Anglican, and Presbyterian—wielded scant sway over the formation and national-level implementation of the international tribunals or national trials or over the network of local *gacaca* courts that were meant to combine accountability, apology, forgiveness, and reconciliation in the wake of Rwanda's genocide of 1994. True, these churches have not been completely passive, issuing declarations of repentance, commending the *gacaca* courts to their followers, and carrying out reconciliation initiatives in civil society. But in comparison to the religious activities detailed above, their political influence has been weak. The reason, we argue, is the same as the reason why Rwandan churches failed to be strong mediators of the Arusha Accords of 1993: they had long been integrated with the Rwandan state—with their Hutu-dominated leadership closely linked with Hutu governments—and espoused a theology that replaced justice with politically passive piety.

Argentina's Catholic Church is another case of a religious actor that exercised little sway on transitional justice—either national trials or the work of the National Commission on the Disappearance of Persons (CONADEP)—due to a legacy of complicit integration. This church's eighty bishops—except a handful of brave dissidents—remained tightly linked with the military junta that fought the Dirty Wars of 1976 to 1983 and committed thousands of acts of torture and extrajudicial killings. Nor was a theology of political reconciliation widely shared within its ranks.[42]

Catholic and Protestant churches in the Czech Republic were also sidelined in the shaping and conduct of transitional justice—here, trials and lustration. Once again, their failure has much to do with the fact they had been integrated with a dictatorship, but in this case far more conflictually. Dominated by their country's Communist regime, they failed to publicly oppose it until the 1980s, and even then did so weakly in comparison to churches in Chile, Guatemala, and South Africa.[43]

Another case of weak religious influence is the former Yugoslavia, where the Croatian Catholic Church, the Serbian Orthodox Church, and the Islamic community of Bosnia were bit players in the International Criminal Tribunal for the former Yugoslavia and lobbied only feebly for truth commissions, which occurred weakly or not at all in Yugoslavia's successor states. During the civil war of 1991 to 1995, these communities played a profoundly mixed role, with some of their clergy urging an end to the shooting and reconciliation but others lending religious sanction to the appeals of nationalist politicians. Compromised and complex in their stance during the war, these religious communities possessed little moral clout to influence the politics of justice after the war.[44]

A final set of cases that fits the pattern of weak influence on transitional justice, a legacy of integration, and the lack of a political theology of reconciliation includes four Orthodox churches. Although some Orthodox churches, and even the ecumenical patriarch, would come to develop a theory and practice of peace and reconciliation as described above, their influence on institutions of transitional justice in the 1970s and 1980s remained weak. The Orthodox Church of Greece did little to encourage the trials of junta leaders after Greece's transition to democracy in 1974. In Bulgaria, Romania, and Russia after the Cold War, little robust transitional justice took place, either punitive justice or truth recovery, and the churches exerted little sway to make it otherwise. Behind this weak influence is roughly the same story that accounted for the Orthodox Church's weak influence on democratization in Chapter Four: a tradition of integration—a conflictual sort under the domination of Communist regimes in Bulgaria, Romania, and Russia, and an acquiescent sort with the Greek junta from 1967 to 1974. Here, though, the missing political theology is one of political reconciliation, not just of human rights and democracy.

More complex and seemingly puzzling for our argument are three other cases of religious actors who exerted little power over transitional justice institutions. The Polish Catholic Church did not lobby strongly either for a truth commission, which never came to pass, or for the more retributive Main Commission for the Examination of Crimes Against the Polish Nation, despite the fact that the church was a paragon of heroic conflictual independence from the mid-1950s up until the collapse of the Communist regime in 1989.[45] But recall our argument that influential advocacy for transitional justice requires both independence and a political theology of reconciliation. It was the political theology that was missing. During the Cold War, human rights, democracy, and ecclesial autonomy dominated the Polish Catholic Church's thinking, giving it strong conceptual resources to oppose the Communist regime but leaving it with little robust thinking about justice in its aftermath—a political theology of reconciliation, for instance.

Puzzling, too, was the Catholic Church of El Salvador, which contained all the right preconditions of influence, having stayed independent of the state during its civil war and containing several leading clergy who proclaimed reconciliation—but in fact exercised only a small influence on its post–civil war truth commission of 1992–1993. The solution to this puzzle is idiosyncratic and underlines our caveat in Chapter Two that political theology and the relationship between religion and state are not the only factors that determine a religious actor's politics. Here, the church was sidelined by the United Nations, which dominated the organization and conduct of El Salvador's truth commission and allowed few other actors, including human rights organizations, to play a role in the process. Religious actors can shape truth commissions powerfully but they are not always essential to their implementation or success.

The Catholic, Anglican, Methodist, and certain factions within the Presbyterian churches of Northern Ireland also exhibit great potential to promote robust institutions of transitional justice. They kept their distance from both governments and opposition movements alike during Northern Ireland's long "troubles" of the 1970s, 1980s, and 1990s and housed top leaders who preached reconciliation. But this case shows that not only are religious actors not necessary for institutions of transitional justice, but neither are they sufficient. Despite the position of the churches, several other political factors— including the powerful British government's reluctance to participate—have stood as a roadblock to truth commissions, trials, or any other transitional justice effort.

CONCLUSION

Civil war settlements and the politics of transitional justice provide numerous settings in which the peace efforts of religious actors can be compared. We have sought to show that religious actors are most successful when they are independent of the state—and, in the case of peace mediation, of opposition forces as well—and espouse a political theology of peace or reconciliation.

Consistent with our caveat in Chapter Two, the cases also show that other variables matter, too. For instance, the absolute size of a religious actor, its size in proportion to the population of a country, and the degree of religiosity of its members can enhance its influence on peace and transitional justice. Archbishop Tutu's ability to lead the South African Truth and Reconciliation Commission in a highly religious fashion, for instance, was due in part to the fact that he operated in a highly religious society. The Vatican's ability to mediate between Argentina and Chile derived in good part from the size and prestige of the Catholic Church in both of these countries. Leadership matters as well. The successful efforts of Desmond Tutu, Juan Gerardi, Joachim Gauck, and Carlos Belo to forge justice and peace were based on a combination of political savvy and an ability to inspire. Finally, the cases reveal that some of the factors that serve to quench religious mediation and influence on transitional justice also lie outside of our argument's framework. A common one is the competing efforts of states and international organizations. Still, religious actors who are best equipped and therefore most likely to mediate a civil war or contribute to their societies' efforts to address past injustices tend to exhibit two clear qualities. They have translated their religious claims into a political theology of reconciliation, and they have maintained a posture of independence from political authorities and opposition factions, sometimes at great cost.

Chapter Eight

TEN RULES FOR SURVIVING GOD'S CENTURY

IN THE THIRD DECADE OF THE TWENTIETH CENTURY, EARLY in the long political career of eventual Portuguese dictator António Salazar, the confident young government minister found himself exchanging heated words with an old school friend, Manuel Gonçalves Cerejeira. Cerejeira, who studied with Salazar at the University of Coimbra, had just become the Catholic archbishop of Lisbon. At a moment of high political tension, Salazar insisted to Cerejeira that as an official of the state he represented "Caesar, just Caesar, and that he was independent and sovereign." Not missing a beat, Cerejeira shot back that as archbishop he represented "God . . . who was independent and sovereign and, what's more, above Caesar." Given their rivalry, Cerejeira must have derived some satisfaction from the fact that, while "Caesar" ruled for an astonishing thirty-six years, until 1968, God's "representative" remained head of the Portuguese Church for an even more astonishing forty-two years, until 1971.

Against the odds, despite a powerful array of secularizing regimes, ideologies, and social trends, God's representatives have outlasted some of their most ferocious twentieth-century rivals. Even more astonishing, in the perennial game of one-upsmanship between religious actors and political authorities, the representatives of God are in the ascendancy and are playing a central role in defining the dominant problems and patterns of world politics in the unfolding twenty-first century. God's partisans are back, they are setting the political agenda, and they are not going away. This is what makes the present century "God's Century."

Ten years after the attacks of September 11, the challenge of devising a stable and satisfactory equilibrium between the determined defenders of Caesar and the indomitable partisans of God remains at the top of the policy agenda in the twenty-first century. How do we understand and manage the politics of global religion in ways that are most likely to yield global freedom, peace, and prosperity, and minimize global violence, cruelty, and oppression? Up to this point, our arguments have been analytical, aimed at describing the world. In this final chapter, we become openly prescriptive, taking stock of what we have learned and proposing a path forward for analysts and practitioners of politics or anyone seeking to survive "God's Century." We offer Ten Rules for doing just that.

If our repeated invocation of "we" strikes some readers as a tad imperial, we acknowledge our limited perspective. We are American political scientists immersed in the political context and policy concerns of the United States. We do not pretend to speak in ways that are equally relevant to every imaginable global audience or policy context. We have kept the problems and challenges faced by American global analysts and foreign policy–makers chiefly in mind and hope that something we say may offer useful insight to these audiences. But we also hope that—with appropriate modifications—what we argue might persuade and guide other individuals and groups inside and outside the United States as well.

RULE ONE: *Acknowledge that religious actors are here to stay.*

The last several decades have vindicated Archbishop Cerejeira's confidence that God's partisans could trump Caesar's heady claims of sovereign superiority. Rather than being overwhelmed by the great modern waves of change, God's representatives have ridden these powerful forces to new heights of independence and capacities for influence that are unlikely to meet serious reversal.

First, the political and social forces of secularization often served to give God's partisans an enclave of independence in which they could preserve their identities and build self-supporting organizations able to play important social and political roles. Even where secularism was most programmatic and determined to weaken or wipe out religious actors—as in the twentieth-century paroxysm of secularist politics that peaked in the fifty years between 1917 and 1967—it often had the effect of strengthening their gathering institutional and ideological resistance to Caesar's excesses (a dynamic evident, for example, in the Muslim Brotherhood's increasing determination to resist escalating Egyptian government repression).

Second, modernization and its attendant processes of industrialization, economic development, and urbanization unleashed people and resources that could be mobilized to create new and potent religious organizations. Particularly, the growth of educated urban middle classes throughout the world created the social base—the foot soldiers—necessary for the formation of independent and politically potent religious institutions. Today, the demographic center of gravity of many religious communities continues to shift from an impoverished, illiterate, and rural mass to an emerging and increasingly sophisticated middle class. And these middle classes, contrary to prediction, do not necessarily abandon their piety when they acquire engineering degrees and bourgeois respectability. In many cases, the opposite occurs: Urban middle classes often adopt a more assertive, self-assured piety, which usually translates into heightened religious activism in public life.

Third, globalization in the form of accelerating immigration and communication has strengthened the independent power of religious groups by intensifying their identity and agency as transnational communities. This transnationalism has made numerous religious communities less vulnerable to manipulation and co-option by dominant governments and groups in any given nation-state or region and more able to play an independent and assertive role on the world stage.

The worldwide quantum leap in religion's capacity for political influence that many analysts have observed since at least the 1970s (and even earlier in some cases) is the cumulative consequence of these and other global trends. Thus empowered, God's partisans have spread across the most important regions and issue areas of world politics and have left their indelible marks— for good and ill. Furthermore, since these trends are likely to continue in both scope and rapidity—especially in the cases of modernization and globalization—the political capacity of religious actors is unlikely to abate in the foreseeable future.

RULE TWO: *Do not assume that the activism of religious actors can or should be confined to a "private sphere."*

Religious actors not only enjoy greater institutional capacity to influence global affairs but also possess a strong conviction that they should use this enhanced capacity to directly influence politics and public life. Of course, politically withdrawn religious sects remain. But in general, religious actors hold sincere convictions about how and why they should transform politics in accordance with God's will, as well as increasingly sophisticated theological blueprints for realizing a more godly politics.

Not content with missionary work or cultural reform, religious actors the world over feel called to lobby, legislate, and govern for God. This springs partly from theological views internal to particular religious traditions. Many Muslims, for example, believe civil authorities are under a divine obligation to adopt *sharia* law. Many Christians, meanwhile, especially in sub-Saharan Africa, believe that civil law should be based on biblical law. As we have noted throughout this book, other powerful political theologies include Engaged Buddhism in East Asia and Southeast Asia and the Hindutva ideology of the Hindu-nationalist movement in India.

The impulse to blend the things of God with the things of Caesar also springs from a more pervasive political shift. Since the late eighteenth century, more and more individuals and groups the world over—including religious individuals and groups—have been shaped by democratic and participatory political ideologies and processes. Partly through the spread of nationalist and anticolonial discourse, peoples almost everywhere came to believe that it was not only right but obligatory to take charge of their political destiny. Particularly between the late nineteenth century and the late twentieth century, therefore, political theologies preaching mere passivity in the face of the "powers that be" fell out of favor. Consequently, even religious traditions that had tended toward political quietism—such as Protestant fundamentalism and black Protestantism in the United States, Pentecostalism in Africa, Catholicism in Latin America, Theravada Buddhism in Sri Lanka and Southeast Asia, and Shiite Islam in Iran—developed theologies that elevate civic activism to a divine duty.

The prevalence of such theologies means that policy issues and proposals once framed almost entirely in terms of "secular" agendas, such as market liberalization or human rights or democratization, are increasingly susceptible to religious reframing. No longer a matter of discussion solely in terms of whether they will yield "freedom" or "development" or "prosperity," such proposals are being debated and considered in terms of whether they will undermine godly morality, traditional religious authority, and divine justice. Proposals for and against the rights of women and of religious minorities in particular cannot be heard except against the background of such religious and cultural concerns.

Today, the resulting sense that religious actors are inevitably shaping public debate is so powerful and pervasive that it unsettles even strongly secularist systems that enjoy long-standing stability and legitimacy, such as France's *laïcité*. There, the formerly uncompromising doctrines that are the legacy of the Jacobins of the French Revolution are being widely questioned, not only by veil-wearing schoolgirls and their parents but also by leading politicians such as President Nicolas Sarkozy, whose 2004 book on religion and public life, *The Republic, Religions, Hope*, shocked many of his fellow citizens by insisting, astonishingly for one of the Republic's leading politicians, "One would be wrong to limit the church's role to spirituality."

RULE THREE: *Learn to live with the fact that the issue is not whether, but when and how, religious actors will enter public life and shape political outcomes.*

The forces driving religious actors to seek greater public influence are beyond anyone's power—save that of God himself—to stop or seriously limit. The trends encouraging the formation of independent religious organizations are unstoppable. The impulse felt by most religious actors to plunge into the fray of political life is inextinguishable.

The challenge, then, is to live with religion's role in public life. To date, the dominant strategies whereby regimes have sought to obviate this challenge have largely failed. One strategy has been the radical secularization of public life through its coercive expulsion from politics and containment within a private sphere; another has been the controlled sacralization of political life through the state-managed support of religious symbols, legislation, and institutions.

The first strategy, historically favored by the revolutionaries of the Left and still practiced in robust form in China and Cuba, grants religious actors limited autonomy within a private sphere but no access to political power, treating religion in much the way one quarantines the diseased, that is, for the purpose of containing and eventually extinguishing a threat to public safety. The second strategy, historically favored by reactionaries on the Right such as Pablo Salazar in Portugal and Francisco Franco in Spain and practiced today by authoritarian governments throughout the Arab world, grants religious actors carefully limited access to political power and privilege but relatively little autonomy. Here the idea is to inoculate society with a mild form of religion in the hope of making it immune to the real thing.

Neither strategy has stopped the drive of religious actors to influence public life on their own terms. The only remaining option, then, is to devise strategies that accommodate the political presence of religious actors in ways that maximize the likelihood that their activism will yield positive rather than negative political outcomes.

RULE FOUR: *Do not exaggerate the power of religious actors in public life, thereby replacing secularization with sacralization . . .*

People like us who write sweeping accounts of religion and world politics should find themselves haunted by the overconfidence that bedeviled an earlier generation of analysts, who predicted without the slightest hesitation that the world was on a fast track to sweep religion—if not the traditional idea of God itself—into the dustbin of history. So unbroken was this consensus that, not accidentally, virtually the only dissenters were religious actors and thinkers, such as Catholic priest and sociologist Andrew Greeley. Perhaps, as a fan of the Chicago Cubs, he had a deep-seated weakness for underdogs. His remarkable 1972 book, *Unsecular Man: The Persistence of Religion*, offered a characteristically pugnacious assault on the conventional wisdom of inevitable and universal secularization.

As much as we sympathize with Greeley's point of view (which held, for example, that whatever religious changes modernity has wrought "make religious questions more critical rather than less critical in the contemporary world"), we earnestly seek to avoid the equal and opposite error of an inevitable and universal "sacralization." We do not argue that the world is destined for theocratic government or that religion is becoming the single master driver of global affairs—leading, some might surmise, to a new and divine "end of history" very different from the secular triumph of liberal capitalism envisioned by Francis Fukuyama. Nor do we argue that religious forces will somehow directly displace or replace rising nation-states such as China and India, whose growing power may well eventually justify the increasing popularity of references to the present century as the "Asian Century," succeeding the previous "American Century." Our point is not that religious actors and ideas will dominate or "win" a zero-sum geostrategic competition against all comers.

Instead, what is called for is a far more nuanced and calibrated perspective. Religious actors will often *not* be the dominant or decisive determinants of political outcomes. But they *will* often play a central and even decisive role in framing the matrix of issues and players from which the dominant outcomes will emerge. As we saw in Chapter Four, religious actors seldom if ever delivered the single knockout punch to an authoritarian regime, but they were often an integral part of the complex of forces that generated democratic progress.

RULE FIVE: . . . *but expect religious actors to play a larger and more pervasive role than conventional wisdom anticipates.*

If religious actors fall well short of political omnipotence, their political impact will almost certainly continue to exceed prevailing expectations in the twenty-first century.

Religious observance was not supposed to become the single biggest predictor of presidential voting preference—greater even than race or income—in the ultramodern twenty-first-century United States. But that is just what it became in the 2004 contest between Republican George W. Bush and Democrat John Kerry. Religious actors and issues were not supposed to force their way onto the political front burner of the most secular cultural zone on earth, Western Europe, many of whose elites believed that the Enlightenment and the French Revolution had made religiopolitical struggle a thing of the past (forgetting perhaps the great nineteenth-century conflicts between the Catholic Church and liberalism we reviewed in Chapter Three). But that is just what they did, partly because of higher fertility rates among more religious people and partly because of continuing immigration from more religious parts of the world—both Muslim-dominated North Africa and Christian-dominated sub-Saharan Africa. Religious and culturally based concerns also shape the attitudes of European elites and average citizens toward the prospect of Muslim-majority Turkey joining the European Union.

Even in "secular" Europe, therefore, the challenge of formulating a new equilibrium between political structures and religious movements is likely to intensify in the coming decades, almost inevitably making the continent of Voltaire and Kant a key battleground in the unfolding of "God's Century." And if this is true in Europe, it is even more true in much of the rest of the world.

In both traditionally religious and traditionally "secular" parts of the world, religious actors will be a defining element in twenty-first-century politics—both the global and regional political competition between major states and the constitutive politics of many major states—in ways conventional wisdom continues to ignore or downplay. For example, nonstate religious actors such as Hamas and Hezbollah have contributed to a shift in the basic balance of power in the Middle East, helping to displace the erstwhile regional supremacy of Saudi Arabia and Egypt in favor of Iran and Syria. Likewise, the stability of numerous other nation-states increasingly depends on the disposition of rising religious actors and communities and how well— or poorly—such states can achieve a viable equilibrium in the face of the challenges these actors pose. This is true of emerging great powers such as China and India as well as of key regional powers such as Indonesia, Nigeria, and Turkey.

How successfully China and India, for example, manage their growing Muslim and Christian communities, which are restive and struggling mightily for greater voice, respect, and autonomy, will prove a major influence on their future stability, prosperity, and, possibly, their territorial integrity. China alone will be home to the world's 19th largest Muslim community by 2030 and is already home to the world's 7th largest Christian community today. These communities are becoming increasingly connected to transnational coreligionists and they will, therefore, become increasingly difficult to contain within an inflexible carapace framed by a repressive Communist state and a monoethnic Han nationalism.

RULE SIX: *Accept that the more governments try to repress or exclude religion from public life, the more such efforts will be self-defeating.*

It is hard to find a more compelling indication of the futility of government repression of religion than an analysis published by the Pew Forum on Religion & Public Life in December 2009. The Pew Forum report found that about 70 percent of the world's people live in states in which there are severe restrictions on religion. Yet many of the societies in which religious restrictions are the greatest—such as China, India, and Vietnam—exhibit high, if not growing, levels of religious vitality and activism. Furthermore, even groups that face some of the most severe political and social opposition in these countries, such as unregistered "house" churches in China or Christian movements among "untouchables," or Dalits, in India, are thriving and pushing their concerns onto the public agenda.

Recent history provides ample demonstration that, as a rule, efforts by governments or powerful groups to restrict religion seldom succeed in stamping out religion's private or public vitality, in the short or long run. Certainly, there are exceptions. Where a government is sufficiently ruthless and resourced, as in the case of the Nazi regime or today's North Korean government, religious actors and communities can be virtually wiped out or at least deprived of any organized presence in society. Short of such exceptionally brutal policies, however, government restrictions tend to unify the groups being repressed, stiffen their will to resist, enhance their organizational flexibility, and elevate their moral authority.

In other words, the more governments try to repress or exclude religious actors from public life in one generation, the more they inadvertently strengthen their capacity to influence public life in the next generation. This dynamic has been evident in the repression of Shiite clerics and groups by the Shah of Iran and Saddam Hussein in Iraq; the repression of the Catholic Church by the Communist regime in Poland; the repression of Christian churches by the apartheid government in South Africa; the repression of the Hindu-nationalist movement by Indira Gandhi in India; and the repression of Tibetan Buddhism by the Communist government in China. Political repression in one generation laid the foundations for public resistance in the next generation.

More effective than hard repression in weakening the autonomy of religious actors has been the soft seduction of co-option. Where religious leaders have been bought off, they have often consensually integrated with political authority, becoming the meek instruments of the state. However, while this policy may succeed in co-opting some religious actors some of the time, it never succeeds in co-opting all of them all of the time. In fact, the very effort to co-opt some religious leaders and groups, even when successful, tends to alienate other religious actors, who recoil from state-approved religion as corrupt and inauthentic. Co-opted Muslim groups and institutions, such as the state-controlled Al-Azhar University in Egypt, are often dismissed by other Muslims as "palace Islamists." Meanwhile, as Quintan Wiktorowicz has shown, groups that lack state sanction, such as the Salafis in Jordan, shun the country's government-controlled mosques and instead win adherents through the proliferation of informal networks and discussion groups.[1]

RULE SEVEN: *Acknowledge that the more governments permit religious actors to be autonomous social actors in a system of consensual independence, the more religion will serve as a "force multiplier" for important social and political goods, including democratization, peacemaking, and reconciliation.*

As we have already noted, the beginning of political wisdom is to recognize that publicly engaged religious actors are here to stay. Strategies of repression or co-option do not work, which leaves a strategy of accommodation as the only remaining option: except where religious actors are inherently violent and destabilizing, assign them a politically and legally protected zone of institutional independence. This involves what the great sociologist Max Weber called "autonomy" and "autocephaly." That is, first give religious actors the freedom to define their own identity, beliefs, and way of life—their own *nomos* ("autonomy"). Second, give religious actors the freedom to define their own leadership structure and appoint their own leaders ("autocephaly").

In other words, place religious actors in a relationship of consensual independence with political authority. Let the state, by conviction and deliberate choice, accept the legitimacy of what many religious actors the world over have been earnestly seeking for decades: not only independence from domination but the opportunity to contribute to public debate and the politics of their societies.

The United States offers one model for liberating God's representatives from Caesar's domination. Unlike the revolutionaries of the Left or the reactionaries of the Right, the republicans who founded the United States respected God without patronizing him.

Despite representing a broad spectrum of religious conviction, ranging from the deism of Thomas Jefferson and Benjamin Franklin to the evangelicalism of Patrick Henry and John Jay, the founders welcomed God as an ally and a cornerstone of their ultramodern political revolution. At the same time, they sought to free religion from its historic dependence on state patronage and vulnerability to state co-option, which they feared would debilitate and corrupt religion and state alike. Immediately after the American Revolution, Christians squabbled with one another, and unlike the federal government, some state governments kept churches dependent on direct government financing. (The last of these state "mini-establishments," in Massachusetts, was abolished only in 1833.) At first, Christian ministers in the new American republic were much like their European counterparts: indolent wards of the state who nonetheless expected a decent share of social and political power as well as the perfect obedience of the masses by virtue of the ministers' position in the social hierarchy.

In the early nineteenth century, however, churches in America became less dependent on state support, and in the absence of state sanctions compelling church attendance, they consciously adapted their message and methods to a society that was increasingly mobile, freethinking, and egalitarian. They thus achieved a growing influence on American society in large part because they were not confined by state controls or co-opted by state support. In short, the new American republic achieved the world's first enduring model of institutional independence between political and religious authority (and to this day, as we noted in Chapter Two, the United States remains the strongest example of church-state separation in the world[2]), resulting in a society that combines high levels of freedom, stability, and religious activism.

We note the American experience not in order to derive an exact model necessarily applicable in every detail to very different cultural and religious contexts. Rather, we note it to underscore the point Alexis de Tocqueville made on observing the American system 175 years ago: unlike the Catholic Church in the France of his day, which was still tethered to the memory and remnants of the *ancien régime*, the churches in America were unshackled from the state and free to be a force for democracy.

In other words, when Caesar liberates God's representatives, he gives society not only a static benefit but a fungible "force multiplier." When religious actors are given substantial independence from the state, they are given the capacity to perform a range of positive functions in society. They promote a widening circle of freedom and expansion of democracy, just as religious groups in American society were in the forefront of the abolitionist movement and the struggle to protect the Cherokee Indians. Or, they are empowered to mediate peace agreements in El Salvador and shape institutions for transitional justice in South Africa. The more freedom religious actors enjoy, the more freedom as well as other social goods religious actors are capable of multiplying—for themselves and others.

As we noted in the course of this book, and in a way that would have pleased Archbishop Cerejeira, religious institutions and communities, not least the archbishop's Catholic Church, have grown increasingly "independent" and "sovereign" since the mid twentieth century. What is more, they have even managed to outmaneuver and outfight the representatives of Caesar in numerous contexts, not only surviving but creating zones of freedom within which they could mount challenges to authoritarian governments of the Left and the Right. As we noted in Chapter Four, in more than 60 percent of the world's countries that have made substantial democratic progress between 1972 and 2009, religious actors played a notable prodemocratic role. And in a majority of these cases, the kind of role religious actors played was prominent, with religious actors joining the vanguard of prodemocratic forces. These religious actors played a major prodemocratic role because they were largely "independent" and "sovereign" actors, in the words of Archbishop Cerejeira. They enjoyed a substantial degree of institutional independence or structural autonomy.

It should be added that the independence of religious actors has other multiplier effects. As Chapter Seven demonstrated, independent religious actors are far more effective in mediating an end to violent conflicts and helping their societies constructively address past injustices. In addition, where religious actors are free to occupy their own space in society, they are more likely to compete with each other for adherents in a religious marketplace, which increases their incentives to offer social services. In addition, when religious actors are no longer a state-owned monopoly, they are under a greater pressure to cater to the inevitably diverse religious preferences of society. This diversification and competition has the effect of producing religious actors inclined to appeal to the broad middle of their societies rather than the extremes, which, in turn, has the effect of encouraging them toward ideological and political moderation. In Egypt, for example, during a period of political liberalization in the late 1990s, some disgruntled young leaders of the Muslim Brotherhood left the organization to form the Wasat (Center) Party—as the name implies, a more centrist and pluralistic movement than the Brotherhood. The party did not take off only because the Egyptian government ended its policy of liberalization. But Wasat's formation illustrates the connection between institutional independence, competition, and moderation.

As we noted earlier, the consequences of opening up more societies to increased independence and activism on the part of religious actors should not be feared. The presence of religious actors in democratic politics does not entail their dominance—far from it. As Charles Kurzman and Ijlal Naqvi noted in their exhaustive analysis of the electoral performance of Islamic parties between 1968 and 2008, such parties have become an increasingly common presence in the politics of many Muslim countries, but they have seldom controlled or dominated electoral outcomes. Overall, Islamist or Islamic-revivalist parties have fared poorly while more moderate parties, committed to democracy, have done well. Furthermore, these scholars found that the electoral success rates of Islamist parties drop even lower in countries with more robust and competitive democratic systems.[3] The pattern holds true for other types of religious parties and politicians as well. Evangelical politicians running largely on evangelical or Christian platforms in Africa and Latin America have seldom performed well in free and fair electoral contests.[4] Where religious actors are institutionally independent and permitted to compete for cultural and political influence alongside other social actors, they enjoy the opportunity to influence society—in mostly positive ways—but almost always lack the ability to take over society.

RULE EIGHT: *Take the religious beliefs and political theologies of religious actors seriously because they interact with political structure and context to explain much of the political behavior of religious actors.*

We argue that it is essential to confront the theological claims of religious people and communities and how those claims translate into political demands. The new atheists argue that religion is irrational, based on fear. While allowing for the pervasiveness of fear and anxiety in human life, this book has demonstrated the genuine presence and motivating power of religious conviction—what we have been calling "political theology"—in the world's politics. In fact, it could be argued that it is the new atheist view of religion itself that is based on irrational fear rather than a clear-eyed understanding that religion assumes numerous and diverse forms, some of which in fact promote good in the world. Furthermore, despite the faith and hope of the new atheism, over 80 percent of the world continues to believe in God, as we pointed out in Chapter One.

We also resist the all-too-common tendency to explain religion away by reducing it to "more basic" economic or social causes. We argue that religion—through its motivating ideas and the mobilizational power of its institutions—is a basic driver of politics in its own right. And the most crucial issue is not the theology of religious actors in general, whether it is tolerant or exclusive in terms of who is eligible for salvation, for example, but rather their teachings on the state and politics.

In other words, the institutional or structural relationship between religious authority and political authority is far from everything. A religious actor may enjoy a perfect degree of institutional independence from political authority but retain a resolutely violent and illiberal political theology. In our view, then, the core driver of the politics of the religious in today's world is not structure or ideology working independently of the other but structure *and* ideology interacting together.

For example, Jillian Schwedler's *Faith in Moderation*, an outstanding comparative study of Islamist political parties in Jordan and Yemen, finds evidence that the major Islamist party in Jordan has moderated in recent years, but the one in Yemen has not. Both parties, the Islamic Action Front in Jordan and the Islah (Reform) Party in Yemen, enjoy some institutional independence from the state, and both have enjoyed some freedom to compete in recent, quasi-democratic elections in the two countries. Political opportunity and participation have not yielded identical effects across the two parties, Schwedler concludes, at least partly because the Islah Party lacks a strong and coherent political theology. Because it lacks a defining discourse, and has a *raison d'être* that is more tribal than ideological or programmatic, it is not capable of democratic evolution or moderation to the same degree as the far more ideological and theologically self-conscious Islamic Action Front. Both institutional independence and political theology are essential to explaining why the Islah Party has not and (in its present form) will not evolve into a more strongly prodemocratic force.

RULE NINE: *Accept that if governments fail to respect the institutional independence of religious actors, especially through systematic repression, the more these governments will encourage pathological forms of religious politics, including religion-based terrorism and religion-related civil wars.*

As we demonstrated in Chapters Five and Six, sustained and systematic efforts to repress religious actors not only tend to fail to secure their objective of weakening religion but also open up a Pandora's box of social and political evils.

We have already noted the powerful and pervasive drive of religious actors to organize their own autonomous life and exercise their own independent influence in the societies of the modern world. Rather than extinguish religion's desire and capacity for influence, modernity at least in some respects has strengthened them. When powerful social actors and governments in particular stand athwart this powerful religious impulse for independence and influence, religious actors are bound to react with intensity. As we noted earlier, the question is not whether they will react but when and how. And, once again, the key to determining how they will react is twofold: the combination of a religious actor's independence from political authority and its political theology.

If a religious actor retains some independence from the state, however embattled and precarious, and if it adheres to a political theology that is essentially peaceable and liberal, however imperfect or incomplete, it is highly unlikely to undertake systematic campaigns of violence against civilians even in the face of severe and sustained government repression. It will instead follow the path of, say, the Catholic Church in Poland or the South African Council of Churches in South Africa.

If, on the other hand, a religious group is subject to severe political repression and exclusion in ways that deprive it of substantial institutional autonomy for a sustained period of time, and if it holds a political theology that sanctions violence against civilians and the legitimacy of a revolutionary takeover of the state, then the religious group in question is likely to respond to its situation by violence, leading either to terrorist acts or full-scale civil war, as the cases of Algeria and Sudan illustrate.

The violence thus set in motion, furthermore, is intended to generate a deepening security dilemma for its victims while enhancing the apparent legitimacy of the attackers. Consider the September 11 terrorist attacks. Ostensibly to defend Muslim lands from "Crusader" oppression and to purify Islamic holy lands and culture of infidel influence, Al Qaeda strikes the heart of the "Crusader" world, America. In response, the United States, led by an overtly Christian president, motivated in part by a historic missionary mentality and supported disproportionately by evangelical Protestants, undertakes an aggressive global "crusade" to destroy Islamist terrorism, which has the effect of making Muslim lands and culture more vulnerable to "infidel" influence. Whatever tactical setbacks it has dealt Al Qaeda as an organization, this aggressive American response to enhance U.S. security has the effect of increasing the credibility of the Islamist caricature of the United States in the Muslim world (as an anti-Muslim "Crusader") and thus of Muslim hostility to the U.S., which in turn has the effect of increasing the worldwide recruitment of Islamist terrorists and, arguably, of diminishing U.S. security.

Unless carefully calibrated, counterterrorist methods are likely to generate a similar dynamic. The efforts of governments to clamp down on religious militancy may well make these governments more vulnerable to religious militancy. Restrictions on religious groups, particularly where they involve systematic subordination and repression, may well deepen rather than soften the radicalization of religion, both because these restrictions further deprive religious actors of their autonomy and because the restrictions will appear to religious actors as further empirical validation of their Manichean political theologies. A vicious downward spiral will result.

RULE TEN: *Appreciate that there is strategic value in pursuing religious freedom in the conduct of foreign policy.*

The foregoing strongly suggests that there is strategic value in pursuing a policy that makes expanding the institutional independence of religious actors a priority. In 1998 the U.S. Congress sought to do just that in passing the International Religious Freedom Act (IRFA). Creating an Office of International Religious Freedom in the State Department as well as an independent commission to monitor and promote religious freedom around the world, the law ensconced religious freedom in the very foreign policy–making apparatus of the United States government. Over the ensuing decade, the office and the commission created by IRFA have spotlighted numerous global violations of the basic human right of religious freedom, including those committed against Muslims in Gujarat, Bahá'ís in Iran, and Christians in China. Upon retiring as the first director of the State Department office, Thomas F. Farr reflected back on the U.S. policy of religious freedom in his book *World of Faith and Freedom.*[5] While he continued to applaud the effort to expose and alleviate the persecution of religious minorities around the world, Farr argued that the U.S. government ought to incorporate religious freedom into its foreign policy much more broadly, making it a staple of its strategies for promoting democracy, reducing terrorism, and many other goals.

We agree. If the U.S. government wishes to navigate its way successfully through "God's Century," enhancing its security and realizing its democratic values, it must come to recognize that religion is far more than the concern of one or two small offices, as important as their work for human rights is. It must come to understand more than it does today the politics of the religious— which religious actors are likely to be its allies, which ones are likely to be its enemies, and which ones might become partners in constructive change; as well as which kinds of regimes treat their religious citizens in a way that is likely to foment civil war and terrorism, and which kinds of regimes treat their religious citizens in a way that promotes their best civic, democratic, productive, and peaceful energies. With such an understanding, the United

States would, for instance, encourage governments in (especially) the Arab Muslim world to adopt policies that permit their religious institutions and actors to enjoy a greater measure of independence from state control and state privilege. Achieving such an understanding means educating officers in the State Department, Defense Department, and National Security Council in the importance of religion far more than currently occurs. Universities and high schools must do their part as well, making the nuanced understanding of religion's role in global politics an essential part of their civics curricula. Only if policymakers in the United States and other Western societies come to understand that religion matters and how religion matters in global politics will they enjoy strategic success in engaging those contexts—including their own countries—where God's political comeback will not soon be reversed.

NOTES

Chapter One
THE TWENTY-FIRST CENTURY AS GOD'S CENTURY

1. "A Bleak Outlook Is Seen for Religion," *New York Times*, February 25, 1968, 3.

2. Richard Hofstadter, *Anti-intellectualism in American Life* (New York: Vintage, 1962), 123. From his vantage point in the early 1960s, Hofstadter was speaking of American fundamentalists, but he could just as well have been speaking of traditional religious believers in much of the rest of the world.

3. Data from Brian J. Grim and Roger Finke, *The Price of Freedom Denied: Religious Persecution and Conflict in the 21st Century* (Cambridge, UK: Cambridge University Press, 2010), chap. 7; and the Pew Global Attitudes Project 2007 at http://pewglobal.org/reports/pdf/258.pdf.

4. Peter L. Berger, "The Desecularization of the World: A Global Overview," in *The Desecularization of the World: Resurgent Religion and World Politics*, ed. Peter L. Berger (Washington, DC: Eerdmans/Ethics and Public Policy Center, 1999), 2.

5. Christopher Hitchens, *God Is Not Great: How Religion Poisons Everything* (New York: Twelve, 2007); Richard Dawkins, *The God Delusion* (New York: Houghton Mifflin, 2006); Daniel C. Dennett, *Breaking the Spell: Religion as a Natural Phenomenon* (New York: Penguin, 2006); and Sam Harris, *The End of Faith: Religion, Terror, and the Future of Reason* (New York: W. W. Norton, 2004).

6. Here we make it clear that we are talking about the *mutual* independence of religious authority and political authority—that is, the independence of religious authority from political authority and vice versa (though the stress of our argument throughout the book is on the importance of religious authority's independence from political authority). To avoid verbosity and repetition, however, we refer to this factor in most of the book simply as "the independence of religious authority and political authority" or "the independence of religious authority from political authority."

7. Peter L. Berger, *The Sacred Canopy: Elements of a Sociological Theory of Religion* (New York: Anchor Books, 1969), 107.

8. James A. Bill, *The Eagle and the Lion: The Tragedy of American-Iranian Relations* (New Haven, CT: Yale University Press, 1988), 417. Italics in original.

9. Neil MacFarquhar, "In Iran, Both Sides Seek to Carry Islam's Banner," *New York Times*, June 21, 2009.

10. Kim-Kwong Chan, "The Christian Community in China: The Leaven Effect," in *Evangelical Christianity and Democracy in Asia*, ed. David Lumsdaine, a volume in the series Evangelical Christianity and Democracy in the Global South, ed. Timothy Samuel Shah (New York and Oxford: Oxford University Press, 2009), 43–86.

Chapter Two
BEHIND THE POLITICS OF RELIGION

1. William P. Alston, "Religion," *Encyclopedia of Philosophy*, vol. 7 (New York: Macmillan, 1972), 140–145.

2. Susanne Hoeber Rudolph, "Introduction: Religion, States, and Transnational Civil Society," in *Transnational Religion and Fading States*, ed. Susanne Hoeber Rudolph and James Piscatori (Boulder, CO: Westview Press, 1997).

3. This definition draws from John Finnis, *Natural Law and Natural Rights* (Oxford, UK: Oxford University Press, 1980), 231–259, and Yves R. Simon, *A General Theory of Authority* (Notre Dame, IN: University of Notre Dame Press, 1991).

4. Quoted in Bruce Lincoln, *Holy Terrors: Thinking about Religion after September 11* (Chicago, IL: University of Chicago Press, 2003), 4.

5. In using the term "political theology," we are aware that it has a history of being used by diverse and prominent authors, among these Carl Schmitt, Johann Baptist Metz, and Francis Fiorenza, all of whose usage of the term differs significantly from ours. For an exploration of the concept, see Hent de Vries and Lawrence Eugene Sullivan, *Political Theologies: Public Religions in a Post-Secular World* (New York: Fordham University Press, 2006).

6. Gilles Kepel, *Jihad: The Trail of Political Islam* (Cambridge, MA: Harvard University Press, 2002), 36–42, 106–135.

7. Whereas "independence of religious and political authority" is our most precise name for this concept, we often use the phrase "independence of religion and state" or something close to this to mean the same thing. Of course, state is itself an equivocal concept and can mean a territorial political entity (Germany, Burma, etc.) as well as governing institutions (as in the phrase "the state is oppressive"). When we speak of independence of religion and state, we mean the latter, i.e., state as governing institutions.

8. David Maland, *Europe in the Seventeenth Century* (London: Macmillan, 1966), 16.

9. Ernst Troeltsch, *The Social Teaching of the Christian Churches*, vol. 2, trans. Olive Wyon (Louisville, KY: Westminster/John Knox Press, 1992).

10. See David Martin, *A General Theory of Secularization* (New York: Harper & Row, 1978); Peter Berger, *The Sacred Canopy: Elements of a Sociological Theory of Religion* (New York: Random House, 1967); Bryan Wilson, *Religion in a Sociological Perspective* (Oxford, UK: Clarendon Press, 1982); and Steve Bruce, *Religion and the Modern World* (Oxford, UK: Oxford University Press, 1996).

11. José Casanova, *Public Religions in the Modern World* (Chicago, IL: University of Chicago Press, 1994).

12. Nils Henrik-Nilsson, "The Lutheran Tradition in Scandinavia," in *The Oxford History of*

Christian Worship, ed. Geoffrey Wainwright and Karen Beth Westerfield Tucker (Oxford, UK: Oxford University Press, 2006).

13. Jonathan Fox, *A World Survey of Religion and the State* (Cambridge, UK: Cambridge University Press, 2007); Brian J. Grim and Roger Finke, "International Religion Indexes: Government Regulation, Government Favoritism, and Social Regulation of Religion," *Interdisciplinary Journal of Research on Religion* 2, no. 1 (2006).

Chapter Three
THE RISE OF POLITICALLY ASSERTIVE RELIGION

1. See, for instance, Steve Bruce, *God Is Dead: Secularization in the West* (Oxford, UK: Blackwell Publishing, 2002).

2. Peter Gyallay-Pap, "Reconstructing the Cambodian Polity: Buddhism, Kingship, and the Quest for Legitimacy," in *Buddhism, Power, and Political Order,* ed. Ian Harris (New York: Routledge, 2007), 76.

3. Donald Eugene Smith, *Religion and Politics in Burma* (Princeton, NJ: Princeton University Press, 1965), 22.

4. John P. Ferguson, "The Quest for Legitimation by Burmese Monks and Kings: The Case of the Shwegyin Sect (19th–20th Centuries)," in *Religion and Legitimation of Power in Thailand, Laos, and Burma,* ed. Bardwell L. Smith (Chambersburg, PA: Anima Books, 1978), 66.

5. Ferguson, "Quest for Legitimation," 68.

6. Donald Eugene Smith, *South Asian Politics and Religion* (Princeton, NJ: Princeton University Press, 1966), 14.

7. Smith, *Religion and Politics in Burma,* 10.

8. Smith, *South Asian Politics and Religion,* 17–18.

9. Ira M. Lapidus, *A History of Islamic Societies* (Cambridge, UK, and New York: Cambridge University Press, 1988), 183–184.

10. D. Mackenzie Brown, *The White Umbrella: Indian Political Thought from Manu to Gandhi* (Berkeley: University of California Press, 1953), 28, quoted in Smith, *Religion and Politics in Burma,* 20.

11. A. L. Basham, *The Wonder That Was India: A Survey of the Culture of the Indian Sub-Continent Before the Coming of the Muslims* (New York: Grove Press, 1959), 81, 86–87.

12. Smith, *South Asian Politics and Religion,* 8–9, 11.

13. Joseph R. Strayer, "The State and Religion: An Exploratory Comparison in Different Cultures: Greece and Rome, the West, Islam," *Comparative Studies in Society and History* 1 (1958), 39.

14. Ramsay MacMullen, *Voting About God in Early Church Councils* (New Haven, CT: Yale University Press, 2006), 19–20.

15. Smith, *South Asian Politics and Religion,* 8.

16. S. N. Eisenstadt, "Religious Organizations and Political Process in Centralized Empires," *Journal of Asian Studies* 21, no. 3 (May 1962), 283, 272.

17. Eisenstadt, "Religious Organizations," 272; Donald Eugene Smith, *Religion and Political Development, an Analytic Study* (Boston, MA: Little, Brown, 1970), 70–75.

18. Eisenstadt, "Religious Organizations," 272.

19. Ira M. Lapidus, "The Separation of State and Religion in the Development of Early Islamic Society," *International Journal of Middle East Studies* 6 (1975), 365.

20. Strayer, "The State and Religion," 39.

21. Strayer, "The State and Religion," 38–43.

22. Eisenstadt, "Religious Organizations," 293–294.

23. Charles Tilly, "Reflections on the History of European State-Making," in *The Formation of National States in Western Europe,* ed. Charles Tilly (Princeton, NJ: Princeton University Press, 1975), 3–84.

24. Brian Tierney, *The Crisis of Church and State, 1050–1300* (Toronto: University of Toronto Press, 1988), 185.

25. Jacques Maritain, "The End of Machiavellianism," in *The Crisis of Modern Times: Perspectives from the Review of Politics, 1939–1962*, ed. A. James McAdams (Notre Dame, IN: University of Notre Dame Press, 2007), 98–127.

26. Daniel Philpott, *Revolutions in Sovereignty: How Ideas Shaped Modern International Relations* (Princeton, NJ: Princeton University Press, 2001).

27. Joseph Lecler, S.J., *The Two Sovereignties: A Study of the Relationship Between Church and State* (New York: Philosophical Library, 1952), 103.

28. Ernst H. Kantorowicz, *The King's Two Bodies: A Study in Mediaeval Political Theology* (Princeton, NJ: Princeton University Press, 1957), 19.

29. Quoting theologian Flacius Illyricus, in Lecler, *The Two Sovereignties*, 104.

30. Lecler, *The Two Sovereignties*, 44.

31. See, for instance, Adrian Hastings, *The Construction of Nationhood: Ethnicity, Religion, and Nationalism* (Cambridge, UK: Cambridge University Press, 1997); Anthony W. Marx, *Faith in Nation: Exclusionary Origins of Nationalism* (New York: Oxford University Press, 2003); Linda Colley, *Britons: Forging the Nation* (New Haven, CT: Yale University Press, 1992).

32. See Philpott, *Revolutions in Sovereignty*, 75–122.

33. Joseph M. Kitagawa, "Buddhism and Asian Politics," *Asian Survey* 2, no. 5 (July 1962), 328.

34. Smith, *Religion and Political Development*, 67.

35. Niyazi Berkes, *The Development of Secularism in Turkey* (Montreal: McGill University Press, 1964), 15.

36. Berkes, *The Development of Secularism in Turkey*, 16.

37. Lynn Avery Hunt, *Politics, Culture, and Class in the French Revolution*, Studies on the History of Society and Culture (Berkeley: University of California Press, 1984).

38. Jean-Jacques Rousseau, *On the Social Contract: With Geneva Manuscript and Political Economy* (New York: St. Martin's Press, 1978).

39. Hunt, *Politics, Culture, and Class*; Simon Schama, *Citizens: A Chronicle of the French Revolution* (New York: Knopf, distributed by Random House, 1989).

40. Michael Burleigh, *Earthly Powers: Religion and Politics in Europe from the French Revolution to the Great War* (London: HarperCollins, 2005).

41. Conor Cruise O'Brien, *Ancestral Voices: Religion and Nationalism in Ireland* (Chicago, IL: University of Chicago Press, 1995), 14ff.

42. Jonathan Israel, *The Dutch Republic: Its Rise, Greatness, and Fall, 1477–1806*, in *Oxford History of Early Modern Europe*, ed. R. J. W. Evans (Oxford, UK: Clarendon Press, 1995), 1115.

43. Israel, *Dutch Republic*, 1125.

44. Owen Chadwick, *The Secularization of the European Mind in the Nineteenth Century: The Gifford Lectures in the University of Edinburgh for 1973–4* (Cambridge, UK, and New York: Cambridge University Press, 1975), 111.

45. Chadwick, *Secularization of the European Mind*, 111–112.

46. Philip Hamburger, *Separation of Church and State* (Cambridge, MA: Harvard University Press, 2002); John T. McGreevy, *Catholicism and American Freedom: A History* (New York: W. W. Norton, 2003).

47. Burleigh, *Earthly Powers*, 315.

48. Theodore Zeldin, *France, 1848–1945: Politics and Anger* (Oxford, UK: Oxford University Press, 1984). See our discussion of current challenges to French secularism in Chapter Eight, "Ten Rules for Surviving God's Century."

49. Chadwick, *Secularization of the European Mind*, 66.

50. O'Brien, *Ancestral Voices*, 16.

51. Martin Wight, *Four Seminal Thinkers in International Theory: Machiavelli, Grotius, Kant, and Mazzini* (Oxford, UK: Oxford University Press, 2005), 89–115.

52. Quoted in Wight, *Four Seminal Thinkers*, 101.

53. Hans Kohn, *Prophets and Peoples: Studies in Nineteenth Century Nationalism* (New York: Collier, 1961), 46–75.

54. Ernest Renan, "What Is a Nation?" (Qu'est-ce qu'une nation?), lecture delivered at the Sorbonne, March 11, 1882.

55. Friedrich Nietzsche, *The Gay Science*, ed. Bernard Williams (Cambridge, UK: Cambridge University Press, 2001), 119–120.

56. Stathis Kalyvas, *The Rise of Christian Democracy in Europe* (Ithaca, NY: Cornell University Press, 1996).

57. Anthony Gill, *The Political Origins of Religious Liberty*, Cambridge Studies in Social Theory, Religion, and Politics (Cambridge, UK, and New York: Cambridge University Press, 2008), 168.

58. Donald Eugene Smith, *Religion and Political Development, an Analytic Study*, (Boston, MA: Little, Brown, 1970), 122–123.

59. M. Searle Bates, *Religious Liberty: An Inquiry* (New York and London: Harper & Bros., 1945), 1.

60. See, for example, Jawaharlal Nehru, *The Discovery of India* (Calcutta: Signet Press, 1946).

61. Jean Lacouture, *The Demigods: Charismatic Leadership in the Third World*, 1st American ed. (New York: Knopf, 1970), 179.

62. On Nehru's antipathy to religion, see, for example, Shashi Tharoor, *Nehru: The Invention of India* (New York: Arcade Publishing, 2003).

63. Reinhold Niebuhr, *Christian Realism and Political Problems* (New York: Scribner, 1953); Reinhold Niebuhr, *The Irony of American History* (New York: Scribner, 1952). On the secularism of leading realist Hans Morgenthau, see Christoph Frei, *Hans J. Morgenthau: An Intellectual Biography* (Baton Rouge: Louisiana State University Press, 2001).

64. Samuel P. Huntington, *Political Order in Changing Societies* (New Haven, CT: Yale University Press, 1968).

65. See, for example, Daniel Lerner, *The Passing of Traditional Society: Modernizing the Middle East* (Glencoe, IL: Free Press, 1958), and Gabriel Abraham Almond and Sidney Verba, *The Civic Culture: Political Attitudes and Democracy in Five Nations* (Princeton, NJ: Princeton University Press, 1963).

66. Michael E. Latham, *Modernization as Ideology: American Social Science and "Nation Building" in the Kennedy Era* (Chapel Hill: University of North Carolina Press, 2000).

67. Lacouture, *Demigods*, 40.

68. Richard P. Mitchell, *The Society of the Muslim Brothers* (New York: Oxford University Press, 1993), xxiii–xxiv.

69. Quoted in "A Bleak Outlook Is Seen for Religion," *New York Times*, February 25, 1968, 3.

70. Thomas Blom Hansen, *The Saffron Wave: Democracy and Hindu Nationalism in Modern India* (Princeton, NJ: Princeton University Press, 1999); Christophe Jaffrelot, *The Hindu Nationalist Movement in India* (New York: Columbia University Press, 1996).

71. Kwesi A. Dickson, "The Church and the Quest for Democracy in Ghana," in *The Christian Churches and the Democratisation of Africa*, ed. Paul Gifford (Leiden, Netherlands: E. J. Brill, 1995), 261–275.

72. Noor Ahmad Baba, *Organisation of Islamic Conference: Theory and Practice of Pan-Islamic Cooperation* (Dhaka, Bangladesh: University Press Limited, 1994), 52–70.

73. Daniel Philpott, "The Catholic Wave," *Journal of Democracy* 15 (2004), 32–46. On the importance of the pope's leadership during the last phase of the Cold War, see John Lewis Gaddis, *The Cold War: A New History* (New York: Penguin Press, 2005).

74. Bruce Desmond Graham, *Hindu Nationalism and Indian Politics: The Origins and Development of the Bharatiya Jana Sangh*, Cambridge South Asian Studies 47 (Cambridge, UK, and New York: Cambridge University Press, 1990).

75. Mark Juergensmeyer, *The New Cold War?: Religious Nationalism Confronts the Secular State* (Berkeley: University of California Press, 1993).

76. Joel A. Carpenter, *Revive Us Again: The Reawakening of American Fundamentalism* (New York: Oxford University Press, 1997).

77. Walpola Rahula, *The Heritage of the Bhikkhu: A Short History of the Bhikkhu in Educational, Cultural, Social, and Political Life* (New York: Grove Press, distributed by Random House, 1974).

78. Ivan Vallier, "The Roman Catholic Church: A Transnational Actor," *International Organization* 25 (1971), 479–502.

79. Rodney Stark and Roger Finke, *Acts of Faith: Explaining the Human Side of Religion* (Berkeley: University of California Press, 2000); and Christian Smith and Michael Emerson, *American Evangelicalism: Embattled and Thriving* (Chicago, IL: University of Chicago Press, 1998).

80. Here we use the categories of Freedom House. See the next chapter (Four) for more detail and explanation. See also Piano Aili, Arch Puddington, and Mark Y. Rosenberg, *Freedom in the World 2006: The Annual Survey of Political Rights and Civil Liberties* (New York: Freedom House, 2006).

81. This is roughly the argument of Mohammed M. Hafez, *Why Muslims Rebel: Repression and Resistance in the Islamic World* (Boulder, CO: Lynne Rienner Publishers, 2003).

82. Peter Singer, *One World: The Ethics of Globalization* (New Haven, CT: Yale University Press, 2002). The strengths and limits of this view are explored in Benjamin R. Barber, *Jihad vs. McWorld* (New York: Ballantine, 1996).

83. Allen D. Hertzke, *Freeing God's Children: The Unlikely Alliance for Global Human Rights* (Lanham, MD: Rowman & Littlefield, 2004).

84. Hassan M. Fattah, "At Mecca Meeting, Cartoon Outrage Crystallized," *New York Times*, February 9, 2006.

85. Christian Democratic parties predate World War II but rose sharply in size and influence after the war.

86. Christian Smith, *The Secular Revolution: Power, Interests, and Conflict in the Secularization of American Public Life* (Berkeley: University of California Press, 2003).

Chapter Four
RELIGION AND GLOBAL DEMOCRATIZATION

1. Michael Slackman, "Memo from Riyadh: Influence of Egypt and Saudi Arabia Fades," *New York Times*, November 11, 2009, A8.

2. Fareed Zakaria, *The Future of Freedom: Illiberal Democracy at Home and Abroad* (New York: W. W. Norton, 2003).

3. Alfred Stepan, *Arguing Comparative Politics* (Oxford, UK: Oxford University Press, 2001), 216.

4. Freedom House ranks every country in the world along a scale of 1, being the freest, to 7, being the least free. Countries that have a ranking of 1 and 2 are considered "Free"; those with 3, 4, and 5, "Partly Free"; and those with 6 and 7, "Not Free." The data are available online at www.freedomhouse.org (accessed May 2010).

5. Charles Kurzman and Ijlal Naqvi, "Islamic Political Parties and Parliamentary Elections," United States Institute of Peace Working Paper (Grant SG-055-06S), January 15, 2009 (revised March 17, 2009); available at http://ducis.jhfc.duke.edu/wp-content/uploads/2009/03/kurzman_20080326.pdf; (accessed May 2010). In their analysis, "more democratic" is based on data from the Polity project, which generates an estimate of democracy for each country that ranges from –10 (least democratic) to +10 (most democratic). Countries with Polity scores of 6–10 are counted as "more democratic"; all countries with lower scores are "less democratic." Kurzman and Naqvi point out, however, that their analysis holds even when Freedom House data are used. Islamic parties participated in 42 percent of elections in Free or Partly Free countries, but only in 18 percent of elections in Not Free countries.

6. Gilles Kepel, *Jihad: The Trail of Political Islam* (Cambridge, MA: Harvard University Press, 2002), 65.

7. Gabriel A. Almond, R. Scott Appleby, and Emmanuel Sivan, *Strong Religion: The Rise of Fundamentalisms Around the World* (Chicago, IL: University of Chicago Press, 2003).

8. Martin Kramer, "The Mismeasure of Political Islam," in *The Islamism Debate,* ed. Martin Kramer (Tel Aviv: Moshe Dayan Center for Middle Eastern and African Studies, 1997), 168.

9. Sudarsan Raghavan, "Egyptian Reform Activists Say U.S. Commitment Is Waning," *Washington Post*, Washington Post Foreign Service, October 9, 2009.

10. This analysis includes only those states with populations greater than 1 million: 32 countries are excluded as a result.

11. M. Steven Fish, "Islam and Authoritarianism," *World Politics* 55, no. 1 (2002), 4–37; Daniela Donno and Bruce M. Russett, "Islam, Authoritarianism, and Female Empowerment: What Are the Linkages?" *World Politics* 56, no. 4 (2004), 582–607.

12. Such cases are consistent with the arguments and evidence in Alfred Stepan and Graeme B. Robertson, "Arab, Not Muslim, Exceptionalism," *Journal of Democracy* 15, no. 4 (2004), 140–146.

13. These countries, along with the net improvement in their combined Freedom House scores, are Albania (+8), Bangladesh (+5), Bosnia-Herzegovina (+5), Burkina Faso (+4), Guinea-

Bissau (+4), Indonesia (+5), Iraq (+3), Kosovo (+5), Kuwait (+3), Kyrgyzstan (+3), Mali (+8), Niger (+3), Nigeria (+3), Pakistan (+3), Senegal (+6), Sierra Leone (+3), and Turkey (+4).

14. Our determination of whether a particular country witnessed any of these forms of pro-democratic religious activism depended on documentation by reliable, third-party observers—such as scholars and other analysts—and never on the claims of religious actors alone. Our assessment is thus limited by the availability of such documentation in a form and language accessible to us. It is entirely possible, if not probable, that some prodemocratic religious activism in some countries—particularly countries in which fieldwork is more difficult or scholarly interest is limited—does not appear on our radar simply because it was undocumented, documented in a form or language inaccessible to us, or we failed to find the relevant and available documentation. One implication of this is that, in all likelihood, *we understate rather than overstate the role of religious actors in global democratization* between 1972 and 2009.

15. Rajiv Chandrasekaran, "How Cleric Trumped U.S. Plan for Iraq: Ayatollah's Call for Vote Forced Occupation Leader to Rewrite Transition Strategy," *Washington Post*, November 26, 2003, A01; and Dawisha Adeed, "The New Iraq: Democratic Institutions and Performance," *Journal of Democracy* 16, no. 3 (July 2005), 37.

16. Christophe Jaffrelot, *The Hindu Nationalist Movement in India* (New York: Columbia University Press, 1996).

17. If we consider that Catholics are roughly one-quarter of the world's population.

18. Lawrence E. Harrison, *The Central Liberal Truth: How Politics Can Change a Culture and Save It from Itself* (Oxford, UK: Oxford University Press, 2006).

19. André Laliberté, "Religious Change and Democratization in Postwar Taiwan: Mainstream Buddhist Organizations and the Kuomintang, 1947–1996," in *Religion in Modern Taiwan: Tradition and Innovation in a Changing Society*, ed. Philip Clart and Charles B. Jones (Honolulu: University of Hawai'i Press, 2003).

20. Rev. Dr. Joshua Young-gi Hong, "Evangelicals and the Democratization of South Korea Since 1987," in *Evangelical Christianity and Democracy in Asia*, ed. David H. Lumsdaine (New York: Oxford University Press, 2009), 185–233; Wi Jo Kang, *Christ and Caesar in Modern Korea: A History of Christianity and Politics* (Albany: State University of New York Press, 1997).

21. Richard Madsen, *Democracy's Dharma: Religious Renaissance and Political Development in Taiwan* (Berkeley: University of California Press, 2007).

22. Samuel P. Huntington, *The Third Wave: Democratization in the Late Twentieth Century* (Norman: University of Oklahoma Press, 1991), 76.

23. Also among these are the Malawian Presbyterian Church, the Mozambican Anglican Church, the Ghanaian Presbyterian Church, Protestant churches in Zambia, the National Council of Churches in South Korea, and evangelical churches in Peru and Nicaragua.

24. These also include Protestant churches in Uganda, Cameroon, and Liberia.

25. "Global Restrictions on Religion," Pew Forum on Religion & Public Life, December 2009, 3.

26. Fish, "Islam and Authoritarianism."

27. See Stepan and Robertson, "Arab, Not Muslim, Exceptionalism," 32.

28. Adrian Karatnycky, "Muslim Countries and the Democracy Gap," *Journal of Democracy* 13, no. 1 (January 2002), 101–104.

29. Vali Nasr, "Rise of 'Muslim Democracy,'" *Journal of Democracy* 16, no. 2 (2005), 14. Open electoral competitions, he documents, have occurred in Bangladesh in 1991, 1996, and 2001; in Indonesia in 1999 and 2004; in Malaysia in 1995, 1999, and 2004; in Pakistan in 1990, 1993, and 1997; and in Turkey in 1995, 1999, and 2002.

30. Jonathan Fox, "World Separation of Religion and State into the 21st Century," *Comparative Political Studies* 39 (2006), 537–569.

Chapter Five
THE "GLOCAL" DIMENSIONS OF RELIGIOUS TERRORISM

1. Ben Fox, "9/11 Defendants: 'We Are Terrorists to the Bone,'" Associated Press Online, March 10, 2009, http://articles.sfgate.com/2009-03-11/news/17211835_1_guantanamo-military-judge-attacks (accessed May 2010).

2. Jess Bravin, "9/11 Defendants Respond to U.S. Government Charges," *Wall Street Journal*, March 11, 2009, A6.

3. Fox, "9/11 Defendants: 'We Are Terrorists to the Bone.'"

4. Robert O. Keohane, "The Globalization of Informal Violence, Theories of World Politics, and 'The Liberalism of Fear'" (Brooklyn, NY, Social Science Research Council), available online at http://www.ssrc.org/sept11/essays/keohane2.htm (accessed April 2010); see "A Nation Challenged; Bin Laden's Statement: 'The Sword Fell,'" *New York Times*, October 8, 2001, B7.

5. Robert Doran, "Apocalyptic Thinking after 9/11: An Interview with René Girard," *Substance: A Review of Theory and Literary Criticism* 37, issue 1 (2008), 20–32, 20–21.

6. Frank J. Buijs, "Muslims in the Netherlands: Social and Political Developments after 9/11," *Journal of Ethnic and Migration Studies* 35, no. 3 (March 2009), 421–438, 422.

7. "Dutch Court Sentences Van Gogh Killer to Life," *New York Times*, July 26, 2005.

8. Anthony Deutsch, "Prosecutors to Charge Van Gogh Killer as Member of Radical Islamic Network," Associated Press, July 28, 2005.

9. See, for example, Bruce Hoffman, "'Holy Terror': The Implications of Terrorism Motivated by a Religious Imperative," *Studies in Conflict and Terrorism* 18, no. 4 (October–December 1995), 271–284, 279–280.

10. Assaf Moghadam, *The Globalization of Martyrdom: Al Qaeda, Salafi Jihad, and the Diffusion of Suicide Attacks* (Baltimore, MD: Johns Hopkins University Press, 2008), 50–54. These numbers include only those suicide attacks in which the perpetrator was identified.

11. Keohane, "The Globalization of Informal Violence."

12. Robert D. Kaplan, "India's New Face," *The Atlantic* 303, no. 3 (April 2009), 74–81, 74.

13. Kaplan, "India's New Face," 74.

14. Kaplan, "India's New Face," 76.

15. For Hoffman, religious terrorism has to be based in sacred text. Because we feel the need to capture secessionist-independence and ethno-religious minority movements in which religion plays a role but is not the core factor over which the parties are fighting, we are more expansive. Hoffman, "'Holy Terror,'" 272.

16. Bruce Hoffman, *Inside Terrorism* (New York: Columbia University Press, 1998), 13–44.

17. "Global Terrorism Database 1" (GTD1). Available online at http://www.start.umd.edu/start/data/gtd/gtd1_and_gtd2.asp.

18. Bruce Hoffman, *Inside Terrorism*, revised ed. (New York: Columbia University Press, 2006), 2.

19. The best literature on religious, communal, and ethnic violence demonstrates this point. See, for example, Donald L. Horowitz, *The Deadly Ethnic Riot* (Berkeley: University of California Press, 2001); Horowitz, *Ethnic Groups in Conflict*, 2nd ed. (Berkeley: University of California

Press, 2000); Horowitz, "Patterns of Ethnic Separatism," *Comparative Studies in Society and History* 23, no. 2 (April 1981), 165–195; Horowitz, "Direct, Displaced, and Cumulative Ethnic Aggression," *Comparative Politics* 6, no. 1 (October 1973), 1–16; Ashutosh Varshney, "Analyzing Collective Violence in Indonesia: An Overview," *Journal of East Asian Studies* 8, issue 3 (September–December 2008), 341–359; Ashutosh Varshney, Mohammad Zulfan Tadjoeddin, and Rizal Panggabean, "Creating Datasets in Information-Poor Environments: Patterns of Collective Violence in Indonesia, 1990–2003," *Journal of East Asian Studies* 8, issue 3 (September–December 2008), 361–394; Varshney, *Ethnic Conflict and Civic Life: Hindus and Muslims in India*, 2nd ed. (New Haven, CT: Yale University Press, 2003); Steven I. Wilkinson, ed., *Religious Politics and Communal Violence* (New York: Oxford University Press, 2005); Wilkinson, *Votes and Violence: Electoral Competition and Ethnic Riots in India* (New York: Cambridge University Press, 2004); and Wilkinson, "India, Consociational Theory, and Ethnic Violence," *Asian Survey* 40, no. 5, "Modernizing Tradition in India" (September–October 2000), 767–791.

20. Dan Isaacs, "What Is Behind Hindu-Christian Violence," BBC News, January 29, 2008, available online at http://news.bbc.co.uk/2/hi/south_asia/7214053.stm (accessed May 2010).

21. Nigeria is split between a 40 percent Christian population and a 50 percent Muslim population but also contains 250 distinct ethnic groups. As a result of ethnic and tribal ties, as well as intrareligious sects and denominations, neither Christianity nor Islam constitutes a clear source of identity on its own.

22. In September 2001, Muslim prayers in the city of Jos provided the impetus for Muslim-Christian fighting that killed 915. Following the appearance of the Danish cartoons depicting the Prophet Mohammed, a February 2006 Muslim protest sparked a wave of revenge attacks that led to both Christian and Muslim rioting throughout the country. In that instance, 157 lost their lives. In the November 2008 incident in Jos, a dispute over the outcome over a local election eventually caused 400 deaths. Facts and figures provided by "Timeline: Ethnic and Religious Unrest in Nigeria," Reuters, February 21, 2009, available online at http://www.alertnet.org/thenews/newsdesk/LU41351.htm (accessed May 2010).

23. Varshney, "Analyzing Collective Violence in Indonesia," 345.

24. Formed around 1993, the organization's original aim was to create an Islamic state in Indonesia. With ties to Al Qaeda, Jemaah Islamiyah has been blamed for carrying out the October 2002 bombings in the city of Bali that killed more than 200 people.

25. Varshney, "Analyzing Collective Violence in Indonesia," 344. These four provinces were West Java, Bali, Bengkulu, and South Kalimantan. Research conducted by Bridget Welsh.

26. Mia Bloom, *Dying to Kill: The Allure of Suicide Terror* (New York: Columbia University Press, 2005), 4; Hoffman, " 'Holy Terror,' " 272; and David C. Rapoport, "Fear and Trembling: Terrorism in Three Religious Traditions," *American Political Science Review* 78, no. 3 (September 1984), 658–677, 659.

27. Hoffman, *Inside Terrorism*, 85.

28. According to data from the National Consortium for the Study of Terrorism and Responses to Terrorism (START), many episodes of terrorism cannot be attributed to a party or cause. See, for example, the chart "Terrorist Incidents by Perpetrator Type, 1998–2004" in "Global Terrorism Database," National Consortium for the Study of Terrorism and Responses to Terrorism (START), University of Maryland and U.S. Department of Homeland Security, available online at http://www.start.umd.edu/data/gtd/ (accessed May 2010).

29. For a discussion of the varied causes of terrorism, see generally Philip Keefer and Norman

Loayza, eds., *Terrorism, Economic Development, and Political Openness* (New York: Cambridge University Press, 2008).

30. Hoffman, *Inside Terrorism*, 85. See also the "Global Terrorism Database," National Consortium for the Study of Terrorism and Responses to Terrorism (START), University of Maryland and U.S. Department of Homeland Security, available online at http://www.start.umd.edu/data/gtd/ (accessed May 2010).

31. Hoffman, *Inside Terrorism*, 85.

32. Our examination of the data supplied in the Global Terrorism Database 2 (GTD2) indicates that Islamic ideology was a factor in 98.08 percent (or 972 of 991) of terrorist incidents carried out by perpetrators classified as religious from 1998 to 2004. See "Global Terrorism Database."

33. See Figures 1–4 in Assaf Moghadam, "Motives for Martyrdom: Al-Qaida, Salafi Jihad, and the Spread of Suicide Attacks," *International Security* 33, no. 3 (Winter 2008–2009), 46–78.

34. Cristoph Reuter, *My Life Is a Weapon: A Modern History of Suicide Bombing*, trans. Helena Ragg-Kirkby (Princeton, NJ: Princeton University Press, 2004), 32.

35. Moghadam, "Motives for Martyrdom," 46–78, 48–49; Assaf Moghadam, "Suicide Terrorism, Occupation, and the Globalization of Martyrdom: A Critique of Dying to Win," *Studies in Conflict and Terrorism* 29, no. 8 (May 2006), 707–729.

36. According to Moghadam's data, "Salafi-jihadist groups were the most dominant perpetrators of suicide missions in Iraq in the five years since the U.S.-led invasion." See Moghadam, "Motives for Martyrdom," 47, 56. See also Mohammed M. Hafez, *Suicide Bombers in Iraq: The Strategy and Ideology of Martyrdom* (Washington, DC: United States Institute of Peace Press, 2007).

37. Hoffman, "'Holy Terror,'" 277.

38. Jessica Stern, *Terror in the Name of God: Why Religious Militants Kill* (New York: Harper-Collins, 2003), 6–7.

39. Hoffman, *Inside Terrorism*, 107–108.

40. Hoffman, *Inside Terrorism*, 111–112.

41. Stern, *Terror in the Name of God*, 9–10.

42. http://www.egm.gov.tr/temuh/terorgrup1.html (accessed May 1, 2010). The other organizations are either dedicated to establishing a separate state for the Kurdish people (e.g., the PKK) and/or a state based in principles of Marxist or Communist ideology.

43. Emrullah Uslu, "From Local Hizbollah to Global Terror: Militant Islam in Turkey," *Middle East Policy* 14, no. 1 (Spring 2007), 124–141, and Süleyman Özören, "Turkish Hizballah (Hizbullah): A Case Study of Radical Terrorism," *Journal of Turkish Weekly*, April 2007 (accessed online March 1, 2010). The group has officially renamed itself Kongra-Gel, although it is still commonly referred to as the PKK.

44. "An Islamist Facing Islamic Terrorism," *The Economist* 369, issue 8352 (November 29, 2003), 46.

45. Claire Berlinski, "In Turkey, a Looming Battle over Islam," *Washington Post,* May 6, 2007, B01.

46. Alexey Malashenko, *Islam for Russia (Ислам Для России)* (Moscow: Carnegie Center, 2007), 8, 16, available at http://carnegieendowment.org/files/pub-35912.pdf (accessed July 2010); and Paul Goble, "Unwritten Russia Directive Blocking Construction of New Mosques," *Eurasia Review*, July 24, 2010, available at http://www.eurasiareview.com/201007245772/unwritten-russia-directive-blocking-construction-of-new-mosques.html (accessed August 2010).

47. Steven Lee Myers, "Growth of Islam in Russia Brings Soviet Response," *New York Times*, November 22, 2005, available at http://www.nytimes.com/2005/11/22/international/europe/22russia.html (accessed May 2010).

48. Myers, "Growth of Islam."

49. Myers, "Growth of Islam."

50. For a more detailed discussion of such sectarian violence, see "Pakistan's Shiite-Sunni Divide," BBC News, June 1, 2004, available online at http://news.bbc.co.uk/2/hi/south_asia/3045122.stm (accessed August 2010).

51. For more on Islam and politics in Pakistan, see C. Christine Fair and Karthik Vaidyanathan, "The Practice of Islam in Pakistan and the Influence of Islam on Pakistani Politics," in *Prospects for Peace in South Asia,* ed. Rafiq Dossani and Henry S. Rowen (Stanford, CA: Stanford University Press, 2005), 75–108.

52. Detailed accounts of these groups' backgrounds can be found in the "Terrorist Organization Profile" portion of START's Web site at http://www.start.umd.edu/start/data_collections/tops/ (accessed February and March 2009).

53. Fair and Vaidyanathan, "The Practice of Islam in Pakistan," 97.

54. Justin Vaïsse, "Veiled Meaning: The French Law Banning Religious Symbols in Public Schools," Brookings Institution, U.S.-France Analysis Series (March 2004), 2, available online at http://www.brookings.edu/articles/2004/03france_vaisse.aspx (accessed May 2010).

55. Jocelyne Cesari, "Young, Muslim, and French—Islam and French Secularism: The Roots of the Conflict," *Wide Angle*, PBS, August 26, 2004, available online at http://www.pbs.org/wnet/wideangle/episodes/young-muslim-and-french/islam-and-french-secularism-the-roots-of-the-conflict/2524/ (accessed May 2010).

56. Vaïsse, "Veiled Meaning," 5. For a detailed discussion of the French law banning such religious symbols, see Xiaorong Li, "What's in a Headscarf?" *Philosophy and Public Policy Quarterly* 24, no. 1/2 (Winter–Spring 2003), 14–17.

57. David Hirschman, "Is France's Burqa Ban Racist?" *Big Think*, July 14, 2010, available online at http://bigthink.com/ideas/20914 (accessed August 4, 2010).

58. See, for example, Ruth Gledhill and Philip Webster, "Archbishop of Canterbury Argues for Islamic Law in Britain," *The Times* (UK), February 8, 2008, available online at http://www.timesonline.co.uk/tol/comment/faith/article3328024.ece (accessed May 2010).

59. We include the case of Northern Ireland in this discussion of terrorism because, despite the damage caused by the conflict, it did not pass the threshold of a civil war. For more on what constitutes a civil war, see Monica Duffy Toft, "Getting Religion? The Puzzling Case of Islam and Civil War," *International Security* 31, no. 4 (Spring 2007), 97–131.

60. "Terrorist Organization Profile: Irish Republican Army (IRA)," START, available online at http://www.start.umd.edu/start/data/tops/terrorist_organization_profile.asp?id=55 (accessed May 2010). See also Mary Jordan and Kevin Sullivan, "Protestants Doubt IRA Disarmament," *Washington Post*, September 27, 2005, A17. For more on past and present efforts to deal with terrorism in Northern Ireland, see James Dingley, ed., *Combating Terrorism in Northern Ireland* (New York: Routledge, 2009).

61. James J. F. Forest, "Conclusion," in *Combating Terrorism in Northern Ireland*, ed. Dingley, 280–301, 294. On January 30, 1972, members of the British Army shot 27 protesters during the Northern Ireland Civil Rights Association march. Thirteen died immediately and one man died later from his injuries. Accounts of what happened are disputed, but it has been widely reported that the soldiers fired into an unarmed group.

62. Dan Balz, "A LOOK AT…Irish Hopes; Now the Hard Part: Building a Peace to Last," *Washington Post*, May 31, 1998, C03.

63. After the killing of two soldiers and a policeman in separate attacks in March 2009, thousands of citizens from the Protestant and Catholic communities in Northern Ireland united to demonstrate against the violence. See Henry McDonald, Esther Addley, and Haroon Siddique, "Peace Protests Across Northern Ireland," *The Guardian*, March 11, 2009, available at http://www.guardian.co.uk/uk/2009/mar/11/northern-ireland-peace-protests (accessed May 2010).

64. Robert L. Hardgrave, Jr., "Hindu Nationalism and the BJP: Transforming Religion and Politics in India," in *Prospects for Peace in South Asia*, ed. Dossani and Rowen, 185–214.

65. For a discussion of Sikh nationalism, see Catarina Kinnvall, *Globalization and Religious Nationalism in India: The Search for Ontological Security* (New York: Routledge, 2006). And for more on the past role of Sikh terrorism, see Mark Juergensmeyer, *The New Cold War?: Religious Nationalism Confronts the Secular State* (Berkeley: University of California Press, 1993), 90–99.

66. John Zubrzycki, "Hindu Nationalists Rule India—But How Long?" *Christian Science Monitor*, May 17, 1996, 6.

67. Ravi Nessman, "Sri Lanka War Near End, but Ethnic Tension Remains," Associated Press, February 5, 2009.

68. Michael Roberts, "Tamil Tiger 'Martyrs': Regenerating Divine Potency?" *Studies in Conflict and Terrorism* 28, no. 6 (2005), 493–514.

69. For details on the constitutional debate, see W. A. Wiswa Warnapala, "The New Constitution of Sri Lanka," *Asian Survey* 13, no. 12 (December 1973), 1179–1192, 1190–1191.

70. See also Emad Shahin, *Political Ascent: Contemporary Islamic Movements in North Africa* (Boulder, CO: Westview Press, 1998).

71. R. Hrair Dekmejian, "The Rise of Political Islamism in Saudi Arabia," *Middle East Journal* 48, no. 4 (Autumn 1994), 627–643.

72. For the following brief summation of the development of modern Islamism in Saudi Arabia, we are particularly indebted to the detailed account that Thomas Hegghammer and Stéphane Lacroix give of this history and the 1979 siege at the Grand Mosque in Mecca. See Hegghammer and Lacroix, "Rejectionist Islamism in Saudi Arabia: The Story of Juhayman al-'Utaybi Revisited," *International Journal of Middle East Studies* 39, no. 1 (2007), 103–122.

73. This represents one intellectual strand of Islamism in Saudi Arabia: "rejectionist Islamism."

74. Hegghammer and Lacroix, "Rejectionist Islamism in Saudi Arabia," 112.

75. Yaroslav Trofimov, *The Siege of Mecca: The Forgotten Uprising in Islam's Holiest Shrine and the Birth of Al Qaeda* (New York: Doubleday, 2007).

76. Trofimov makes this argument. See, generally, his *Siege of Mecca*. For more, see Dekmejian, "The Rise of Political Islamism in Saudi Arabia," 628, and Joseph A. Kechichian, "Islamic Revivalism and Change in Saudi Arabia," *Muslim World* 80, no. 1 (January 1990), 1–16, 9–12.

77. Hegghammer and Lacroix, "Rejectionist Islamism in Saudi Arabia," 113.

78. Seth G. Jones and Martin C. Libicki, *How Terrorist Groups End: Lessons for Countering al Qa'ida* (Pittsburgh: RAND Corporation, 2008), 36.

79. Jones and Libicki, *How Terrorist Groups End*, xiv.

80. Jones and Libicki, *How Terrorist Groups End*, 19.

81. Jones and Libicki, *How Terrorist Groups End*, 35.

82. Jones and Libicki, *How Terrorist Groups End*, 36–37.

83. Stern, *Terror in the Name of God*, 283.

84. Thomas Hegghammer, "Introduction: Abdallah Azzam, Imam of Jihad," in *Al Qaeda in Its*

Own Words, ed. Gilles Kepel and Jean-Pierre Milelli (Cambridge, MA: Belknap Press of Harvard University Press, 2008), 81–101, 101.

85. Hegghammer, "Introduction: Abdallah Azzam, Imam of Jihad," 92, 101.

86. Hegghammer, "Introduction: Abdallah Azzam, Imam of Jihad," 97.

Chapter Six
Religious Civil Wars: Nasty, Brutish, and Long

1. Data on terrorism in Afghanistan comes from START's second Global Terrorism Database, or GTD2 (College Park, MD: National Consortium for the Study of Terrorism and Responses to Terrorism, updated March 2009), available online at http://www.start.umd.edu/start/data/gtd/ (accessed May 2010).

2. These groups, all Islamic in ideology, were the Taliban, Jahesh-ol-Muslimeen, Hezb-e-Islami, Al Qaeda, and Saif-ul-Muslimeen.

3. *Country Reports on Terrorism 2007* (Washington, DC: United States Department of State, April 2008), 132.

4. Office of the Director of National Intelligence, *2008 Report on Terrorism* (Washington, DC: National Counterterrorism Center, April 30, 2009), 10.

5. Hamid Karzai, Statement at the 62nd U.N. General Assembly, New York, September 25, 2007, cited in *Country Reports on Terrorism 2007*, 131.

6. David Kilcullen, *The Accidental Guerrilla: Fighting Small Wars in the Midst of a Big One* (Oxford, UK, and New York: Oxford University Press, 2009).

7. Nasreen Ghufran, "The Taliban and the Civil War Entanglement in Afghanistan," *Asian Survey* 41, no. 3 (May–June 2001), 465.

8. Zalmay Khalilzad, "Afghanistan in 1994: Civil War and Disintegration," *Asian Survey* 35, no. 2, "A Survey of Asia in 1994: Part II" (February 1995), 147.

9. Rasul Bakhsh Rais, "Conflict in Afghanistan: Ethnicity, Religion, and Neighbours," *Ethnic Studies Report* 17, no. 1 (January 1999), 1–12, 6.

10. Rais, "Conflict in Afghanistan," 7.

11. Ghufran, "The Taliban and the Civil War Entanglement in Afghanistan," 464.

12. Amy Waldman, "No TV, No Chess, No Kites: Taliban's Code, from A to Z," *New York Times,* November 11, 2001, A1, B5.

13. James Dobbins, "Ending Afghanistan's Civil War," testimony presented before the House Armed Services Committee on January 30, 2007 (Pittsburgh: RAND Corporation, 2007), 1.

14. Monica Duffy Toft, "Getting Religion? The Puzzling Case of Islam and Civil War," *International Security* 31, no. 4 (Spring 2007), 98.

15. Toft, "Getting Religion?" 116.

16. See data presented in Monica Duffy Toft, "Religion, Civil War, and International Order," BCSIA Discussion Paper, Discussion Paper 2006-03 (Cambridge, MA: Belfer Center for Science and International Affairs, July 2006), 9. Jonathan Fox also confirms the increasing influence of religion in conflict for the period 1945–2001. See Fox, "The Rise of Religious Nationalism and Conflict: Ethnic Conflict and Revolutionary Wars, 1945–2001," *Journal of Peace Research* 41, no. 6 (November 2004), 715–731.

17. Toft, "Getting Religion?" 113.

18. See, for example: Mark Mazzetti, "A Shifting Enemy: U.S. Generals Say Civil War, Not Insurgency, Is Greatest Threat," *New York Times,* November 17, 2006, A8; and Sheryl Gay Stolberg, "In Baltics, Bush Blames Qaeda for Iraq Violence and Declines to Call Situation Civil War," *New York Times,* November 28, 2006, A18.

19. Adapted from Monica Duffy Toft, "Population Shifts and Civil War: A Test of Power Transition Theory," *International Interactions* 33, no. 3 (2007), 253.

20. Monica Duffy Toft, *Securing the Peace: The Durable Settlement of Civil Wars* (Princeton, NJ: Princeton University Press, 2010), 120.

21. Steven R. David, "Saving America from the Coming Civil Wars," *Foreign Affairs* 78, no. 1 (January–February 1999), 111.

22. David, "Saving America from the Coming Civil Wars," 103–104.

23. Toft, "Religion, Civil War, and International Order," 9. Again, religion was "central" when combatants fought over whether a particular religion would be the source of governance for a state (or a region of that state). In contrast, religion was "peripheral" when combatants merely identified with a particular religion and grouped themselves by tradition.

24. Toft, "Religion, Civil War, and International Order," 9.

25. See Table 1 in Toft, "Getting Religion?" 114.

26. Toft, "Getting Religion?" 97.

27. See Table 5 in Toft, "Religion, Civil War, and International Order," 15.

28. Assaf Moghadam, "A Global Resurgence of Religion?" Working Paper Series, Weatherhead Center for International Affairs, no. 03-03 (Cambridge, MA: Weatherhead Center for International Affairs, Harvard University, 2003), 65.

29. Jack L. Snyder, *From Voting to Violence: Democratization and Nationalist Conflict* (New York: W. W. Norton, 2000).

30. Assaf Moghadam, "Motives for Martyrdom: Al-Qaeda, Salafi Jihad, and the Spread of Suicide Attacks," *International Security* 33, no. 3 (Winter 2008–2009), 54. See, generally, Moghadam, "The New Martyrs Go Global," *Boston Globe,* November 18, 2005, A19; Marc Sageman, *Leaderless Jihad: Terror Networks in the Twenty-First Century* (Philadelphia: University of Pennsylvania Press, 2008); and Gabriel Weimann, *Terrorism on the Internet: The New Arena, The New Challenges* (Washington, DC: United States Institute of Peace Press, 2006).

31. For more on these issues, see Toft, "Getting Religion?" 107–112.

32. Ivan Arreguín-Toft, *How the Weak Win Wars: A Theory of Asymmetric Conflict* (New York: Cambridge University Press, 2005).

33. On Islamic strategic thinkers' views on how to defeat the West, see Jarret M. Brachman and William F. McCants, "Stealing al-Qa'ida's Playbook," *Studies in Conflict and Terrorism* 29, no. 4 (June 2006), 309–321.

34. See Robert L. Hardgrave, Jr., "Hindu Nationalism and the BJP: Transforming Religion and Politics in India," in *Prospects for Peace in South Asia,* ed. Rafiq Dossani and Henry S. Rowen (Stanford, CA: Stanford University Press, 2005), 185–214.

35. Anurag Pandey, "Communalism and Separatism in India: An Analysis," *Journal of Asian and African Studies* 42, issue 6 (2007), 533–549, 545.

36. Chen Jian, "The Tibetan Rebellion of 1959 and China's Changing Relations with India and the Soviet Union," *Journal of Cold War Studies* 8, no. 3 (Summer 2006), 56.

37. Jian, "The Tibetan Rebellion of 1959," 61.

38. Jian, "The Tibetan Rebellion of 1959," 78.

39. Jian, "The Tibetan Rebellion of 1959," 75. For more on the suppression and destruction of religion in Tibet, see George N. Patterson, "The Situation in Tibet," *China Quarterly*, no. 6 (April–June 1961), 82.

40. Jian, "The Tibetan Rebellion of 1959," 57.

41. Jian, "The Tibetan Rebellion of 1959," 100.

42. Jian, "The Tibetan Rebellion of 1959," 80.

43. For a discussion on the dangers posed by the Tibetan conflict to neighboring states, see Patterson, "The Situation in Tibet," 86.

44. Phillip Carter, "There Are Four Iraq Wars: How Many of Them Can We Win?" Slate.com, February 9, 2007, at http://www.slate.com/?id=2159460 (accessed May 2010).

45. Francis M. Deng, "Sudan—Civil War and Genocide: Disappearing Christians of the Middle East," *Middle East Quarterly* 8, no. 1 (Winter 2001), 13.

46. See, for example, Randolph Martin, "Sudan's Perfect War," *Foreign Affairs* 81, no. 2 (March–April 2002), 120.

47. Lee Smith, "Sudan's Osama: The Islamist Roots of the Darfur Genocide," Slate.com, August 5, 2004, at http://www.slate.com/id/2104814/ (accessed May 2010).

48. For a fuller account of the lead-up to the First Chechen War, see Monica Duffy Toft, *The Geography of Ethnic Violence: Identity, Interests, and the Indivisibility of Territory* (Princeton, NJ: Princeton University Press, 2003), 70–79.

49. Boris Yeltsin, *Midnight Diaries*, trans. Catherine A. Fitzpatrick (New York: PublicAffairs, 2000), 58–59. Italics added.

50. Emil Souleimanov and Ondrej Ditrych, "The Internationalisation of the Russian-Chechen Conflict: Myths and Reality," *Europe-Asia Studies* 60, no. 7 (September 2008), 1201.

51. See also Marat Grebennikov, "Proliferation of Islamic Extremism in the Caucasus: New Challenges to Multilateral Security and Political Stability" (thesis for the Graduate School of International Studies, University of Denver, 2004), 39.

52. Souleimanov and Ditrych, "The Internationalisation of the Russian-Chechen Conflict," 1200.

53. Matthew Evangelista, *The Chechen Wars: Will Russia Go the Way of the Soviet Union?* (Washington, DC: Brookings Institution Press, 2002).

54. Evangelista, *The Chechen Wars*, 180.

55. "And they call it peace," *The Economist* 386, issue 8569 (March 1, 2008), 54.

56. Katrien Hertog, "A Self-Fulfilling Prophecy: The Seeds of Islamic Radicalisation in Chechnya," *Religion, State, and Society* 33, no. 3 (September 2005), 241.

57. Evangelista, *The Chechen Wars*, 72.

58. Hertog, "A Self-Fulfilling Prophecy," 241.

59. Toft, *The Geography of Ethnic Violence*, 68.

60. Evangelista, *The Chechen Wars*, 91.

61. Evangelista, *The Chechen Wars*, 71, 91.

62. "Russia's Dagestan: Conflict Causes," International Crisis Group, Europe Report no. 192, June 3, 2008, 1.

63. Monica Duffy Toft and Yuri Zhukov, "Religious Violence in the Caucasus: Global Jihad or Local Grievance?" Paper presented at the International Studies Association Conference, New Orleans, LA, February 2010.

64. Hertog, "A Self-Fulfilling Prophecy," 245.

65. Despite this moderation, religion was still a central factor in the Tajik civil war.

66. "Allah's Shadow," *The Economist* 368, issue 8334 (July 26, 2003), 4–6.

67. Mohammed M. Hafez, *Why Muslims Rebel: Repression and Resistance in the Islamic World* (Boulder, CO: Lynne Rienner Publishers, 2003), 202.

68. Mark Juergensmeyer, *Global Rebellion: Religious Challenges to the Secular State, from Christian Militias to Al Qaeda* (Berkeley: University of California Press, 2008), 99.

69. T. Jeremy Gunn makes this argument in his "Shaping an Islamic Identity: Religion, Islamism, and the State in Central Asia," *Sociology of Religion* 64, no. 3, special issue (Autumn 2003), 402–403, 399–400.

70. See, for example, Gunn, "Shaping an Islamic Identity."

71. Robert G. Kaiser, "Tajiks Upbeat About 'Most Backward' Republic," *Washington Post*, August 1, 2002, A20.

72. "Hopes for Peace Pact Gain in Tajikistan," *New York Times*, May 19, 1997, A4.

73. Hafez, *Why Muslims Rebel*, 203.

74. Fabio Oliva, "Between Contribution and Disengagement: Post-conflict Elections and the OSCE Role in the Normalization of Armed Groups and Militarized Political Parties in Bosnia and Herzegovina, Tajikistan, and Kosovo," *Helsinki Monitor: Security and Human Rights* 18, no. 3 (2007), 206.

75. Hafez, *Why Muslims Rebel*, 1.

76. For detailed discussions of the Algerian civil war, see, for example, Shireen Hunter, *The Algerian Crisis: Origins, Evolution, and Lessons for the Maghreb and Europe* (Brussels: Centre for European Policy Studies, 1996); and Andrew Pierre and William B. Quandt, *The Algerian Crisis: Policy Options for the West* (Washington, DC: Carnegie Endowment for International Peace, 1996).

77. Daniel Philpott, "Explaining the Political Ambivalence of Religion," *American Political Science Review* 101, no. 3 (August 2007), 519.

78. Judith Miller, "The Islamic Wave," *New York Times*, May 31, 1992, Section 6, 23.

79. "Terrorist Organization Profiles," National Consortium for the Study of Terrorism and Responses to Terrorism (START), University of Maryland and U.S. Department of Homeland Security, available online at http://www.start.umd.edu/start/data/tops/terrorist_organization_profile.asp?id=288 (accessed February and March 2009).

80. Caryle Murphy, "Algeria's Secular Army, Islamic Militants Battle for Power," *Washington Post*, January 25, 1994, A14.

81. Craig C. Smith, "Islam and Democracy: Algerians Try to Blaze a Trail," *New York Times*, April 14, 2004, A4.

82. For more on the connection between political suppression and the use of violence, see Mohammed M. Hafez, "From Marginalization to Massacres: A Political Process Explanation of GIA Violence in Algeria," in *Islamic Activism: A Social Movement Theory Approach*, ed. Quintan Wiktorowicz (Bloomington: Indiana University Press, 2004), 37–60.

83. Hafez, *Why Muslims Rebel*, 42.

84. See Hafez, *Why Muslims Rebel*, 78.

85. Roger Cohen, "State of Fear: A Special Report," *New York Times*, December 28, 1996, Section 1, 1.

86. Hafez, *Why Muslims Rebel*, 121. As Hafez notes, the Islamic Armed Group (Groupe Islamique Armé, GIA) was never willing to compromise with secular political forces.

87. Juergensmeyer, *Global Rebellion*, 80–81.

88. Craig Whitlock, "Algerian Program Offers Amnesty, but Not Answers About Past," *Washington Post*, September 17, 2006, A17.

89. Hafez, *Why Muslims Rebel*, 30.

90. "Reconciliation, up to a point," *The Economist* 380, issue 8493 (September 2, 2006).

91. Katrin Bennhold and Souad Mekhennet, "Familiar Threats Constrict Press Freedom in Algeria," *New York Times*, December 28, 2007, A8.

92. See, for example, Monica Duffy Toft, "Why Islam Lies at the Heart of Iraq's Civil War," *Christian Science Monitor* 100, issue 131 (June 2, 2008).

93. Thomas Friedman has noted this as well. See Friedman, "Ten Months or Ten Years," *New York Times*, November 29, 2006, A29.

94. Quoted in Carter, "There Are Four Iraq Wars."

95. See Office of Reconstruction and Humanitarian Assistance, "A Unified Mission Plan for Post Hostilities Iraq," draft, version 2, April 3, 2003. See also Toft, *Securing the Peace*, chap. 9, "Conclusion."

96. Mark Juergensmeyer suggests this argument. See Juergensmeyer, *Terror in the Mind of God: The Global Rise of Religious Violence* (Berkeley: University of California Press, 2003), 243–249.

97. Philip Jenkins, "Mystical Power," *Boston Globe*, January 25, 2009, available online at http://www.boston.com/bostonglobe/ideas/articles/2009/01/25/mystical_power/?s_campaign=8315 (accessed May 2010).

98. Jenkins, "Mystical Power."

99. Jenkins, "Mystical Power."

100. For more on Islam and democracy, see, for example, Abdulaziz Sachedina, *The Islamic Roots of Democratic Pluralism* (New York: Oxford University Press, 2001).

101. Angel Rabasa, Cheryl Benard, Lowell H. Schwartz, and Peter Sickle, *Building Moderate Muslim Networks* (Pittsburgh: RAND Corporation, 2007), 74.

102. Rabasa et al., *Building Moderate Muslim Networks*, 73.

Chapter Seven
MILITANTS FOR PEACE AND JUSTICE

1. Cameron Hume, *Ending Mozambique's War: The Role of Mediation and Good Offices* (Washington, DC: United States Institute of Peace Press, 1994), 3–4.

2. Hume, *Ending Mozambique's War*, 3–4, 15.

3. See Chester A. Crocker, "Foreword," in *Ending Mozambique's War*, by Cameron Hume, x–xi.

4. Andrew Mack, *Global Patterns of Political Violence* (New York: International Peace Academy, 2007), and Monica Duffy Toft, *Securing the Peace: The Durable Settlement of Civil Wars* (Princeton, NJ: Princeton University Press, 2010).

5. R. Scott Appleby, *The Ambivalence of the Sacred: Religion, Violence, and Reconciliation* (Lanham, MD: Rowman & Littlefield, 2000), 121.

6. Scott Thomas, *The Global Resurgence of Religion and the Transformation of International Relations: The Struggle for the Soul of the Twenty-First Century* (New York: Palgrave Macmillan, 2004), 161–166.

7. See Mary Ann Glendon, *A World Made New: Eleanor Roosevelt and the Universal Declaration of Human Rights* (New York: Random House, 2001).

8. Daniel Philpott and Timothy Samuel Shah, "Faith, Freedom, and Federation: The Role of Religious Ideas and Institutions in European Political Convergence," in *Religion in an Expanding Europe*, ed. Timothy A. Byrnes and Peter J. Katzenstein (Cambridge, UK: Cambridge University Press, 2006), 34–64; Brent F. Nelsen, James L. Guth, and Cleveland Fraser, "Does Religion Matter? Christianity and Public Support for the European Union," *European Union Politics* 2, no. 2 (2001), 191–217.

9. Anastasios Yannoulatos, *Facing the World: Orthodox Christian Essays on Global Concerns*, trans. Pavlos Gottfried (Crestwood, NY: St. Vladimir's Seminary Press, 2003); His All Holiness Ecumenical Patriarch Bartholomew, *Encountering the Mystery: Understanding Orthodox Christianity Today* (New York: Doubleday, 2008). We are also indebted to a personal communication from Elizabeth Prodromou, May 29, 2009.

10. Ian Harris, ed., *Buddhism and Politics in Twentieth-Century Asia* (London: Pinter Publishers, 1999); Christopher Queen, "Buddhism and World Order," unpublished report, Harvard Project on Religion and Global Politics, 2005; Donald K. Swearer, *The Buddhist World of Southeast Asia* (Albany: State University of New York Press, 1995).

11. See Tsjeard Bouta, S. Ayse Kadayifci-Orellana, and Mohammed Abu-Nimer, *Faith-Based Peace-Building: Mapping and Analysis of Christian, Muslim, and Multi-Faith Actors* (Washington, DC: Netherlands Institute of International Relations "Clingdael" in cooperation with Salam Institute for Peace and Justice, 2005).

12. "Underground Woman: Sakena Yacoobi and the Afghan Institute of Learning," in *Peacemakers in Action: Profiles of Religion in Conflict Resolution*, ed. David Little (Cambridge, UK: Cambridge University Press, 2007), 382–401.

13. See Rajmohan Gandhi, "Hinduism and Peacebuilding," in *Religion and Peacebuilding*, ed. Harold Coward and Gordon S. Smith (Albany: State University of New York Press, 2004), 45–68.

14. Appleby, *The Ambivalence of the Sacred*, 50–54.

15. "Warriors and Brothers: Imam Muhammad Ashafa and Pastor James Wuye," in *Peacemakers in Action*, ed. Little, 247–277.

16. For several collections of essays that describe peacemaking or peace-building activities that generally occur on the level of civil society, see Douglas Johnston, ed., *Faith-Based Diplomacy: Trumping Realpolitik* (Oxford, UK: Oxford University Press, 2003); Little, ed., *Peacemakers in Action*; Douglas Johnston and Cynthia Sampson, eds., *Religion: The Missing Dimension of Statecraft* (New York: Oxford University Press, 1994); and Coward and Smith, eds., *Religion and Peacebuilding*.

17. John Paul Lederach, "Five Qualities of Practice in Support of Reconciliation Processes," in *Forgiveness and Reconciliation: Religion, Public Policy, and Conflict Transformation*, ed. Raymond G. Helmick, S.J., and Rodney L. Petersen (Philadelphia: Templeton Foundation Press, 2001), 183–193.

18. Samuel P. Huntington, *The Third Wave: Democratization in the Late Twentieth Century* (Norman: University of Oklahoma Press, 1991), 73.

19. Toft, *Securing the Peace*, 7. Different figures, but ones yielding the same conclusion, come from Charles T. Call and Elizabeth M. Cousens: "The trend toward negotiated settlements after the Cold War also created entry points for international peacekeeping: between 1946 and 1990, twice as many conflicts ended through victory than through negotiations, whereas between 1995 and 2004, negotiated settlements were three times as likely to end war as outright victory," they write. They add in a footnote that "between 1994 and 2004, out of 48 wars ended, 36 con-

cluded with negotiation compared to victory." See Charles T. Call and Elizabeth M. Cousens, "Ending Wars and Building Peace: International Responses to War-Torn Societies," *International Studies Quarterly* 9 (2008), 5.

20. *A More Secure World: Our Shared Responsibility: Report of the Secretary-General's High-Level Panel on Threats, Challenges, and Change* (New York: United Nations, 2004), 33–34.

21. See Uppsala Conflict Data Program, available at http://www.pcr.uu.se/research/UCDP/data_and_publications/datasets.htm.

22. Sometimes locating exactly when a peace agreement took place is complex. For instance, the Peace Agreement Dataset shows that sixteen peace agreements took place in Guatemala between 1990 and 1996. Usually, what this indicates is a single complex peace process in which different dimensions of a conflict are settled through separate peace agreements. In other cases, a conflict might reignite and then become settled through a subsequent agreement or cease-fire. In Burundi, the 2000 Arusha Agreements were a fairly comprehensive settlement to a round of civil war that began in 1993 and took some 200,000 to 250,000 lives. But it did not settle the conflict among all factions, some eighteen of which were fighting against the government. It took a series of several subsequent agreements up through 2009 to bring remaining factions out of the field.

23. See "The St. Egidio Platform for a Peaceful Solution of the Algerian Crisis," available at http://www.santegidio.org/news/rassegna/00000/19980530_peaceworks2_EN.htm.

24. Lisa Lindsley, "The Beagle Channel Settlement: Vatican Mediation Resolves a Century-Old Dispute," *Journal of Church and State* 29 (1987), 435–455; Thomas Princen, "International Mediation—The View from the Vatican; Lessons from Mediating the Beagle Channel Dispute," *Negotiation Journal* 3, issue 4 (1987), 347–366.

25. Paul Jeffrey, *Recovering Memory: Guatemalan Churches and the Challenge of Peacemaking* (Uppsala, Sweden: Life & Peace Institute, 1998); Jeffrey Klaiber, *The Church, Dictatorship, and Democracy in Latin America* (Maryknoll, NY: Orbis Books, 1998), 216–238.

26. Carlos Fernández, Mauricio García-Durán, and Fernando Sarmiento, "Peace Mobilization in Colombia, 1978–2002," *Accord: Alternatives to War: Colombia's Peace Processes* 14 (2004), 18–23.

27. Marie L. Besancon, "Blessed Are the Peacemakers: Senator Danforth as Special Envoy to the Sudan," Kennedy School of Government Case Program, Harvard University, 2009.

28. Michael Comerford, "The Angolan Churches from the Bicesse to the Luena Peace Agreements (1991–2002): The Building of a Peace Agenda and the Road to Ecumenical Dialogue," *Journal of Religion in Africa* 37, no. 4 (2007), 491–522.

29. Mike Tharp, "In the Shadows of Somalia," *U.S. News and World Report* 114, no. 1 (January 11, 1993), 32.

30. Klaiber, *The Church, Dictatorship, and Democracy in Latin America*, 193–215; John M. Kirk, *Politics and the Catholic Church in Nicaragua* (Gainesville: University Press of Florida, 1992), 151–169; Bruce Nichols, "Religious Conciliation Between the Sandinistas and the East Coast Indians of Nicaragua," in *Religion, the Missing Dimension of Statecraft*, ed. Johnston and Sampson, 64–87.

31. Timothy Longman, "Church Politics and the Genocide in Rwanda," *Journal of Religion in Africa* 31, no. 2 (May 2001), 166, 171, 180.

32. Brandon Hamber and Richard A. Wilson, "Symbolic Closure through Memory, Reparation, and Revenge in Post-Conflict Societies," *Journal of Human Rights* 1, no. 1 (March 2002), 40.

33. Mark Gevisser, "The Witnesses," *New York Times Magazine*, June 22, 1997.

34. Recovery of Historical Memory Project, *Guatemala: Never Again!* (Maryknoll, NY: Orbis Books, 1999), xxv.

35. Desmond Tutu, *No Future Without Forgiveness* (New York: Random House, 1999).

36. The term "transitional justice" arose originally in Latin America to describe the dilemma of whether to prosecute human rights violators in military dictatorships after transitions to democracy. The term has since broadened to include truth commissions, reparations, and other measures that societies adopt to deal with the past. The broad version of the term gives rise to a dilemma, though, namely, that measures similar to these are often adopted many years after a transition and sometimes even before a transition—during a civil war, for instance. Spain, for example, began to debate dealing with the injustices of the dictatorship of Francisco Franco in the early 2000s, despite the fact that Franco had died in 1975. International criminal tribunals of the past fifteen years have undertaken to indict leaders of military factions as war criminals while armed conflicts are still taking place. Our own imperfect recommendation is to retain the term "transitional justice" but allow it to encompass the temporal and substantive breadth of its several component practices.

37. For helpful sources on the liberal peace, see Roland Paris, *At War's End: Building Peace After Civil Conflict* (Cambridge, UK: Cambridge University Press, 2004); and Oliver P. Richmond, "The Problem of Peace: Understanding the 'Liberal Peace,'" *Conflict, Security & Development* 6, no. 3 (2006), 291–314.

38. Michael Hayes and David Tombs, eds., *Truth and Memory: The Church and Human Rights in El Salvador and Guatemala* (Leominster, UK: Gracewing, 2001), 34, 104–108, 111, 125; Paul Jeffrey, "Telling the Truth," *Christian Century* 112, no. 25 (August 30, 1995), 28–63; and Klaiber, *The Church, Dictatorship, and Democracy in Latin America*, 216–38.

39. Alexandra Barahona de Brito, *Human Rights and Democratization in Latin America: Uruguay and Chile* (Oxford, UK: Oxford University Press, 1997), 106–113, 55–60; Michael Fleet and Brian H. Smith, *The Catholic Church and Democracy in Chile and Peru* (Notre Dame, IN: University of Notre Dame Press, 1997), 160–166.

40. Beth Dougherty, "Searching for Answers: Sierra Leone's Truth and Reconciliation Commission," *African Studies Quarterly* 8, no. 1 (2004); Jeffrey Klaiber, "Peru's Truth Commission and the Churches," *Bulletin of Missionary Research* 28, no. 4 (2004); Arnold S. Kohen, "The Catholic Church and the Independence of Timor-Leste," in *Bitter Flowers, Sweet Flowers: Timor-Leste, Indonesia, and the World Community*, ed. Richard Tanter, Mark Selden, and Stephen R. Shalom (Lanham, MD: Rowman & Littlefield, 2001).

41. A. James McAdams, "The Double Demands of Reconciliation: The Case of Unified Germany," in *The Politics of Past Evil*, ed. Daniel Philpott (Notre Dame, IN: University of Notre Dame Press, 2006), 127–149; McAdams, *Judging the Past in Unified Germany* (Cambridge, UK: Cambridge University Press, 2001), 23–54; and Anne Sa'adah, *Germany's Second Chance: Truth, Justice, and Democratization* (Cambridge, MA: Harvard University Press, 1998), 143–188.

42. Klaiber, *The Church, Dictatorship, and Democracy in Latin America*, 75–91.

43. Sabrina P. Ramet, *Nihil Obstat: Religion, Politics, and Social Change in East-Central Europe and Russia* (Durham, NC: Duke University Press, 1998), 112–119.

44. David A. Steele, "Christianity in Bosnia-Herzegovina and Kosovo: From Ethnic Captive to Reconciling Agent," in *Faith-Based Diplomacy*, ed. Johnston (Oxford, UK: Oxford University Press, 2003), 126–129.

45. We hold to this claim despite allegations in recent years that some Polish church leaders collaborated with the secret police of the Communist regime.

Chapter Eight
TEN RULES FOR SURVIVING GOD'S CENTURY

1. Quintan Wiktorowicz, *The Management of Islamic Activism: Salafis, the Muslim Brotherhood, and State Power in Jordan* (Albany: State University of New York Press, 2001).

2. Jonathan Fox, *A World Survey of Religion and the State* (Cambridge, UK: Cambridge University Press, 2007).

3. Charles Kurzman and Ijlal Naqvi, "Islamic Political Parties and Parliamentary Elections," United States Institute of Peace Working Paper (Grant SG-055-06S), January 15, 2009 (revised March 17, 2009), available at http://ducis.jhfc.duke.edu/wp-content/uploads/2009/03/kurzman_20080326.pdf (accessed May 2010).

4. C. Mathews Samson, "From War to Reconciliation: Guatemalan Evangelicals and the Transition to Democracy, 1982–2001," in *Evangelical Christianity and Democracy in Latin America*, ed. Paul Freston (Oxford, UK: Oxford University Press, 2008), 63–96; Cyril Imo, "Evangelicals, Muslims, and Democracy: With Particular Reference to the Declaration of Sharia in Northern Nigeria," and Isabel Apawo Phiri, "President Frederick Chiluba and Zambia: Evangelicals and Democracy in a 'Christian Nation,'" in *Evangelical Christianity and Democracy in Africa*, ed. Terence O. Ranger (Oxford, UK: Oxford University Press, 2008), chaps. 1 and 3, respectively.

5. Thomas F. Farr, *World of Faith and Freedom: Why International Religious Liberty Is Vital to American National Security* (Oxford, UK: Oxford University Press, 2008).

BIBLIOGRAPHY

Adeed, Dawisha. "The New Iraq: Democratic Institutions and Performance." *Journal of Democracy* 16, no. 3 (July 2005), 35–49.

Aili, Piano, Arch Puddington, and Mark Y. Rosenberg. *Freedom in the World 2006: The Annual Survey of Political Rights and Civil Liberties.* New York: Freedom House, 2006.

"Allah's Shadow." *The Economist* 368, issue 8334 (July 26, 2003).

Almond, Gabriel Abraham, and Sidney Verba. *The Civic Culture: Political Attitudes and Democracy in Five Nations.* Princeton, NJ: Princeton University Press, 1963.

Almond, Gabriel A., R. Scott Appleby, and Emmanuel Sivan. *Strong Religion: The Rise of Fundamentalisms Around the World.* Chicago, IL: University of Chicago Press, 2003.

Alston, William P. "Religion." *Encyclopedia of Philosophy,* vol. 7. New York: Macmillan, 1972.

"And they call it peace." *The Economist* 386, issue 8569 (March 1, 2008).

Appleby, R. Scott. *The Ambivalence of the Sacred: Religion, Violence, and Reconciliation.* Lanham, MD: Rowman & Littlefield, 2000.

Arreguín-Toft, Ivan. *How the Weak Win Wars: A Theory of Asymmetric Conflict.* New York: Cambridge University Press, 2005.

Baba, Noor Ahmad. *Organisation of Islamic Conference: Theory and Practice of Pan-Islamic Cooperation.* Dhaka, Bangladesh: University Press Limited, 1994.

Balz, Dan. "A LOOK AT . . . Irish Hopes; Now the Hard Part: Building a Peace to Last." *Washington Post,* May 31, 1998, C03.

Barahona de Brito, Alexandra. *Human Rights and Democratization in Latin America: Uruguay and Chile.* Oxford, UK: Oxford University Press, 1997.

Barber, Benjamin R. *Jihad vs. McWorld.* New York: Ballantine, 1996.

Basham, A. L. *The Wonder That Was India: A Survey of the Culture of the Indian Sub-Continent Before the Coming of the Muslims.* New York: Grove Press, 1959.

Bates, M. Searle. *Religious Liberty: An Inquiry.* New York and London: Harper & Bros., 1945.

Bennhold, Katrin, and Souad Mekhennet. "Familiar Threats Constrict Press Freedom in Algeria." *New York Times,* December 28, 2007, A8.

Berger, Peter L. "The Desecularization of the World: A Global Overview." In *The Desecularization of the World: Resurgent Religion and World Politics,* edited by Peter L. Berger. Washington, DC: Eerdmans/Ethics and Public Policy Center, 1999, 1–18.

———. *The Sacred Canopy: Elements of a Sociological Theory of Religion.* New York: Random House, 1967.

Berkes, Niyazi. *The Development of Secularism in Turkey.* Montreal: McGill University Press, 1964.

Berlinski, Claire. "In Turkey, a Looming Battle Over Islam." *Washington Post,* May 6, 2007, B01.

Besancon, Marie L. "Blessed Are the Peacemakers: Senator Danforth as Special Envoy to the Sudan." Kennedy School of Government Case Program, Harvard University, 2009.

Bill, James A. *The Eagle and the Lion: The Tragedy of American-Iranian Relations.* New Haven, CT: Yale University Press, 1988.

"A Bleak Outlook Is Seen for Religion." *New York Times,* February 25, 1968, 3.

Bloom, Mia. *Dying to Kill: The Allure of Suicide Terror.* New York: Columbia University Press, 2005.

Bouta, Tsjeard, S. Ayse Kadayifci-Orellana, and Mohammed Abu-Nimer. *Faith-Based Peace-Building: Mapping and Analysis of Christian, Muslim, and Multi-Faith Actors.* Washington, DC: Netherlands Institute of International Relations "Clingdael" in cooperation with Salam Institute for Peace and Justice, 2005.

Brachman, Jarret M., and William F. McCants. "Stealing al-Qa'ida's Playbook." *Studies in Conflict and Terrorism* 29, no. 4 (June 2006), 309–321.

Bravin, Jess. "9/11 Defendants Respond to U.S. Government Charges." *Wall Street Journal,* March 11, 2009, A6.

Brown, D. Mackenzie. *The White Umbrella: Indian Political Thought from Manu to Gandhi.* Berkeley: University of California Press, 1953.

Bruce, Steve. *God Is Dead: Secularization in the West.* Oxford, UK: Blackwell Publishing, 2002.

———. *Religion and the Modern World.* Oxford, UK: Oxford University Press, 1996.

Buijs, Frank J. "Muslims in the Netherlands: Social and Political Developments After 9/11." *Journal of Ethnic and Migration Studies* 35, no. 3 (March 2009), 421–438.

Burleigh, Michael. *Earthly Powers: Religion and Politics in Europe from the French Revolution to the Great War.* London: HarperCollins, 2005.

Call, Charles T., and Elizabeth M. Cousens. "Ending Wars and Building Peace: International Responses to War-Torn Societies." *International Studies Quarterly* 9 (2008), 1–21.

Carpenter, Joel A. *Revive Us Again: The Reawakening of American Fundamentalism.* New York: Oxford University Press, 1997.

Carter, Phillip. "There Are Four Iraq Wars: How Many of Them Can We Win?" Slate.com. February 9, 2007. Available at http://www.slate.com/id/2159460 (accessed May 2010).

Casanova, José. *Public Religions in the Modern World.* Chicago, IL: University of Chicago Press, 1994.

Central Intelligence Agency. *The World Factbook.* Available at: http:www.cia.gov/library/publications/the-world-factbook/ (accessed May 2010).

Cesari, Jocelyne. "Young, Muslim, and French—Islam and French Secularism: The Roots of the Conflict." *Wide Angle,* PBS, August 26, 2004. Available at http://www.pbs.org/wnet/wideangle/episodes/young-muslim-and-french/islam-and-french-secularism-the-roots-of-the-conflict/2524/ (accessed May 2010).

Chadwick, Owen. *The Secularization of the European Mind in the Nineteenth Century; The Gifford Lectures in the University of Edinburgh for 1973–4.* Cambridge, UK, and New York: Cambridge University Press, 1975.

Chan, Kim-Kwong. "The Christian Community in China: The Leaven Effect." In *Evangelical Christianity and Democracy in Asia,* edited by David Lumsdaine. A volume in the series Evangelical Christianity and Democracy in the Global South, edited by Timothy Samuel Shah. New York and Oxford: Oxford University Press, 2009, 43–86.

Chandrasekaran, Rajiv. "How Cleric Trumped U.S. Plan for Iraq: Ayatollah's Call for Vote Forced Occupation Leader to Rewrite Transition Strategy." *Washington Post,* November 26, 2003, A01.

Cohen, Roger. "State of Fear: A Special Report." *New York Times,* December 28, 1996, Section 1, 1.

Colley, Linda. *Britons: Forging the Nation.* New Haven, CT: Yale University Press, 1992.

Comerford, Michael. "The Angolan Churches from the Bicesse to the Luena Peace Agreements (1991–2002): The Building of a Peace Agenda and the Road to Ecumenical Dialogue." *Journal of Religion in Africa* 37, no. 4 (2007), 491–522.

Country Reports on Terrorism 2007. Washington, DC: United States Department of State, April 2008.

Coward, Harold and Gordon S. Smith, eds. *Religion and Peacebuilding.* Albany: State University of New York Press, 2004.

Crocker, Chester A. "Foreword." In *Ending Mozambique's War: The Role of Mediation and Good Offices,* by Cameron Hume. United States Institute of Peace Press, 1994, x–xi.

David, Steven R. "Saving America from the Coming Civil Wars." *Foreign Affairs* 78, no. 1 (January–February 1999), 103–116.

Dawkins, Richard. *The God Delusion.* New York: Houghton Mifflin, 2006.

Dekmejian, R. Hrair. "The Rise of Political Islamism in Saudi Arabia." *Middle East Journal* 48, no. 4 (Autumn 1994), 627–643.

Deng, Francis M. "Sudan—Civil War and Genocide: Disappearing Christians of the Middle East." *Middle East Quarterly* 8, no. 1 (Winter 2001), 13–21.

Dennett, Daniel C. *Breaking the Spell: Religion as a Natural Phenomenon.* New York: Penguin, 2006.

Deutsch, Anthony. "Prosecutors to Charge Van Gogh Killer as Member of Radical Islamic Network." Associated Press, July 28, 2005.

de Vries, Hent, and Lawrence Eugene Sullivan. *Political Theologies: Public Religions in a Post-Secular World.* New York: Fordham University Press, 2006.

Dickson, Kwesi A. "The Church and the Quest for Democracy in Ghana." In *The Christian Churches and the Democratisation of Africa,* edited by Paul Gifford. Leiden, Netherlands: E. J. Brill, 1995, 261–275.

Dingley, James, ed. *Combating Terrorism in Northern Ireland.* New York: Routledge, 2009.

Dobbins, James. "Ending Afghanistan's Civil War." Testimony presented before the House Armed Services Committee on January 30, 2007. Pittsburgh: RAND Corporation, 2007.

Donno, Daniela, and Bruce M. Russett. "Islam, Authoritarianism, and Female Empowerment: What Are the Linkages?" *World Politics* 56, no. 4 (2004), 582–607.

Doran, Robert. "Apocalyptic Thinking after 9/11: An Interview with René Girard." *Substance: A Review of Theory and Literary Criticism* 37, issue 1 (2008), 20–32.

Dougherty, Beth. "Searching for Answers: Sierra Leone's Truth and Reconciliation Commission." *African Studies Quarterly* 8, no. 1 (2004), 39–56.

"Dutch Court Sentences Van Gogh Killer to Life." *New York Times,* July 26, 2005.

Eisenstadt, S. N. "Religious Organizations and Political Process in Centralized Empires." *Journal of Asian Studies* 21, no. 3 (May 1962), 271–294.

Evangelista, Matthew. *The Chechen Wars: Will Russia Go the Way of the Soviet Union?* Washington, DC: Brookings Institution Press, 2002.

Fair, C. Christine, and Karthik Vaidyanathan. "The Practice of Islam in Pakistan and the Influence of Islam on Pakistani Politics." In *Prospects for Peace in South Asia*, edited by Rafiq Dossani and Henry S. Rowen. Stanford, CA: Stanford University Press, 2005, 75–108.

Farr, Thomas F. *World of Faith and Freedom: Why International Religious Liberty Is Vital to American National Security.* Oxford, UK: Oxford University Press, 2008.

Fattah, Hassan M. "At Mecca Meeting, Cartoon Outrage Crystallized." *New York Times*, February 9, 2006.

Ferguson, John P. "The Quest for Legitimation by Burmese Monks and Kings: The Case of the Shwegyin Sect (19th–20th Centuries)." In *Religion and Legitimation of Power in Thailand, Laos, and Burma*, edited by Bardwell L. Smith. Chambersburg, PA: Anima Books, 1978, 66–86.

Fernández, Carlos, Mauricio García-Durán, and Fernando Sarmiento. "Peace Mobilization in Colombia, 1978–2002." *Accord: Alternatives to War: Colombia's Peace Processes* 14 (2004), 18–23.

Finnis, John. *Natural Law and Natural Rights.* Oxford, UK: Oxford University Press, 1980.

Fish, M. Steven. "Islam and Authoritarianism." *World Politics* 55, no. 1 (2002), 4–37.

Fleet, Michael, and Brian H. Smith. *The Catholic Church and Democracy in Chile and Peru.* Notre Dame, IN: University of Notre Dame Press, 1997.

Forest, James J. F. "Conclusion." In *Combating Terrorism in Northern Ireland*, edited by James Dingley. New York: Routledge, 2009, 280–301.

Fox, Ben. "9/11 Defendants: 'We Are Terrorists to the Bone.'" Associated Press Online, March 10, 2009. Available at http://articles.sfgate.com/2009-03-11/news/17211835_1_guantanamo-military-judge-attacks (accessed May 2010).

Fox, Jonathan. "The Rise of Religious Nationalism and Conflict: Ethnic Conflict and Revolutionary Wars, 1945–2001." *Journal of Peace Research* 41, no. 6 (November 2004), 715–731.

———. "World Separation of Religion and State into the 21st Century." *Comparative Political Studies* 39 (2006), 537–569.

———. *A World Survey of Religion and the State.* Cambridge, UK: Cambridge University Press, 2007.

Frei, Christoph. *Hans J. Morgenthau: An Intellectual Biography.* Baton Rouge: Louisiana State University Press, 2001.

Friedman, Thomas. "Ten Months or Ten Years." *New York Times*, November 29, 2006, A29.

Gaddis, John Lewis. *The Cold War: A New History.* New York: Penguin Press, 2005.

Gandhi, Rajmohan. "Hinduism and Peacebuilding." In *Religion and Peacebuilding*, edited by Harold Coward and Gordon S. Smith. Albany: State University of New York Press, 2004, 45–68.

Gevisser, Mark. "The Witnesses." *New York Times Magazine*, June 22, 1997.

Ghufran, Nasreen. "The Taliban and the Civil War Entanglement in Afghanistan." *Asian Survey* 41, no. 3 (May–June 2001), 462–487.

Gill, Anthony. *The Political Origins of Religious Liberty.* Cambridge Studies in Social Theory, Religion, and Politics. Cambridge, UK, and New York: Cambridge University Press, 2008.

Gledhill, Ruth, and Philip Webster. "Archbishop of Canterbury Argues for Islamic Law in Britain." *The Times* (UK), February 8, 2008. Available at http://www.timesonline.co.uk/tol/comment/faith/article3328024.ece (accessed May 2010).

Glendon, Mary Ann. *A World Made New: Eleanor Roosevelt and the Universal Declaration of Human Rights.* New York: Random House, 2001.

"Global Restrictions on Religion." Pew Forum on Religion & Public Life, December 2009, 3. Available at http://pewforum.org/newassets/images/reports/restrictions/restrictionsfull report.pdf (accessed May 2010).

"Global Terrorism Database 1" (GTD1). Available at http://www.start.umd.edu/start/data/gtd/ gtd1_and_gtd2.asp (accessed May 2010).

Goble, Paul. "Unwritten Russia Directive Blocking Construction of New Mosques." *Eurasia Review,* July 24, 2010. Available at http://www.eurasiareview.com/201007245772/unwritten-russia-directive-blocking-construction-of-new-mosques.html (accessed August 2010).

Graham, Bruce Desmond. *Hindu Nationalism and Indian Politics: The Origins and Development of the Bharatiya Jana Sangh.* Cambridge South Asian Studies 47. Cambridge, UK, and New York: Cambridge University Press, 1990.

Grebennikov, Marat. "Proliferation of Islamic Extremism in the Caucasus: New Challenges to Multilateral Security and Political Stability." Thesis for the Graduate School of International Studies, University of Denver, 2004.

Grim, Brian J., and Roger Finke. "International Religion Indexes: Government Regulation, Government Favoritism, and Social Regulation of Religion." *Interdisciplinary Journal of Research on Religion* 2, no. 1 (2006), 1–40.

———. *The Price of Freedom Denied: Religious Persecution and Conflict in the 21st Century.* Cambridge, UK: Cambridge University Press, 2010.

Gunn, T. Jeremy. "Shaping an Islamic Identity: Religion, Islamism, and the State in Central Asia." *Sociology of Religion* 64, no. 3, special issue (Autumn 2003), 389–410.

Gutmann, Amy, and Dennis Thompson. "The Moral Foundations of Truth Commissions." In *Truth v. Justice: The Morality of Truth Commissions,* edited by Robert Rotberg and Dennis Thompson. Princeton, NJ: Princeton University Press, 2000, 22–44.

Gyallay-Pap, Peter. "Reconstructing the Cambodian Polity: Buddhism, Kingship, and the Quest for Legitimacy." In *Buddhism, Power, and Political Order,* edited by Ian Harris. New York: Routledge, 2007, 71–103.

Hafez, Mohammed M. "From Marginalization to Massacres: A Political Process Explanation of GIA Violence in Algeria." In *Islamic Activism: A Social Movement Theory Approach,* edited by Quintan Wiktorowicz. Bloomington: Indiana University Press, 2004, 37–60.

———. *Suicide Bombers in Iraq: The Strategy and Ideology of Martyrdom.* Washington, DC: United States Institute of Peace Press, 2007.

———. *Why Muslims Rebel: Repression and Resistance in the Islamic World.* Boulder, CO: Lynne Rienner Publishers, 2003.

Hamber, Brandon, and Richard A. Wilson. "Symbolic Closure through Memory, Reparation, and Revenge in Post-Conflict Societies." *Journal of Human Rights* 1, no. 1 (March 2002), 35–53.

Hamburger, Philip. *Separation of Church and State.* Cambridge, MA: Harvard University Press, 2002.

Hansen, Thomas Blom. *The Saffron Wave: Democracy and Hindu Nationalism in Modern India.* Princeton, NJ: Princeton University Press, 1999.

Hardgrave, Robert L., Jr. "Hindu Nationalism and the BJP: Transforming Religion and Politics in India." In *Prospects for Peace in South Asia,* edited by Rafiq Dossani and Henry S. Rowen. Stanford, CA: Stanford University Press, 2005, 185–214.

Harris, Ian, ed. *Buddhism and Politics in Twentieth-Century Asia*. London: Pinter Publishers, 1999.

Harris, Sam. *The End of Faith: Religion, Terror, and the Future of Reason*. New York: W. W. Norton, 2004.

Harrison, Lawrence E. *The Central Liberal Truth: How Politics Can Change a Culture and Save It from Itself*. Oxford, UK: Oxford University Press, 2006.

Hastings, Adrian. *The Construction of Nationhood: Ethnicity, Religion, and Nationalism*. Cambridge, UK: Cambridge University Press, 1997.

Hayes, Michael, and David Tombs, eds. *Truth and Memory: The Church and Human Rights in El Salvador and Guatemala*. Leominster, UK: Gracewing, 2001.

Hegghammer, Thomas. "Introduction: Abdallah Azzam, Imam of Jihad." In *Al Qaeda in Its Own Words*, edited by Gilles Kepel and Jean-Pierre Milelli. Cambridge, MA: Belknap Press of Harvard University Press, 2008, 81–101.

Hegghammer, Thomas, and Stéphane Lacroix. "Rejectionist Islamism in Saudi Arabia: The Story of Juhayman al-'Utaybi Revisited." *International Journal of Middle East Studies* 39, no. 1 (2007), 103–122.

Henrik-Nilsson, Nils. "The Lutheran Tradition in Scandinavia." In *The Oxford History of Christian Worship*, edited by Geoffrey Wainwright and Karen Beth Westerfield Tucker. Oxford, UK: Oxford University Press, 2006.

Hertog, Katrien. "A Self-Fulfilling Prophecy: The Seeds of Islamic Radicalisation in Chechnya." *Religion, State, and Society* 33, no. 3 (September 2005), 239–252.

Hertzke, Allen D. *Freeing God's Children: The Unlikely Alliance for Global Human Rights*. Lanham, MD: Rowman & Littlefield, 2004.

Hirschman, David. "Is France's Burqa Ban Racist?" *Big Think*, July 14, 2010. Available at http://bigthink.com/ideas/20914 (accessed August 4, 2010).

His All Holiness Ecumenical Patriarch Bartholomew. *Encountering the Mystery: Understanding Orthodox Christianity Today*. New York: Doubleday, 2008.

Hitchens, Christopher. *God Is Not Great: How Religion Poisons Everything*. New York: Twelve, 2007.

Hoffman, Bruce. " 'Holy Terror': The Implications of Terrorism Motivated by a Religious Imperative." *Studies in Conflict and Terrorism* 18, no. 4 (October–December 1995), 271–284.

———. *Inside Terrorism*. New York: Columbia University Press, 1998, 2006.

Hofstadter, Richard. *Anti-intellectualism in American Life*. New York: Vintage, 1962.

Hong, Rev. Dr. Joshua Young-gi. "Evangelicals and the Democratization of South Korea Since 1987." In *Evangelical Christianity and Democracy in Asia*, edited by David H. Lumsdaine. New York: Oxford University Press, 2009, 185–233.

"Hopes for Peace Pact Gain in Tajikistan." *New York Times*, May 19, 1997, A4.

Horowitz, Donald L. *The Deadly Ethnic Riot*. Berkeley: University of California Press, 2001.

———. "Direct, Displaced, and Cumulative Ethnic Aggression." *Comparative Politics* 6, no. 1 (October 1973), 1–16.

———. *Ethnic Groups in Conflict*. 2nd ed. Berkeley: University of California Press, 2000.

———. "Patterns of Ethnic Separatism." *Comparative Studies in Society and History* 23, no. 2 (April 1981), 165–195.

Hume, Cameron. *Ending Mozambique's War: The Role of Mediation and Good Offices*. Washington, DC: United States Institute of Peace Press, 1994.

Hunt, Lynn Avery. *Politics, Culture, and Class in the French Revolution.* Studies on the History of Society and Culture. Berkeley: University of California Press, 1984.

Hunter, Shireen. *The Algerian Crisis: Origins, Evolution, and Lessons for the Maghreb and Europe.* Brussels: Centre for European Policy Studies, 1996.

Huntington, Samuel P. *Political Order in Changing Societies.* New Haven, CT: Yale University Press, 1968.

———. *The Third Wave: Democratization in the Late Twentieth Century.* Norman: University of Oklahoma Press, 1991.

Imo, Cyril. "Evangelicals, Muslims, and Democracy: With Particular Reference to the Declaration of Sharia in Northern Nigeria." In *Evangelical Christianity and Democracy in Africa,* edited by Terence O. Ranger. Oxford, UK: Oxford University Press, 2008, 37–66.

Isaacs, Dan. "What Is Behind Hindu-Christian Violence." BBC News, January 29, 2008. Available at http://news.bbc.co.uk/2/hi/south_asia/7214053.stm (accessed May 2010).

"An Islamist Facing Islamic Terrorism." *The Economist* 369, issue 8352 (November 29, 2003).

Israel, Jonathan. *The Dutch Republic: Its Rise, Greatness, and Fall, 1477–1806.* In *Oxford History of Early Modern Europe,* edited by R. J. W. Evans. Oxford, UK: Clarendon Press, 1995.

Jaffrelot, Christophe. *The Hindu Nationalist Movement in India.* New York: Columbia University Press, 1996.

Jeffrey, Paul. *Recovering Memory: Guatemalan Churches and the Challenge of Peacemaking.* Uppsala, Sweden: Life & Peace Institute, 1998.

———. "Telling the Truth." *Christian Century* 112, no. 25 (August 30, 1995).

Jenkins, Philip. "Mystical Power." *Boston Globe,* January 25, 2009. Available at http://www.boston.com/bostonglobe/ideas/articles/2009/01/25/mystical_power/?s_campaign=8315 (accessed May 2010).

Jian, Chen. "The Tibetan Rebellion of 1959 and China's Changing Relations with India and the Soviet Union." *Journal of Cold War Studies* 8, no. 3 (Summer 2006), 54–101.

Johnston, Douglas, ed. *Faith-Based Diplomacy: Trumping Realpolitik.* Oxford, UK: Oxford University Press, 2003.

Johnston, Douglas, and Cynthia Sampson, eds. *Religion: The Missing Dimension of Statecraft.* New York: Oxford University Press, 1994.

Jones, Seth G., and Martin C. Libicki. *How Terrorist Groups End: Lessons for Countering al Qa'ida.* Pittsburgh: RAND Corporation, 2008.

Jordan, Mary, and Kevin Sullivan. "Protestants Doubt IRA Disarmament." *Washington Post,* September 27, 2005, A17.

Juergensmeyer, Mark. *Global Rebellion: Religious Challenges to the Secular State, from Christian Militias to Al Qaeda.* Berkeley: University of California Press, 2008.

———. *The New Cold War?: Religious Nationalism Confronts the Secular State.* Berkeley: University of California Press, 1993.

———. *Terror in the Mind of God: The Global Rise of Religious Violence.* Berkeley: University of California Press, 2003.

Kaiser, Robert G. "Tajiks Upbeat About 'Most Backward' Republic." *Washington Post,* August 1, 2002, A20.

Kalyvas, Stathis. *The Rise of Christian Democracy in Europe.* Ithaca, NY: Cornell University Press, 1996.

Kang, Wi Jo. *Christ and Caesar in Modern Korea: A History of Christianity and Politics.* Albany: State University of New York Press, 1997.

Kantorowicz, Ernst H. *The King's Two Bodies: A Study in Mediaeval Political Theology.* Princeton, NJ: Princeton University Press, 1957.

Kaplan, Robert D. "India's New Face." *The Atlantic* 303, no. 3 (April 2009), 74–81.

Karatnycky, Adrian. "Muslim Countries and the Democracy Gap." *Journal of Democracy* 13, no. 1 (January 2002), 101–104.

Karzai, Hamid. Statement at the 62nd U.N. General Assembly, New York. September 25, 2007. In *Country Reports on Terrorism 2007.* Washington, DC: United States Department of State, April 2008.

Kechichian, Joseph A. "Islamic Revivalism and Change in Saudi Arabia." *Muslim World* 80, no. 1 (January 1990), 1–16.

Keefer, Philip, and Norman Loayza, eds. *Terrorism, Economic Development, and Political Openness.* New York: Cambridge University Press, 2008.

Keohane, Robert O. "The Globalization of Informal Violence, Theories of World Politics, and 'The Liberalism of Fear.'" Brooklyn, NY, Social Science Research Council. Available at http://www.ssrc.org/sept11/essays/keohane2.htm (accessed May 2010).

Kepel, Gilles. *Jihad: The Trail of Political Islam.* Cambridge, MA: Harvard University Press, 2002.

Khalilzad, Zalmay. "Afghanistan in 1994: Civil War and Disintegration." *Asian Survey* 35, no. 2, "A Survey of Asia in 1994: Part II" (February 1995), 147–152.

Kilcullen, David. *The Accidental Guerrilla: Fighting Small Wars in the Midst of a Big One.* Oxford, UK, and New York: Oxford University Press, 2009.

Kinnvall, Catarina. *Globalization and Religious Nationalism in India: The Search for Ontological Security.* New York: Routledge, 2006.

Kirk, John M. *Politics and the Catholic Church in Nicaragua.* Gainesville: University Press of Florida, 1992, 151–169.

Kitagawa, Joseph M. "Buddhism and Asian Politics." *Asian Survey* 2, no. 5 (July 1962), 1–11.

Klaiber, Jeffrey. *The Church, Dictatorship, and Democracy in Latin America.* Maryknoll, NY: Orbis Books, 1998.

———. "Peru's Truth Commission and the Churches." *Bulletin of Missionary Research* 28, no. 4 (2004).

Kohen, Arnold S. "The Catholic Church and the Independence of Timor-Leste." In *Bitter Flowers, Sweet Flowers: Timor-Leste, Indonesia, and the World Community,* edited by Richard Tanter, Mark Selden, and Stephen R. Shalom. Lanham, MD: Rowman & Littlefield, 2001.

Kohn, Hans. *Prophets and Peoples: Studies in Nineteenth Century Nationalism.* New York: Collier, 1961.

Kramer, Martin. "The Mismeasure of Political Islam." In *The Islamism Debate,* edited by Martin Kramer. Tel Aviv: Moshe Dayan Center for Middle Eastern and African Studies, 1997, 161–173.

Kurzman, Charles, and Ijlal Naqvi. "Islamic Political Parties and Parliamentary Elections." United States Institute of Peace Working Paper (Grant SG-055-06S), January 15, 2009 (revised March 17, 2009). Available at http://ducis.jhfc.duke.edu/wp-content/uploads/2009/03/kurzman_20080326.pdf (accessed May 2010).

Lacouture, Jean. *The Demigods: Charismatic Leadership in the Third World.* 1st American ed. New York: Knopf, 1970.

Laliberté, André. "Religious Change and Democratization in Postwar Taiwan: Mainstream Buddhist Organizations and the Kuomintang, 1947–1996." In *Religion in Modern Taiwan: Tradition and Innovation in a Changing Society,* edited by Philip Clart and Charles B. Jones. Honolulu: University of Hawai'i Press, 2003.

Lapidus, Ira M. *A History of Islamic Societies.* Cambridge, UK, and New York: Cambridge University Press, 1988.

———. "The Separation of State and Religion in the Development of Early Islamic Society." *International Journal of Middle East Studies* 6 (1975), 363–385.

Latham, Michael E. *Modernization as Ideology: American Social Science and "Nation Building" in the Kennedy Era.* Chapel Hill: University of North Carolina Press, 2000.

Lecler, Joseph, S.J. *The Two Sovereignties: A Study of the Relationship Between Church and State.* New York: Philosophical Library, 1952.

Lederach, John Paul. "Five Qualities of Practice in Support of Reconciliation Processes." In *Forgiveness and Reconciliation: Religion, Public Policy, and Conflict Transformation,* edited by Raymond G. Helmick, S.J., and Rodney L. Petersen. Philadelphia: Templeton Foundation Press, 2001, 183–193.

Lerner, Daniel. *The Passing of Traditional Society: Modernizing the Middle East.* Glencoe, IL: Free Press, 1958.

Li, Xiaorong. "What's in a Headscarf?" *Philosophy and Public Policy Quarterly* 24, no. 1/2 (Winter–Spring 2003), 14–17.

Lincoln, Bruce. *Holy Terrors: Thinking about Religion after September 11.* Chicago, IL: University of Chicago Press, 2003.

Lindsley, Lisa. "The Beagle Channel Settlement: Vatican Mediation Resolves a Century-Old Dispute." *Journal of Church and State* 29 (1987), 435–455.

Little, David, ed. *Peacemakers in Action: Profiles of Religion in Conflict Resolution.* Cambridge, UK: Cambridge University Press, 2007.

Longman, Timothy. "Church Politics and the Genocide in Rwanda." *Journal of Religion in Africa* 31, no. 2 (May 2001), 163–186.

MacFarquhar, Neil. "In Iran, Both Sides Seek to Carry Islam's Banner." *New York Times,* June 21, 2009.

Mack, Andrew. *Global Patterns of Political Violence.* New York: International Peace Academy, 2007.

MacMullen, Ramsay. *Voting About God in Early Church Councils.* New Haven, CT: Yale University Press, 2006.

Madsen, Richard. *Democracy's Dharma: Religious Renaissance and Political Development in Taiwan.* Berkeley: University of California Press, 2007.

Maland, David. *Europe in the Seventeenth Century.* London: Macmillan, 1966.

Malashenko, Alexey. *Islam for Russia (Ислам Для России).* Moscow: Carnegie Center, 2007. Available at http://carnegieendowment.org/files/pub-35912.pdf (accessed July 2010).

Maritain, Jacques. "The End of Machiavellianism." In *The Crisis of Modern Times: Perspectives from the Review of Politics, 1939–1962,* edited by A. James McAdams. Notre Dame, IN: University of Notre Dame Press, 2007, 98–127.

Martin, David. *A General Theory of Secularization.* New York: Harper & Row, 1978.

Martin, Randolph. "Sudan's Perfect War." *Foreign Affairs* 81, no. 2 (March–April 2002), 111–127.

Marx, Anthony W. *Faith in Nation: Exclusionary Origins of Nationalism.* New York: Oxford University Press, 2003.

Mazzetti, Mark. "A Shifting Enemy: U.S. Generals Say Civil War, Not Insurgency, Is Greatest Threat." *New York Times,* November 17, 2006, A8.

McAdams, A. James. "The Double Demands of Reconciliation: The Case of Unified Germany." In *The Politics of Past Evil,* edited by Daniel Philpott. Notre Dame, IN: University of Notre Dame Press, 2006, 127–149.

———. *Judging the Past in Unified Germany*. Cambridge, UK: Cambridge University Press, 2001.

McDonald, Henry, Esther Addley, and Haroon Siddique. "Peace Protests Across Northern Ireland." *The Guardian*, March 11, 2009. Available at http://www.guardian.co.uk/uk/2009/mar/11/northern-ireland-peace-protests (accessed May 2010).

McDonald, Mark. "Fighting Intensifies in Sri Lanka." *New York Times*, April 6, 2009. Available at http://www.nytimes.com/2009/04/07/world/asia/07lanka.html (accessed May 2010).

McGreevy, John T. *Catholicism and American Freedom: A History*. New York: W. W. Norton, 2003.

Miller, Judith. "The Islamic Wave." *New York Times*, May 31, 1992, Section 6, 23.

Mitchell, Richard P. *The Society of the Muslim Brothers*. New York: Oxford University Press, 1993, xxiii–xxiv.

Moghadam, Assaf. *The Globalization of Martyrdom: Al Qaeda, Salafi Jihad, and the Diffusion of Suicide Attacks*. Baltimore, MD: Johns Hopkins University Press, 2008, 50–54.

———. "A Global Resurgence of Religion?" Working Paper Series, Weatherhead Center for International Affairs, no. 03-03. Cambridge, MA: Weatherhead Center for International Affairs, Harvard University, 2003.

———. "Motives for Martyrdom: Al-Qaeda, Salafi Jihad, and the Spread of Suicide Attacks." *International Security* 33, no. 3 (Winter 2008–2009), 46–78.

———. "The New Martyrs Go Global." *Boston Globe*, November 18, 2005, A19.

———. "Suicide Terrorism, Occupation, and the Globalization of Martyrdom: A Critique of Dying to Win." *Studies in Conflict and Terrorism* 29, no. 8 (May 2006), 707–729.

A More Secure World: Our Shared Responsibility: Report of the Secretary-General's High-Level Panel on Threats, Challenges, and Change. New York: United Nations, 2004.

Murphy, Caryle. "Algeria's Secular Army, Islamic Militants Battle for Power." *Washington Post*, January 25, 1994, A14.

Myers, Steven Lee. "Growth of Islam in Russia Brings Soviet Response." *New York Times*, November 22, 2005. Available at http://www.nytimes.com/2005/11/22/international/europe/22russia.html (accessed May 2010).

Nasr, Vali. "Rise of 'Muslim Democracy.'" *Journal of Democracy* 16, no. 2 (2005), 13–27.

"A Nation Challenged; Bin Laden's Statement: 'The Sword Fell.'" *New York Times*, October 8, 2001, B7.

National Consortium for the Study of Terrorism and Responses to Terrorism (START). "Terrorist Incidents by Perpetrator Type, 1998–2004" chart in "Global Terrorism Database." University of Maryland and U.S. Department of Homeland Security. Available at http://www.start.umd.edu/data/gtd/ (accessed May 2010).

National Consortium for the Study of Terrorism and Responses to Terrorism (START). "Terrorist Organization Profiles." University of Maryland and U.S. Department of Homeland Security. Available at http://www.start.umd.edu/start/data_collections/tops/terrorist_organization_profile.asp?id=288 (accessed February and March 2009).

Nehru, Jawaharlal. *The Discovery of India*. Calcutta: Signet Press, 1946.

Nelsen, Brent F., James L. Guth, and Cleveland Fraser. "Does Religion Matter? Christianity and Public Support for the European Union." *European Union Politics* 2, no. 2 (2001), 191–217.

Nessman, Ravi. "Sri Lanka War Near End, but Ethnic Tension Remains." Associated Press, February 5, 2009.

Nichols, Bruce. "Religious Conciliation Between the Sandinistas and the East Coast Indians of Nicaragua." In *Religion, the Missing Dimension of Statecraft*, edited by Douglas Johnston and Cynthia Sampson. Oxford, UK: Oxford University Press, 1994, 64–87.

Niebuhr, Reinhold. *Christian Realism and Political Problems*. New York: Scribner, 1953.

———. *The Irony of American History*. New York: Scribner, 1952.

Nietzsche, Friedrich. *The Gay Science*. Edited by Bernard Williams. Cambridge, UK: Cambridge University Press, 2001.

O'Brien, Conor Cruise. *Ancestral Voices: Religion and Nationalism in Ireland*. Chicago, IL: University of Chicago Press, 1995.

Office of the Director of National Intelligence. *2008 Report on Terrorism*. Washington, DC: National Counterterrorism Center, April 30, 2009.

Office of Reconstruction and Humanitarian Assistance. "A Unified Mission Plan for Post Hostilities Iraq." Draft, version 2, April 3, 2003.

Oliva, Fabio. "Between Contribution and Disengagement: Post-conflict Elections and the OSCE Role in the Normalization of Armed Groups and Militarized Political Parties in Bosnia and Herzegovina, Tajikistan, and Kosovo." *Helsinki Monitor: Security and Human Rights* 18, no. 3 (2007), 192–207.

Özören, Süleyman. "Turkish Hizballah (Hizbullah): A Case Study of Radical Terrorism." *Journal of Turkish Weekly*, April 2007. Available at http://www.turkishweekly.net/article/28/turkish-hizballah-a-case-study-of-radical-terrorism.html (accessed March 1, 2010).

Pandey, Anurag. "Communalism and Separatism in India: An Analysis." *Journal of Asian and African Studies* 42, issue 6 (2007), 533–549.

"Pakistan's Shiite-Sunni Divide." BBC News, June 1, 2004. Available at http://news.bbc.co.uk/2/hi/south_asia/3045122.stm (accessed August 2010).

Paris, Roland. *At War's End: Building Peace After Civil Conflict*. Cambridge, UK: Cambridge University Press, 2004.

Patterson, George N. "The Situation in Tibet." *China Quarterly*, no. 6 (April–June 1961), 81–86.

Pew Global Attitudes Project 2007. Available at http://pewglobal.org/reports/pdf/258.pdf (accessed May 2010).

Philpott, Daniel. "The Catholic Wave." *Journal of Democracy* 15 (2004), 32–46.

———. "Explaining the Political Ambivalence of Religion." *American Political Science Review* 101, no. 3 (August 2007), 505–525.

———. *Revolutions in Sovereignty: How Ideas Shaped Modern International Relations*. Princeton, NJ: Princeton University Press, 2001.

Philpott, Daniel, and Timothy Samuel Shah. "Faith, Freedom, and Federation: The Role of Religious Ideas and Institutions in European Political Convergence." In *Religion in an Expanding Europe*, edited by Timothy A. Byrnes and Peter J. Katzenstein. Cambridge, UK: Cambridge University Press, 2006, 34–64.

Phiri, Isabel Apawo. "President Frederick Chiluba and Zambia: Evangelicals and Democracy in a 'Christian Nation.' " In *Evangelical Christianity and Democracy in Africa*, edited by Terence O. Ranger. Oxford, UK: Oxford University Press, 2008, 95–130.

Pierre, Andrew, and William B. Quandt. *The Algerian Crisis: Policy Options for the West*. Washington, DC: Carnegie Endowment for International Peace, 1996.

Princen, Thomas. "International Mediation—The View from The Vatican; Lessons from Mediating the Beagle Channel Dispute." *Negotiation Journal* 3, issue 4 (1987), 347–366.

Queen, Christopher. "Buddhism and World Order." Unpublished report. Harvard Project on Religion and Global Politics, 2005.

Rabasa, Angel, Cheryl Benard, Lowell H. Schwartz, and Peter Sickle. *Building Moderate Muslim Networks.* Pittsburgh: RAND Corporation, 2007.

Raghavan, Sudarsan. "Egyptian Reform Activists Say U.S. Commitment Is Waning." *Washington Post,* Washington Post Foreign Service, October 9, 2009.

Rahula, Walpola. *The Heritage of the Bhikkhu: A Short History of the Bhikkhu in Educational, Cultural, Social, and Political Life.* New York: Grove Press, distributed by Random House, 1974.

Rais, Rasul Bakhsh. "Conflict in Afghanistan: Ethnicity, Religion, and Neighbours." *Ethnic Studies Report* 17, no. 1 (January 1999), 1–12.

Ramet, Sabrina P. *Nihil Obstat: Religion, Politics, and Social Change in East-Central Europe and Russia.* Durham, NC: Duke University Press, 1998.

Rapoport, David C. "Fear and Trembling: Terrorism in Three Religious Traditions." *American Political Science Review* 78, no. 3 (September 1984), 658–677.

"Reconciliation, up to a point." *The Economist* 380, issue 8493 (September 2, 2006).

Recovery of Historical Memory Project. *Guatemala: Never Again!* Maryknoll, NY: Orbis Books, 1999.

Renan, Ernest. "What Is a Nation?" (Qu'est-ce qu'une nation?). Lecture delivered at the Sorbonne, March 11, 1882. Available at http://www.cooper.edu/humanities/core/hss3/e_renan .html (accessed May 2010).

Reuter, Cristoph. *My Life is a Weapon: A Modern History of Suicide Bombing.* Translated by Helena Ragg-Kirkby. Princeton, NJ: Princeton University Press, 2004.

Richmond, Oliver P. "The Problem of Peace: Understanding the 'Liberal Peace.'" *Conflict, Security & Development* 6, no. 3 (2006), 291–314.

Roberts, Michael. "Tamil Tiger 'Martyrs': Regenerating Divine Potency?" *Studies in Conflict Terrorism* 28, no. 6 (2005), 493–514.

Rousseau, Jean-Jacques. *On the Social Contract: With Geneva Manuscript and Political Economy.* New York: St. Martin's Press, 1978.

Rudolph, Susanne Hoeber. "Introduction: Religion, States, and Transnational Civil Society." In *Transnational Religion and Fading States,* edited by Susanne Hoeber Rudolph and James Piscatori. Boulder, CO: Westview Press, 1997, 1–24.

"Russia's Dagestan: Conflict Causes." International Crisis Group, Europe Report no. 192, June 3, 2008.

Sa'adah, Anne. *Germany's Second Chance: Truth, Justice, and Democratization.* Cambridge, MA: Harvard University Press, 1998.

Sachedina, Abdulaziz. *The Islamic Roots of Democratic Pluralism.* New York: Oxford University Press, 2001.

Sageman, Marc. *Leaderless Jihad: Terror Networks in the Twenty-First Century.* Philadelphia: University of Pennsylvania Press, 2008.

Samson, C. Mathews. "From War to Reconciliation: Guatemalan Evangelicals and the Transition to Democracy, 1982–2001." In *Evangelical Christianity and Democracy in Latin America,* edited by Paul Freston. Oxford, UK: Oxford University Press, 2008, 63–96.

Schama, Simon. *Citizens: A Chronicle of the French Revolution.* New York: Knopf, distributed by Random House, 1989.

Shahin, Emad. *Political Ascent: Contemporary Islamic Movements in North Africa.* Boulder, CO: Westview Press, 1998.

Simon, Yves R. *A General Theory of Authority.* Notre Dame, IN: University of Notre Dame Press, 1991.

Singer, Peter. *One World: The Ethics of Globalization.* New Haven, CT: Yale University Press, 2002.

Slackman, Michael. "Memo from Riyadh: Influence of Egypt and Saudi Arabia Fades." *New York Times,* November 11, 2009, A8.

Smith, Christian. *The Secular Revolution: Power, Interests, and Conflict in the Secularization of American Public Life.* Berkeley: University of California Press, 2003.

Smith, Christian, and Michael Emerson. *American Evangelicalism: Embattled and Thriving.* Chicago, IL: University of Chicago Press, 1998.

Smith, Craig C. "Islam and Democracy: Algerians Try to Blaze a Trail." *New York Times,* April 14, 2004, A4.

Smith, Donald Eugene. *Religion and Political Development, an Analytic Study.* The Little, Brown Series in Comparative Politics. Boston, MA: Little, Brown, 1970.

———. *Religion and Politics in Burma.* Princeton, NJ: Princeton University Press, 1965.

———. *South Asian Politics and Religion.* Princeton, NJ: Princeton University Press, 1966.

Smith, Lee. "Sudan's Osama: The Islamist Roots of the Darfur Genocide." Slate.com, August 5, 2004. Available at http://www.slate.com/id/2104814/ (accessed May 2010).

Snyder, Jack L. *From Voting to Violence: Democratization and Nationalist Conflict.* New York: W. W. Norton, 2000.

Souleimanov, Emil, and Ondrej Ditrych. "The Internationalisation of the Russian-Chechen Conflict: Myths and Reality." *Europe-Asia Studies* 60, no. 7 (September 2008), 1199–1222.

Stark, Rodney, and Roger Finke. *Acts of Faith: Explaining the Human Side of Religion.* Berkeley: University of California Press, 2000.

"The St. Egidio Platform for a Peaceful Solution of the Algerian Crisis." Available at http://www.santegidio.org/news/rassegna/00000/19980530_peaceworks2_EN.htm (accessed May 2010).

Steele, David A. "Christianity in Bosnia-Herzegovina and Kosovo: From Ethnic Captive to Reconciling Agent." In *Faith-Based Diplomacy: Trumping Realpolitik,* edited by Douglas Johnston. Oxford, UK: Oxford University Press, 2003, 126–129.

Stepan, Alfred. *Arguing Comparative Politics.* Oxford, UK: Oxford University Press, 2001.

Stepan, Alfred, and Graeme B. Robertson. "Arab, Not Muslim, Exceptionalism." *Journal of Democracy* 15, no. 4 (2004), 140–146.

Stern, Jessica. *Terror in the Name of God: Why Religious Militants Kill.* New York: HarperCollins, 2003.

Stolberg, Sheryl Gay. "In Baltics, Bush Blames Qaeda for Iraq Violence and Declines to Call Situation Civil War." *New York Times,* November 28, 2006, A18.

Strayer, Joseph R. "The State and Religion: An Exploratory Comparison in Different Cultures: Greece and Rome, the West, Islam." *Comparative Studies in Society and History* 1 (1958), 38–43.

Swearer, Donald K. *The Buddhist World of Southeast Asia.* Albany: State University of New York Press, 1995.

"Tamil Tiger Planes Raid Colombo." BBC News, February 21, 2009. Available at http://news.bbc.co.uk/2/hi/south_asia/7902392.stm (accessed May 2010).

Tharoor, Shashi. *Nehru: The Invention of India.* New York: Arcade Publications, 2003.

Tharp, Mike. "In the Shadows of Somalia." *U.S. News and World Report* 114, no. 1 (January 11, 1993), 32–37.

Thomas, Scott. *The Global Resurgence of Religion and the Transformation of International Relations: The Struggle for the Soul of the Twenty-First Century.* New York: Palgrave Macmillan, 2004.

Tierney, Brian. *The Crisis of Church and State, 1050–1300.* Toronto: University of Toronto Press, 1988.

Tilly, Charles. "Reflections on the History of European State-Making." In *The Formation of National States in Western Europe,* edited by Charles Tilly. Princeton, NJ: Princeton University Press, 1975, 3–84.

"Timeline: Ethnic and Religious Unrest in Nigeria." Reuters, February 21, 2009. Available at http://www.alertnet.org/thenews/newsdesk/LU41351.htm (accessed May 2010).

Toft, Monica Duffy. *The Geography of Ethnic Violence: Identity, Interests, and the Indivisibility of Territory.* Princeton, NJ: Princeton University Press, 2003.

———. "Getting Religion? The Puzzling Case of Islam and Civil War." *International Security* 31, no. 4 (Spring 2007), 97–131.

———. "Population Shifts and Civil War: A Test of Power Transition Theory." *International Interactions* 33, no. 3 (July 2007), 243–269.

———. "Religion, Civil War, and International Order." BCSIA Discussion Paper, Discussion Paper 2006-03. Cambridge, MA: Belfer Center for Science and International Affairs, July 2006.

———. *Securing the Peace: The Durable Settlement of Civil Wars.* Princeton, NJ: Princeton University Press, 2010.

———. "Why Islam Lies at the Heart of Iraq's Civil War." *Christian Science Monitor* 100, issue 131 (June 2, 2008). Available at http://www.csmonitor.com/Commentary/Opinion/2008/0602/p09s01-coop.html (accessed May 1, 2010).

Toft, Monica Duffy, and Yuri Zhukov. "Religious Violence in the Caucasus: Global Jihad or Local Grievance?" Paper presented at the International Studies Association Conference, New Orleans, LA, February 2010.

Troeltsch, Ernst. *The Social Teaching of the Christian Churches.* Vol. 2. Translated by Olive Wyon. Louisville, KY: Westminster/John Knox Press, 1992.

Trofimov, Yaroslav. *The Siege of Mecca: The Forgotten Uprising in Islam's Holiest Shrine and the Birth of Al Qaeda.* New York: Doubleday, 2007.

Turkish government terrorism site. Available at http://www.egm.gov.tr/temuh/terorgrup1.html (accessed May 1, 2010).

Tutu, Desmond. *No Future Without Forgiveness.* New York: Random House, 1999.

"Underground Woman: Sakena Yacoobi and the Afghan Institute of Learning." In *Peacemakers in Action: Profiles of Religion in Conflict Resolution,* edited by David Little. Cambridge, UK: Cambridge University Press, 2007, 382–401.

Uppsala Conflict Data Program. Available at http://www.pcr.uu.se/research/UCDP/data_and_publications/datasets.htm (accessed May 2010).

Uslu, Emrullah. "From Local Hizbollah to Global Terror: Militant Islam in Turkey." *Middle East Policy* 14, no. 1 (Spring 2007), 124–141.

Vaïsse, Justin. "Veiled Meaning: The French Law Banning Religious Symbols in Public Schools."

Brookings Institution, U.S.-France Analysis Series (March 2004). Available at http://www
.brookings.edu/articles/2004/03france_vaisse.aspx (accessed May 2010).

Vallier, Ivan. "The Roman Catholic Church: A Transnational Actor." *International Organization*
25 (1971), 479–502.

Van de Voorde, Cécile. "Sri Lankan Terrorism: Assessing and Responding to the Threat of the
Liberation Tigers of Tamil Eelam (LTTE)." *Police Practice and Research* 6, no. 2 (May 2005),
181–199.

Varshney, Ashutosh. "Analyzing Collective Violence in Indonesia: An Overview." *Journal of East
Asian Studies* 8, issue 3 (September–December 2008), 341–359.

———. *Ethnic Conflict and Civic Life: Hindus and Muslims in India*. 2nd ed. New Haven, CT:
Yale University Press, 2003.

Varshney, Ashutosh, Mohammad Zulfan Tadjoeddin, and Rizal Panggabean. "Creating Datasets in Information-Poor Environments: Patterns of Collective Violence in Indonesia,
1990–2003." *Journal of East Asian Studies* 8, issue 3 (September–December 2008), 361–394.

Warnapala, W. A. Wiswa. "The New Constitution of Sri Lanka." *Asian Survey* 13, no. 12
(December 1973), 1179–1192.

Waldman, Amy. "No TV, No Chess, No Kites: Taliban's Code, from A to Z." *New York Times*,
November 11, 2001, A1.

"Warriors and Brothers: Imam Muhammad Ashafa and Pastor James Wuye." In *Peacemakers
in Action: Profiles of Religion in Conflict Resolution*, edited by David Little. Cambridge, UK:
Cambridge University Press, 2007, 247–277.

Weimann, Gabriel. *Terrorism on the Internet: The New Arena, the New Challenges*. Washington,
DC: United States Institute of Peace Press, 2006.

Whitlock, Craig. "Algerian Program Offers Amnesty, but Not Answers About Past." *Washington
Post*, September 17, 2006, A17.

Wight, Martin. *Four Seminal Thinkers in International Theory: Machiavelli, Grotius, Kant, and
Mazzini*. Oxford, UK: Oxford University Press, 2005.

Wiktorowicz, Quintan. *The Management of Islamic Activism: Salafis, the Muslim Brotherhood,
and State Power in Jordan*. Albany: State University of New York Press, 2001.

Wilkinson, Steven I. "India, Consociational Theory, and Ethnic Violence." *Asian Survey* 40, no.
5, "Modernizing Tradition in India" (September–October 2000), 767–791.

———. ed. *Religious Politics and Communal Violence*. New York: Oxford University Press, 2005.

———. *Votes and Violence: Electoral Competition and Ethnic Riots in India*. New York: Cambridge University Press, 2004.

Wilson, Bryan. *Religion in a Sociological Perspective*. Oxford, UK: Clarendon Press, 1982.

Yannoulatos, Anastasios. *Facing the World: Orthodox Christian Essays on Global Concerns*.
Translated by Pavlos Gottfried. Crestwood, NY: St. Vladimir's Seminary Press, 2003.

Yeltsin, Boris. *Midnight Diaries*. Translated by Catherine A. Fitzpatrick. New York: Public-
Affairs, 2000.

Zakaria, Fareed. *The Future of Freedom: Illiberal Democracy at Home and Abroad*. New York:
W. W. Norton, 2003.

Zeldin, Theodore. *France, 1848–1945: Politics and Anger*. Oxford, UK: Oxford University Press,
1984.

Zubrzycki, John. "Hindu Nationalists Rule India—But How Long?" *Christian Science Monitor*,
May 17, 1996, 6.

ACKNOWLEDGMENTS

THIS BOOK BEGAN IN 2000 with the discussions of a working group of scholars on "Religion and Global Politics" at Harvard University. The participants included Samuel P. Huntington, Bryan Hehir, David Little, Jessica Stern, and the three of us. Convinced that religion mattered in global politics far more than academia or the Western media had recognized, we resolved to develop a research agenda to explore the connection. Then came September 11, 2001, leaving no doubt that religion mattered in global politics and giving our work a new urgency. In 2002 the group's work became a research initiative generously funded by the Weatherhead Center for International Affairs at Harvard University and the Smith Richardson Foundation. *God's Century* is the culmination of this initiative.

This book results from genuine collaboration. Through e-mails, phone calls, and numerous visits and meetings dating back to July 2007, we brainstormed, discussed, argued, and persuaded. The product is more than the sum of its authors, both in the sense that each of us brought expertise to the table that none of the others had, but also in that together we developed ideas that resulted uniquely from our interaction and engagement. There is no adequate way to order our names in a way that reflects the depth of our cooperation and collaboration; it could just as easily have been other than what it is.

We wish to thank those who assisted the initiative and the book over these years. First, we thank those institutions that provided the financial and logistical support that made this work possible. These include the Smith Richardson Foundation, the Carnegie Corporation of New York, the Henry R. Luce Initiative on Religion and International Affairs, the Alexander von Humboldt Foundation, the Weatherhead Center for International Affairs and the Edmond J. Safra Foundation Center for Ethics at Harvard University, the Pew Forum on Religion and Public Life, the Institute on Culture, Religion, and World Affairs at Boston University, the U.S. Commission on International Religious Freedom, the Institute for Advanced Studies in Culture at the University of Virginia, and the Joan B. Kroc Institute for International Peace Studies at Notre Dame. Among these organizations, providing particularly crucial support for the project were Marin Strmecki, senior vice president of the Smith Richardson Foundation; Allan Song, program officer of the Smith Richardson Foundation; Steven Bloomfield, executive director of the Weatherhead Center for International Affairs; and Scott Appleby, director of the Kroc Institute. The advisory board of the Religion and Global Politics project offered critical feedback and other forms of support as well. They include Scott Appleby, Robert Barro, Peter Berger, Houchang Chehabi, James Cooney, Jorge Dominguez, Sohail Hashmi, Robert Hefner, Ayesha Jalal, James Johnson, Douglas Johnston, Mark Juergensmeyer, Luis Lugo, Paul Marshall, Elizabeth Prodromou, Christopher Queen, Lamin Sanneh, Thomas Simons, Stanley Tambiah, Constantin Von Barloewen, and Tu Weiming. We thank Francis Fukuyama, who shared his reflections on religion and identity politics at the final workshop for the project in May 2007. We owe a special thanks to Jim Kurth for his enthusiasm, encouragement, and depth of insight from the beginning of this project.

For crucial administrative support, we thank Beth Baiter and James Clem at the Weatherhead Center and Evelyn Hsieh and Meghan Tinsley at Harvard's Kennedy School.

The book owes much to the efforts of a number of colleagues along the way who provided insightful comments and helpful suggestions on how to improve it. We thank in particular Bill Carroll, Benjamin Judkins, Marjam Künkler, Ahmet Kuru, Assaf Moghadam, Sebastian Schmidt, and Chris Soper. We are also indebted to Jack Snyder, who read multiple drafts of our chapters and provided quick and incisive feedback. We also presented portions of the book at a number of conferences and university seminars, including the American Political Science Association, the International Studies Association, and Columbia University, Georgetown University, Harvard University, Princeton University, the University of California–Berkeley, the University of Chicago, the University of Virginia, and Yale University.

Able research assistance was plentiful. We are grateful to Stephanie Aberger, Dan Brown, Peter Campbell, Edgar Chen, Katie Day, Robert Dowd, Julia Fitzpatrick, Colleen Gilg, Catherine Harrington, Laurie Johnston, Stephen Joyce, Ben Kaplan, Dana Lee, Jessica Lieberman, Kevin Loria, David Lumsdaine, Gwen McCarter, Kevin McCormick, Sarah Mehta, Sarah Miller, Rachel Mumford, Julia Kirby, Elizabeth Mullen, Paul Nauert, Alexander Pickett, Robert Portada, Eli Sasaran, John Skakun, Jonathan Smith, Carolyn Sweeney, Erin Urquhart, and Afiya Whisby.

We wish to thank our editor at W. W. Norton, Roby Harrington, for believing in and continuously supporting the book project from its inception, as well as members of Norton's editorial and production staff, including Aaron Javsicas, Carly Fraser, and Cait Callahan.

Finally, we thank our families for their patience and unflappable support, especially our spouses: Ivan Arreguín-Toft; Diana Philpott; and Rebecca Samuel Shah.

We dedicate this book to Samuel P. Huntington, who was a mentor, teacher, and encouraging friend to each of us. Throughout the Religion in Global Politics project, he was characteristically generous, charming, constructively and wittily critical, and visionary. He was also one of the greatest political scientists, and indeed analysts of politics, of his generation. It was his singular perspicacity and his ability to think outside of the usual ruts that enabled him to see that religion was reshaping global politics in a way and at a time that few others did. His courage and uncanny ability to communicate enabled the entire world—truly—to engage in a conversation about the subject. Sam passed away on December 24, 2008, while we were still drafting this book. It is fitting that we dedicate *God's Century* to his memory as a tribute to his life's work and foresight.

INDEX

Page numbers in *italics* refer to figures and tables. Page numbers beginning with 225 refer to notes.